718

KU-323-751

פירוש

ArtScroll Judaica Classics®

Inspiration

translated and arranged by
Rabbi Shimon Finkelman

from the Hebrew "Yirah VeDa'as"
which was compiled by
Rabbi Yosef Weiss

יראה ודעת

and Insight
Volume II

DISCOURSES ON THE HOLIDAYS AND OTHER THEMES
BY THE MANCHESTER ROSH YESHIVAH,
RABBI YEHUDAH ZEV SEGAL, ZT"L

Published by
Mesorah Publications, ltd

FIRST EDITION
First Impression . . . August 1993

Published and Distributed by
MESORAH PUBLICATIONS, Ltd.
Brooklyn, New York 11232

Distributed in Israel by
MESORAH MAFITZIM / J. GROSSMAN
Rechov Harav Uziel 117
Jerusalem, Israel

Distributed in Europe by
J. LEHMANN HEBREW BOOKSELLERS
20 Cambridge Terrace
Gateshead, Tyne and Wear
England NE8 1RP

Distributed in Australia & New Zealand by
GOLD'S BOOK & GIFT CO.
36 William Street
Balaclava 3183, Vic., Australia

Distributed in South Africa by
KOLLEL BOOKSHOP
22 Muller Street
Yeoville 2198
Johannesburg, South Africa

ARTSCROLL JUDAICA CLASSICS®
Inspiration and Insight Vol. II
© Copyright 1993, by MESORAH PUBLICATIONS, Ltd.
4401 Second Avenue / Brooklyn, N.Y. 11232 / (718) 921-9000

ALL RIGHTS RESERVED.

No part of this book may be reproduced
in any form — including photocopying and retrieval systems —
without written permission from the copyright holder,
except by a reviewer who wishes to quote brief passages in connection with a review
written for inclusion in magazines or newspapers.

THE RIGHTS OF THE COPYRIGHT HOLDER WILL BE STRICTLY ENFORCED.

ISBN:
0-89906-435-3 (hard cover)
0-89906-436-1 (paperback)

Typography by CompuScribe at ArtScroll Studios, Ltd.
4401 Second Avenue / Brooklyn, N.Y. 11232 / (718) 921-9000

Printed in the United States of America by Noble Book Press Corp.
Bound by Sefercraft Inc., Quality Bookbinders, Brooklyn, N.Y.

Dedicated to the memory of

the Manchester Rosh Yeshiva,

הגאון והצדיק
הרב יהודה זאב הלוי סג״ל זצוק״ל

He was *rebbi,* mentor and father
to his family, to scores of *talmidim,*
and to countless Jews across the globe.
In our own lives, he was a source
of guidance, solace and inspiration.
He enriched our lives beyond words.
We are grateful for having had the privilege
of basking in his radiance. May his teachings
continue to inspire us and may he intercede
in Heaven for the benefit of *Klal Yisrael.*

Moshe Sholom and Gittle Devorah Grussgott
Dovid Zvi and Shifra Neumann

לעלוי נשמת

התינוקת

מינדל אסתר ע"ה בת משה יהודה כ"ץ הי"ו

נפטרה ז' טבת תשנ"ג

Her passing left us griefstricken,

but we took comfort in

HaRav Segal's words of consolation.

He made our pain his own

and this too, was a source of strength

in our time of sorrow.

תנצב"ה

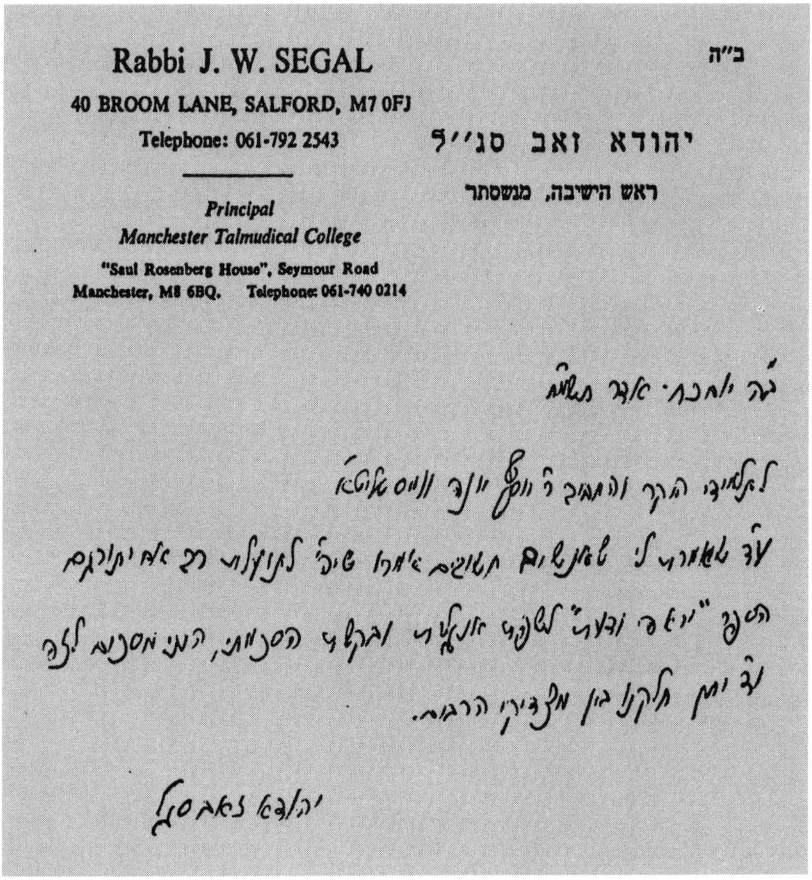

Rabbi J. W. SEGAL

40 BROOM LANE, SALFORD, M7 0FJ

Telephone: 061-792 2543

Principal

Manchester Talmudical College

"Saul Rosenberg House", Seymour Road
Manchester, M8 6BQ.   Telephone: 061-740 0214

ב"ה

יהודא זאב סג"ל

ראש הישיבה, מנשסתר

[handwritten Hebrew note]

ב"ה יום כח אדר תשמ"ח

לתלמידי היקר והחביב ר' יוסף יונה ווייס שליט"א

ע"ד שאמרת לי שאנשים חשובים אמרו שיהי' לתועלת רב אם יתורגם
הספר ,,יראה ודעת" לשפת אנגלית ובקשת הסכמתי, הנני מסכים לזה וד'
יתן חלקנו בין מצדיקי הרבים.

יהודא זאב סגל

Rabbi M. Z. Ehrentreu מאיר צבי הכהן עהרנטרייא

40 Broom Lane, Salford M7 0FJ ראש ישיבת מנשסתר, וראש הכולל דרישיבת מנשסתר
Manchester, England. Tel: 061 792 2543

יום א' מימי הגבלה תשנ"ג

החיים והשלו' לכ' הרב יוסף יונה וייס שליט"א

שמחתי מאד לשמוע שאתה עומד להוציא לאור שיחותיו של הראש ישיבה זצוק"ל — חלק השני בשפת אנגלית.

הראש ישיבה זצוק"ל כבר בחייו היה מסכים להדפיס שיחותיו והיה מחזק להמשיך בעבודה זו להתעורר בחיזוק עמל התורה, ועבודה ותיקון המדות. וגם התעורר ברבים ענין שמירת הלשון בכל תפוצות ישרא'.

ואני תפילה אשר חפץ ה' בידנו יצליח שהספר יביא התועלת המכוונת.

והנני מברכך שזכות זיכו הרבים וזכות הראש ישיבה זצוק"ל תעמוד לך ולמשפחתך. ונזכה לראות הרמת קרן התורה וישרא' במהרה.

ברוב ברכה

מאיר צבי הכהן עהרנטרייא

∽§ Table of Contents

৽ Publisher's Preface

Rabbi Yehudah Zev Segal was a legend in his lifetime. During his last decade and a half particularly, Rabbi Segal's influence spread far beyond his native England to Jewish communities all across the world.

As an eminent Torah scholar and revered *tzaddik*, Rabbi Segal was sought out everywhere for his counsel, blessings and prayers. His warmth, concern and genuine love for every Jew imbued his petitioners with a feeling that mere words cannot convey. He was a primary force in the worldwide awakening toward study of the Chofetz Chaim's classic code on the laws of *lashon hara* (forbidden speech).

It is against this backdrop that Rabbi Segal's *shmuessen* (ethical discourses) have had so great an impact. His words are down-to-earth, powerful and uplifting; they inspire the reader toward spiritual striving, and make him confident that he *can* succeed. Rabbi Segal's discourses convey a sense of who he was — a spiritual giant who keenly understood human nature, and who utilized his vast Torah knowledge to help others develop their strengths and overcome their weaknesses.

The first volume of **Inspiration and Insight,** discourses on the weekly *parashah*, was published in 1990 to popular acclaim. This long-awaited second volume, written and arranged by Rabbi Shimon Finkelman, further preserves the memory and teachings of this great Torah personality, who passed away suddenly on 22 Shevat, 5753/1993. The book contains discourses on the *yomim tovim*, *teshuvah*, general ethical themes, and moving eulogies of recent Torah luminaries. In total, it is a priceless word portrait of the ethical world of the Jew.

Credit for this volume goes to Rabbi Yosef Weiss, a student and disciple of the *Rosh Yeshivah*, who compiled the Hebrew edition and coordinated this English rendition. Rabbi Weiss is a rebbi at Yeshivah Ohr Chodosh of Lakewood, N.J.

We are confident that this volume will be a powerful force toward the eternal goals to which Rabbi Segal devoted his life.

◄§ Foreword
by Rabbi Yosef Weiss

As I take pen in hand to write briefly concerning the awesome loss all of us have suffered — the passing of the *Rosh Yeshivah* הַגָּאוֹן וְהַצַּדִּיק הָרַב יְהוּדָה זְאֵב סג׳׳ל זצוק׳׳ל — my heart grieves and my eyes well with tears. This feeling is shared by the *Rosh Yeshivah's* family, to whom he was bound by a powerful love; by his *talmidim*, whose feelings toward him, as they drank from his wisdom and developed under his watchful guidance, was that of sons to a father, with souls bound to one another; and by the scores of individuals all across the globe who sought the *Rosh Yeshivah's* counsel, *tefillos* and *berachos*, and came away strengthened in faith, prepared to go about their service of Hashem with renewed spirit and hope.

What follows is an attempt to convey, in some small way and in general terms, the rich spiritual legacy which the *Rosh Yeshivah* has left us, for the benefit of all who strive to learn from his pure and lofty path of *avodas Hashem*.

In eulogizing his mentor, HaRav Yechezkel Levenstein זצ׳׳ל, the *Rosh Yeshivah* cited a passage from the daily *tefillah:* אַשְׁרֵי אִישׁ שֶׁיִּשְׁמַע לְמִצְוֹתֶיךָ וְתוֹרָתְךָ וּדְבָרְךָ יָשִׂים עַל לִבּוֹ, *Praiseworthy is the person who obeys Your commandments and takes to his heart Your teaching and Your word.* The *Rosh Yeshivah* noted that a person may, through the course of his lifetime, accumulate many *mitzvos* and hours of Torah study, but he is deemed praiseworthy only if he *takes to his heart* the service of Hashem.

Any *mitzvah* which the *Rosh Yeshivah* performed was done with שִׂימַת הַלֵּב, *attentiveness of heart.* Every word of Torah over which he toiled was pondered well to discern the will of Hashem that was inherent in it. He taught us that each *mitzvah* was a distinct form of *avodah*, Divine service, that its performance endows one with *kedushah*, sanctity, and that it should be done with proper *kavanah*, intent, as taught by *Chazal*.

The *Rosh Yeshivah* studied Torah with awesome, ceaseless *hasmadah* (diligence). His every moment was dedicated to plumbing the depths of Torah. He strove to achieve a clarity in every word of the text at hand, and he reviewed each topic as many times as was necessary to master it. He fulfilled the command, *And you shall speak of them [words of Torah] . . . when you go on the way (Devarim 6:7)*, as he reviewed his studies whenever he traveled, whether on foot or by means of transportation. He even had a fixed study session during the few minute's drive from the Manchester Yeshivah to his home.

The idea of "relaxing" was foreign to him. He did everything with intensity. When speaking on the phone he would involve himself totally in the caller's problem. When the conversation ended, the *Rosh Yeshivah* would immediately resume his learning from where he had left off without wasting a moment. He exhorted his *talmidim* to ensure that their own study sessions not be marred by idle conversation or any other type of unnecessary interruption.

Each word uttered by the *Rosh Yeshivah* in *tefillah* was weighed, said with proper intent and carefully enunciated. To the *Rosh Yeshivah*, the *siddur* was a work of *mussar*. He pondered the meaning of the *tefillos* and drew lessons from them. Every *tefillah* or *berachah*, including such oft-recited *berachos* as *asher yatzar* and *shehakol*, was read from a *siddur* (to aid concentration) slowly and with intensity.

In observing the *Rosh Yeshivah* as he prayed, one could see that the needs of *Klal Yisrael*, both on a communal and individual level, weighed heavily upon him. His typical daily *Shemoneh Esrei* was uttered with heartfelt tears.

The *Rosh Yeshivah* always strove to help his fellow Jews in any way possible. Before he performed an act of *chesed*, he would concentrate on the fulfillment of the *mitzvah* וְאָהַבְתָּ לְרֵעֲךָ כָּמוֹךָ, *Love your neighbor as yourself (Vayikra 19:18)*. He would listen as someone poured out his troubles and heartaches, and would be נוֹשֵׂא בְּעוֹל עִם חֲבֵירוֹ, *share his friend's burden* to the point that his distress was readily apparent. And another person's joy was his joy.

He would seek ways to perform even small, seemingly insignificant, acts of *chesed* in such a way that others would not know the identity of their benefactor. The *Rosh Yeshivah* would stress that, as with any *mitzvah*, an act of *chesed* endows a Jew with *kedushah*.

He was a living embodiment of David *HaMelech's* words: שִׁוִּיתִי ה' לְנֶגְדִּי תָמִיד, *I have set Hashem before me always* (*Tehillim* 16:8). Throughout the day, the *Rosh Yeshivah* would actively acknowledge his awareness of being in Hashem's Presence. In the morning, immediately upon awakening and reciting *Modeh Ani*, he would sit up and say, "*Baruch Hashem*, I have awakened healthy; I give thanks for every single breath." While donning his attire, he would recite the two paragraphs of *Ani Ma'amin* in which one acknowledges belief in God's system of reward and punishment, and G-d's knowledge of our every deed and thought. He once startled a *talmid* by saying, "Get ready!" "For what?" asked the *talmid*. The *Rosh Yeshivah* replied, "Heaven is photographing everything you do. Be careful."

He expended enormous effort in the area of *shemiras halashon*. He stressed the importance of daily study of *Sefer Chofetz Chaim*, and to this end established a calendar by which two *halachos* in *Sefer Chofetz Chaim* and one page in *Sefer Shemiras HaLashon* would be studied each day. Today, this system of daily study is followed in cities around the world. So precious was the *luach* (calendar) to him, that the *Rosh Yeshivah* requested that it be placed in the *aron* in which he was buried. He said, "It will be my passport to *Olam Habah*."

When petitioners would come before him, the *Rosh Yeshivah* would ask them if they had a fixed study session in these laws, and he would offer them a *luach*. He encouraged the study of *hilchos shemiras halashon* in family settings, especially at the Friday night *seudah*, and he called on yeshivos and Beis Yaakovs to make the study of these crucial laws part of the school curriculum. The *Rosh Yeshivah* would say that one must study the laws of *shemiras halashon* his entire life.

When people would phone the *Rosh Yeshivah* to relate personal travails, he would advise them to study the laws of *shemiras halashon* regularly, and would add that in this merit the Chofetz Chaim would intercede on their behalf.

As mentioned above, the *Rosh Yeshivah* strove to fulfill every *mitzvah* with absolute perfection. Nevertheless, he would caution us not to practice *chumros*, stringencies in observance, which go beyond the letter of the law, if such performance would cause hardship or heartache to others — especially a parent or spouse. He would say that two *mitzvos* in which one surely should seek stringencies are כַּבֵּד אֶת אָבִיךָ וְאֶת אִמֶּךָ, *Honor your father and your mother* and וְאָהַבְתָּ לְרֵעֲךָ כָּמוֹךָ, *Love your neighbor as yourself.*

Though only a *talmid*, I can state unequivocally that the *Rosh Yeshivah* demanded of himself that he live by the lofty concepts which formed the core of his *shmuessen* (discourses). Indeed, it seemed to us that his every word and deed was a perfect reflection of Hashem's will as expressed in the Torah. The *Rosh Yeshivah* was a living testimony to the fact that even in our day it is possible for a person to attain awesome levels of Torah knowledge, *yiras Hashem* and *kedushah*.

May the *Rosh Yeshivah* serve as a *meilitz yosher* for his beloved family, *talmidim*, and all of *Klal Yisrael*; and may he intercede before the Throne of Glory so that we may witness the coming of *Mashiach*, speedily and in our time.

❦ ❦ ❦

It is with deep gratitude to *Hashem Yisbarach* that we present this second English volume of *shmuessen* of the *Rosh Yeshivah* זצ"ל. *Baruch Hashem*, the first volume of *Inspiration and Insight* has been well received, and it is in response to the public's appreciation of that volume that we have prepared the material presented herein.

While the first volume was arranged according to the weekly *parashah*, much of this second volume focuses on the seasons of the Jewish year. The second section of this work contains discourses on general themes, and the third is a collection of *hespeidim* (eulogies) of *gedolei Yisrael* delivered by the *Rosh Yeshivah*. It was the *Rosh Yeshivah*'s custom during the month of Elul to delve into the words of *Rabbeinu Yonah*'s classic, *Sha'arei Teshuvah*. Excerpts of the *Rosh Yeshivah*'s comments to *Sha'arei Teshuvah*, which compose the fourth section of this work, have been culled from the second volume of סֵפֶר יִרְאָה וָדַעַת, the Hebrew collection of the *Rosh Yeshivah's shmuessen*.

It should be pointed out that when the *Rosh Yeshivah* was consulted regarding the idea of producing an English work, he made clear that the *shmuessen* need not be translated literally; rather, they should be adapted in a manner that would be of optimum benefit to the English-reading public. In the Hebrew volumes, where the discourses are arranged by topic only, discourses are virtually unchanged from the *Rosh Yeshivah's* original Yiddish presentation. In the English version, however, the order of the subject matter was often rearranged. Also, in many instances, concepts have been expanded upon for the sake of clarity. The footnotes contain supplementary material added by the translator and are not found in the original Hebrew.

❦   ❦   ❦

I wish to take this opportunity to once again express my appreciation to my *chaver*, RABBI SHIMON FINKELMAN, for his fine English rendition of the *Rosh Yeshivah's* thoughts. I can honestly say that Reb Shimon's work has given me added appreciation for the words of the *Rosh Yeshivah*. May *HaKodosh Baruch Hu* bless him and his family with כָּל טוּב, and may he continue to be מַרְבִּיץ תּוֹרָה for many years to come.

My appreciation to RABBI NOSSON SCHERMAN and RABBI MEIR ZLOTOWITZ for undertaking the publication of this work. My thanks to the graphics master RABBI SHEAH BRANDER, as well as to the entire staff of ArtScroll/Mesorah Publications.

R' MOSHE SHOLOM GRUSSGOTT and R' DOVID ZVI NEUMANN have been instrumental in making the publication of this work possible. Their many years of selfless dedication toward the needs of the *Rosh Yeshivah* have been an inspiration to myself and others, and serve as a classic illustration of a *talmid's* devotion to a *rebbi*. May their efforts לְזַכּוֹת אֶת הָרַבִּים bring an abundance of blessing to them and their families.

In both the Hebrew and English editions of this work I benefited from the guidance of HARAV YISROEL ZVI BRODY שליט״א, *Rav of Beis*

Medrash Shaarei Orah in Brooklyn and formerly *Dayan* in Manchester. May he continue to guide me and others בְּדֶרֶךְ ה׳ for many years to come.

I would like to express my deep appreciation to RABBI BINYOMIN FRIEDLAND and RABBI YOSEF GELBWACHS, *Roshei Yeshivah* of *Yeshivah Ohr Chodosh* in Lakewood, N.J., who guide their *yeshivah* with *mesiras nefesh* as well as true love and devotion toward their *talmidim*. I am indeed fortunate to be a part of such a wonderful *mosad*. May *HaKadosh Baruch Hu* grant them the strength to continue their *avodas hakodesh* for many years to come.

❧ ❧ ❧

I take this opportunity to thank those who have had a profound influence on my personal growth and development. My parents, MR. AND MRS. ELIEZER WEISS, survived the flames of the Holocaust to dedicate themselves with heart and soul to raising children who would carry on the *mesorah* of their respective families. They spared no effort in my *chinuch* and that of my older brother, REB SHLOMO, who guided me along the דֶּרֶךְ הַתּוֹרָה וְהַיִּרְאָה.

My in-laws, RABBI AND MRS. CHAIM YAAKOV DAVIS of London, have made their home a true meeting place of *chachamim*. They also epitomize the attribute of *chesed*, as they forever give of themselves for the sake of the community and individuals alike. May they all be granted long life and good health and enjoy much *nachas* from their entire families.

My wife TOVA תחי׳, through her goodness of heart and love of Torah, has been a constant source of support to me. May *Hashem Yisbarach* repay her with long life and good health, and may we together merit to raise our children to תּוֹרָה, חוּפָּה, וּמַעֲשִׂים טוֹבִים.

❧ ❧ ❧

It is impossible for me to thank adequately the many *Rebbeim* who have taught me Torah over the years and inspired me to strive for achievement in Torah and *yiras shamayim*. I would, however, like to mention the following *talmidei chachamim* שליט״א, who head the *yeshivos* in which I have studied since my *mesivta* days began:

HARAV YERUCHAM SHAIN, *Rosh Yeshivah* of the *Adelphia Yeshivah*, and the *Menahel*, HARAV DOVID TRENK; HARAV SIMCHA SCHUSTAL and HARAV MEIR HERSHKOWITZ, *Roshei Yeshivah* of *Yeshivah Bais Binyomin*, and the *Menahel*, HARAV DOVID HERSH MEYER; the revered *Mashgiach* of *Beth Medrash Govoha*, HARAV NOSSON WACHTFOGEL; and the *Roshei Yeshivah:* HARAV ARYEH MALKIEL KOTLER, HARAV YERUCHOM OLSHIN, HARAV DOVID SCHUSTAL and HARAV YISRAEL NEUMAN. May they all merit to see their *talmidim* follow in their ways.

I close with a *tefillah* that this volume of *Inspiration and Insight* achieve the same degree of acceptance in the Torah community as did the first, and may it serve to enhance *k'vod shamayim*.

Inspiration and Insight

PART I

Jewish Holidays

The Gift of Shabbos

בָּרוּךְ אַתָּה ה׳. . .אֲשֶׁר קִדְּשָׁנוּ בְּמִצְוֹתָיו, וְרָצָה בָנוּ, וְשַׁבַּת קָדְשׁוֹ
בְּאַהֲבָה וּבְרָצוֹן הִנְחִילָנוּ . . .

*Blessed are You, Hashem . . . Who sanctified us with
His commandments, found favor in us, and with love
and favor gave us His Shabbos as a heritage . . . (from
the Friday night Kiddush).*

⊰§ Fitting Receptacles

At a time when the rest of the world was steeped in idol worship,
Avraham *Avinu*, and then Yitzchak and Yaakov, clung to
Hashem, Blessed is He, with love and devotion. Thus did they
become the Patriarchs of God's chosen nation, and thus did Hashem
deliver their descendants from the servitude of Egypt to stand at the
foot of Mount Sinai and receive the Torah.

Our nation's exalted status is beautifully expressed in the
Shemoneh Esrei of *Yom Tov*:

> *You have chosen us from among all the nations; You
> loved us and found favor in us; You exalted us above all
> the tongues and You sanctified us with Your command-
> ments. You drew us close, our King, to Your service and
> proclaimed Your great and Holy Name upon us.*

There is a noteworthy distinction between the two texts which we have cited. On *Yom Tov*, we first mention וְרָצִיתָ בָּנוּ, *and You found favor in us*, which is followed by וְקִדַּשְׁתָּנוּ, *and You sanctified us*. This sequence is easily understood. Because Hashem found favor in us, He therefore sanctified us.

However, in the Friday night *kiddush*, this order is reversed; there, we express praise of Hashem אֲשֶׁר קִדְּשָׁנוּ בְּמִצְוֹתָיו, *Who sanctified us with His mitzvos*, וְרָצָה בָּנוּ, *and found favor in us*. This requires explanation. Is it not *because* Hashem took pleasure in us — that is, in our ancestors — that He sanctified us with His commandments? Why, then, does אֲשֶׁר קִדְּשָׁנוּ בְּמִצְוֹתָיו precede וְרָצָה בָּנוּ?

As the time for the redemption from Egypt neared, the Jews had sunk in the forty-ninth level of *tumah*, spiritual impurity. Had they sunk yet further, it would have been impossible for them to have been extricated from the spiritual filth in which they were mired. Hashem, in His infinite mercy, provided *B'nei Yisrael* with that which earned them great merit and ignited their spiritual revival.

> It is written (Yechezkel 16:8), "I passed over you and I saw you — Behold, the moment was one of love"; the time had come to [fulfill the] oath that I had sworn to Avraham that I would redeem his children. But they had no mitzvos with which to involve themselves so that [in their merit] they could be redeemed! — as it is written, "... but you were naked and bare [i.e., devoid of the merit of mitzvos]."
>
> He therefore gave them two mitzvos, the blood of the Pesach offering and the blood of milah, as they were circumcised on that night. Thus it is written, "[I passed over you and I saw you] wallowing in your blood [בְּדָמָיִךְ]" — in two bloods[1] (Rashi to Sh'mos 12:6).

Virtually overnight, *B'nei Yisrael* rose from the morass of idol worship to become sanctified by God as His Chosen People. Moreover, their hasty departure toward the wilderness was indicative of the awesome level of *emunah*, faith, that they had attained.

---

1. See Volume I, discourse to *Parashas Bo*.

Regarding this the prophet states (Yirmiyahu 2:2), "[So said Hashem]: I remember for your sake the kindness of your youth, the love of your bridal days, how you followed Me in a wilderness in an unsown land." What reward is stated afterward? "Israel is sanctified before Hashem, the choicest of His crop" (Rashi to Sh'mos 12:39).

All this could not have occurred without the spiritual uplift which the performance of *korban Pesach* and *bris milah* provided. Just as these *mitzvos* were a necessary prelude to the Redemption, so, too, was their performance a necessary prelude to the Jews' being given the *mitzvah* of Shabbos.[2]

We know that Hashem has endowed the Jew with the power to confer *kedushah*, sanctity, upon a given object. Through mere utterance, a Jew confers *kedushah* upon his animal, making it fit to be offered upon God's altar as a *korban*. One who derives personal benefit from this animal is guilty of *me'ilah*, unlawful benefit from consecrated property.

The *kedushah* of Shabbos, which is sanctified by Hashem Himself, is on an entirely different plane. The Torah states:

וַיְבָרֶךְ אֱלֹהִים אֶת יוֹם הַשְּׁבִיעִי וַיְקַדֵּשׁ אוֹתוֹ.
God blessed the seventh day and sanctified it (Bereishis 2:3).

To quote *Aruch HaShulchan* (*Orach Chaim* 242:1), "The sanctity of Shabbos is superior to all sanctities, and its blessing is superior to all blessings. Therefore, it was sanctified and blessed from the beginning of creation, as it is written, 'God blessed the seventh day and sanctified it.' " Without the *mitzvos* of *korban Pesach* and *bris milah*, the Jews could not have attained the spiritual level necessary to bask in the light of the holy Shabbos.

We can liken this to a strong medication which a doctor administers in the hope that it will cure his patient. He begins with a small dose and carefully monitors its effect. If the effect is positive, then he will increase the dosage to an amount that will be sufficient

---

2. Shabbos, along with certain other *mitzvos*, was given to the Jews at Marah shortly after the Exodus (*Sanhedrin* 56b).

to bring about a complete cure. Similarly, *B'nei Yisrael* received their first "doses" of spiritual medicine through *korban Pesach* and *bris milah* and this readied them to receive the awesome *kedushah* of Shabbos.

This, then, is the meaning of the *kiddush* text cited above: *Blessed are You, Hashem . . . Who sanctified us with His commandments* — the commandments of *Pesach* and *milah* — and thereby, *found favor in us and with love and favor gave us His Shabbos as a heritage . . .*[3]

►§ Hidden Treasure

> *HaKadosh Baruch Hu said to Moshe: "I have a precious gift hidden in My treasure house — its name is Shabbos and it is My desire that Israel be granted it. Go inform them of this" (Beitzah 16a).*

A treasure house contains one's most precious possessions, cherished items of inestimable value. Shabbos is Hashem's precious gift to us and it is our obligation to treat it as such, both in the way in which we experience it and the way in which we prepare for it.

---

3. R' Eliyahu Lopian makes the following observation. *Rambam* (*Hilchos Beis HaBechirah* 6:15) rules that the sanctity with which the Temple Mount was endowed at the time of the construction of the *Beis HaMikdash* remains forever. Whence did this sanctity stem? *Rambam* writes: "Shlomo [*HaMelech*] sanctified the Temple Courtyard and Jerusalem both for that time and for the future." Shlomo's efforts caused the manifestation of a *kedushah*, sanctity, that would remain on the Temple Mount forever.

Rambam further states (7:7):

> Although, due to our sins, the Temple still lies in ruins, one must treat that site with the same awe that was accorded it when the Temple stood . . . as it is written, *You shall observe My Shabbos and you shall have awe for My sanctuary* (*Vayikra* 26:2). Just as observance of Shabbos is eternal, so is awe of the Temple eternal; though it is destroyed, its sanctity remains.

While the Torah compares the sanctity of the *Beis HaMikdash* to that of Shabbos, there is a vast difference between the two. The *Beis HaMikdash* acquired its sanctity through human effort. The sanctity of Shabbos flows directly from God, Who "blessed the seventh day and sanctified it." Now, if the Torah is so concerned lest we enter the Temple area in a state of unpreparedness, or lest we behave disrespectfully when even *facing* that place — how careful must we be with regard to the sanctity of Shabbos (*Lev Eliyahu*)!

The *Arizal* writes that the sanctity of Shabbos begins to descend to the world on Friday at midday. In fact, the word עֶרֶב in עֶרֶב שַׁבָּת is related to the word תַּעֲרוּבוֹת, *mixtures*. *Erev Shabbos* is a mixture of sorts, for though it is a weekday, its afternoon contains some of the sanctity of the approaching Shabbos.[4]

Rambam (*Hilchos Shabbos* 30:1-2) states:

> *What did the Sages mean by* כָּבוֹד (*to honor the Shabbos*)? *It is a mitzvah for a person to wash his face, hands and feet with warm water on Erev Shabbos in honor of Shabbos, then to wrap himself in a garment of tzitzis and sit with awe as he waits to greet the Shabbos — as if he would be going out to greet a king. The early Sages would gather their disciples on Erev Shabbos, wrap themselves and say, "Come, let us go out to greet the Shabbos king."*

Erev Shabbos should not be spent on trivial matters that have no connection with Shabbos preparations. Rather, one should go about his physical preparations for the day and then immerse himself in spiritual preparation through *tefillah* and Torah study.

Mesechta Megillah concludes with the following: "The Rabbis taught: Moshe decreed for Israel that they should inquire about and expound upon the matters of the day — the laws of Pesach on Pesach, the laws of Shavuos on Shavuos, and the laws of Succos on Succos" (*Megillah* 32a). The commentators raise a difficulty: Earlier, the *Gemara* (29b) stated that one "inquires about the laws of Pesach *thirty days before* Pesach." Why, then, does the *Gemara* subsequently state that this obligation is limited to the *Yom Tov* itself?

We can resolve this as follows. The obligation to begin studying the laws thirty days before the *Yom Tov* is for practical purposes, to be well-versed in the laws of the *Yom Tov* so that its *mitzvos* can be observed properly. The requirement to study the laws on the *Yom Tov* itself is for an entirely different purpose, as we shall explain.

With regard to the *korban chatas*, sin offering, the Torah states זֹאת תּוֹרַת הַחַטָּאת, *this is the Torah [i.e., teaching] of the chatas*. From

---

4. *Zera Kodesh* writes that we begin the Friday night *kiddush* with the words יוֹם הַשִּׁשִׁי, *the sixth day*, because the sixth day is a bridge between Shabbos and the rest of the week.

this terminology, *Chazal* (*Menachos* 110a) derive that whoever involves himself in the study of the *chatas* is regarded as if he had actually offered a *chatas*. This concept applies to other *mitzvos* as well. The spiritual light of every *mitzvah* is bound up with the Written and Oral Torah portions which discuss that *mitzvah*. When one studies the laws of a *Yom Tov* on that *Yom Tov*, he become infused with the sanctity of the day in a most unique way. This is why Moshe decreed that one should study the laws of each *Yom Tov* during the *Yom Tov* itself.

The awesome light of the holy day of Shabbos is bound up with *Mesechta Shabbos*, its commentaries and codes. It is therefore of great benefit to establish a fixed study session in these texts on the day of Shabbos.

Of course, one should be meticulous in fulfilling the *halachic requirement* to "read for himself each week, that week's *parashah* twice and its *Targum* [*Onkelos*] once [שְׁנַיִם מִקְרָא וְאֶחָד תַּרְגוּם]" (*Shulchan Aruch, Orach Chaim* 285:1). This, too, serves to bring upon oneself the *kedushah* of Shabbos.[5]

May we merit to experience Shabbos in accordance with its laws and may the day's *kedushah* inspire us to dedicate the days that follow to the service of Hashem and His Torah.

---

5. The *Arizal* (as cited in *Kaf HaChaim* ch. 250) writes that reviewing the *parashah* prior to Shabbos — particularly on the morning of *Erev Shabbos* — is a means through which the *kedushah* of Shabbos manifests itself upon that individual when Shabbos begins.

The *Gemara* (*Berachos* 8b) states that in merit of reviewing the *parashah* each week, one's days and years will be lengthened.

Absorbing the Day's Sanctity

◆§ Proper Observance

But My Sabbaths you are to observe; for it is a sign between Me and you for your generations, to know that I am Hashem Who sanctifies you (Sh'mos 31:13).

And you shall observe the Shabbos, for it is holy unto you (ibid. v. 14).

And the Children of Israel shall observe the Shabbos (ibid. v. 16).

C*hazal* teach that were all of Israel to properly observe two consecutive Sabbaths, they would immediately be redeemed (*Shabbos* 118b). *Maharal* explains: In the blessing of *Havdalah*, we praise Hashem Who "separates between ... Israel and the nations, between the seventh day and the six weekdays." These two separations are intertwined: Were the Jewish nation to properly observe Shabbos on two consecutive weeks and in doing so demonstrate a clear and absolute separation of this exalted day from the other days of the week, then a clear and absolute separation of the Jewish people from their gentile neighbors would follow naturally and redemption would arrive.

What is meant by "proper" Shabbos observance? Surely, this is more than mere abstention from forbidden labor. *S'fas Emes* comments that the three expressions of שְׁמִירַת שַׁבָּת, *Shabbos observance*, in the above Scriptural verses allude to the sanctification of Shabbos in thought, deed and word, מַחֲשָׁבָה, דִּבּוּר and מַעֲשֶׂה.

As is derived from another Scriptural verse (*Yeshayahu* 58:13), on Shabbos one may not even mention plans for the weekday which involve labor that is prohibited on Shabbos (see *Orach Chaim* 307).

Observance in thought is likewise derived from Scripture. The Torah states, *Six days you are to work and accomplish all your tasks, but the seventh day is Shabbos to Hashem* (*Exodus* 20:9-10). *Rashi* (citing *Mechilta*) interprets: "*Six days you are to work* — when Shabbos comes it should be in your eyes as if all your work has been completed; you should not give thought to your work." A Jew who directs his thoughts on this day toward spiritual matters, and not the mundane, further strengthens the bond between Shabbos, himself and his Creator.

⋖§ Proper Preparation

To experience Shabbos in the most desired way, one cannot wait for sundown on Friday to begin turning his thoughts Heavenward. The Torah states, זָכוֹר אֶת יוֹם הַשַּׁבָּת לְקַדְּשׁוֹ, Remember the Shabbos day to hallow it (*Exodus* 20:8). *Mechilta* derives from the word זָכוֹר, remember, that Shabbos should be in one's thoughts throughout the week. "R' Yitzchak says, Do not count days as others count them, rather you should count every weekday in relation to Shabbos." *Ramban* elaborates: Other nations do not consider the days of the week to be interrelated. This is why they call the days by separate names, each after a different heavenly force [i.e., Sunday after the sun, Monday after the moon, etc.]. Israel, however, counts all days in reference to Shabbos. As we preface the *Song of the Day* at the conclusion of *Shacharis*, "Today is the first day of the Shabbos ... Today is the second day ... " Through constant remembrance of Shabbos, one will forever be cognizant of the existence of Hashem, Who created the world in six days and rested, as it were, on the seventh.

Moreover, our remembrance should be one of לְקַדְּשׁוֹ, *to sanctify it*: "[One should bear in mind] that the cessation of work [on this day] is because it is a hallowed day, a day on which to turn away from our preoccupations with the vanities of life, and grant delight to our souls by following God's path and hearing His word from the mouths of sages and prophets, as it is written: 'Why do you go to him [i.e., the prophet] today? — it is not Rosh Chodesh or Shabbos!' (*Melachim* 4:23) — for such was their way" (*Ramban*, *ibid.*).

The Jewish calendar is a never-ending spiral. If throughout the week a Jew anticipates the spirituality of the coming Shabbos, then his Shabbos will surely be an uplifting experience. However, the degree of anticipation depends on how the previous Shabbos was experienced.

> *Reish Lakish said: On the eve of Shabbos, The Holy one, Blessed is He, grants each person an additional soul; at the conclusion of Shabbos, it is taken from him, as it is written (Exodus 31:17):* שָׁבַת וַיִּנָּפַשׁ [וּבַיּוֹם הַשְּׁבִיעִי], *"[and on the seventh day] He ceased and rested." (Homiletically, this can be interpreted):* כֵּיוָן שֶׁשָּׁבַת, *Once he [i.e. a Jew] has rested, then* וַוי אָבְדָה נֶפֶשׁ *Woe! The (additional) soul is lost! (Beitzah 16a).*

The root of וַיִּנָּפַשׁ is נֶפֶשׁ, which is usually translated as *soul*, but which can also mean *desire*.[1] Shabbos represents the pinnacle of *dveikus*, spiritual attachment, to the extent that if one attaches himself to Shabbos, he attaches himself to the One Above. The *neshamah yeseirah*, additional soul, with which every Jew is endowed on Shabbos allows for this intense attachment. Moreover, *Chiddushei HaRim* writes that each week as the sanctity of Shabbos is about to descend to this world, Moshe *Rabbeinu* himself awakens the soul of every Jew to welcome the holy day of Shabbos.[2] Thus, as Shabbos begins, a Jew should be able to naturally perceive the day's sanctity. If, when Shabbos arrives, this perception is absent, it is due to lack of proper preparation and other spiritual shortcomings.[3]

---

1. See *Bereishis* 23:8.

2. *Chiddushei HaRim* bases this on the following passage: "HaKadosh Baruch Hu said to Moshe, 'I have a precious gift hidden in My treasure house - its name is Shabbos and it is my desire that Israel be granted it. Go inform them of this.' " (*Beitzah* 16a). *Chiddushei HaRim* interprets this to mean that Moshe was instructed to *inform them of this* in every generation, at the onset of each Shabbos.

3. In *Zichru Toras Moshe*, R' Avraham Danzig (author of *Chayei Adam*) writes: "One should realize — and can experience for himself — that when he will focus his thoughts properly and when the awe of God will truly fill his heart so that his deeds be pleasing [to God], then surely after he will immerse himself [in a *mikveh*] with proper intent to accept upon himself the sanctity of Shabbos, he will perceive the additional soul within himself."

R' Eliyahu Lopian was wont to quote the above passage. He shyly admitted that, at times, he could actually perceive the added soul within himself as Shabbos began.

Those who knew R' Lopian recall the noticeable change that would come over him when Shabbos began. His radiant complexion reflected both an inner excitement and the sanctity of the added soul that shone from within.

During his last days, as he lay in a semi-coma, R' Lopian's face reddened on Friday evening as always, and his lips murmured the *Kabbalas Shabbos* prayers.

⋙ Shabbos Desecration

The severity of *chilul Shabbos*, desecration of Shabbos, is evident from the fact that the Scriptural punishment for willful transgression is *sekilah*, stoning.[4] Moreover, *Chazal* decreed that the *mitzvah* of *shofar* not be performed when Rosh Hashanah falls on Shabbos lest a person involved in the study of the laws inadvertently carry the *shofar* through a public thoroughfare as he seeks the guidance of an expert (*Rosh Hashanah* 29b). *Chazal* deemed it correct to have all of *Klal Yisrael* not fulfill this *mitzvah* lest a single Jew be guilty of inadvertent *chilul Shabbos*.

The severity of *chilul Shabbos* is predicated on the awesome sanctity of Shabbos. Because the day's sanctity is so great, therefore its desecration is so severe.

Another reason for the severity of *chilul Shabbos* is the unique status of Shabbos among the *mitzvos*. *Rambam* (*Hilchos Shabbos* 30:15) states: "Shabbos and [the prohibition against] idol worship are each equivalent to all other *mitzvos* combined. Shabbos is the eternal sign between the Holy One and ourselves. Therefore, one who transgresses any other *mitzvah* is counted among the sinners of Israel; however, one who publicly violates Shabbos is like an idol worshiper."

---

4. According to the majority opinion (*Mishnah Sanhedrin* 9:3), *sekilah* is the most severe of the four methods of capital punishment which one may be subject to for transgression of a Biblical law.

In his preface to the third volume of *Mishnah Berurah*, which deals exclusively with the laws of Shabbos, the *Chofetz Chaim* writes:

> The Torah states: "*Remember the Shabbos day to sanctify it ... for in six days, Hashem made the heavens and the earth ...*" (*Exodus* 20:8). *The Torah is telling us that Shabbos is a fundament of Jewish faith, for it makes known that the universe is a creation. Since God is Creator of all, He is therefore Master over all, and we are His servants and are obligated to do His will and to serve Him with our entire body, soul and resources — for all belongs to Him. Twelve times the Torah admonishes us to keep Shabbos. Our Sages have taught: "Whoever observes Shabbos is considered as if he has kept the entire Torah, and whoever desecrates Shabbos is considered as if he has denied the entire Torah" — for, as we have said, Shabbos is a fundament of Jewish belief.*
>
> *One should know that the two hundred and forty-eight positive commandments, which God obligated us to remember and keep, correspond to the two hundred and forty-eight limbs in the human body. Now, the human body is comprised of a variety of limbs; certain limbs are not crucial to sustain life. While losing a hand or foot is an exceedingly great loss, nevertheless, man can survive such a loss. However, man cannot survive without his head, or with a heart that has been damaged beyond repair, for the source of life stems from these parts.*
>
> *So it is with mitzvos, regarding which it is written, "... that man shall carry them out and by which he shall live" (Vayikra 18:5), and, "... it is your life and the length of your days" (Devarim 30:20), and other verses which teach us that one's existence in the World to Come hinges on his observance of Torah [in this world]... Failure to observe those mitzvos which correspond to the mind and heart causes the soul's primary source of vitality to be lost. Belief in God and His Torah, and the observance of Shabbos which is a*

*fundament of faith, are the very lifeblood of the soul's
existence both in this world and the Hereafter.*

Each festival of the Jewish calendar has its own unique spiritual
aura and blessing. Pesach is a time most auspicious for personal
redemption from the enslavement of one's earthly desires, for it was
at that time of year that the Jews gained their redemption from their
overlords in Egypt. Shavuos is a time most auspicious for attaining a
greater attachment to Torah study.

Shabbos is a day of מְנוּחַת אֱמֶת וֶאֱמוּנָה, *rest of truth and faith* (from
the *Minchah Shemoneh Esrei*). Observance of Shabbos is a testimony
to Hashem's having created all that exists. It is a day most auspicious
for the individual Jew to reach a heightened level of *emunah*.
However, to accomplish this, one must relate to the day's sanctity in
the proper manner, by keeping Shabbos in his thoughts throughout
the week, enhancing his own *kedushah* during the weekdays
through the performance of *mitzvos*, and experiencing the holy day
of Shabbos in a way that strictly adheres to the guidelines set forth by
the Torah. May we observe Shabbos in the desired manner and
thereby merit the יֹום שֶׁכֻּלוֹ שַׁבָּת, *Day of Everlasting Shabbos*, through
the coming of *Mashiach*, speedily and in our time.

The Tests of Life

⋞ Lapse Amid the Miracles

וּבְנֵי יִשְׂרָאֵל יוֹצְאִים בְּיָד רָמָה.

And the children of Israel went out with an upraised hand (Sh'mos 14:8).

With an upraised hand — with great and renowned might (Rashi citing Mechilta).

The greatness of their might lay in its renown, meaning, that they did not run away in secret; rather, they made their presence known and left amid joy and song, with drums and harps, in the way of those who are redeemed (Ramban).

The Jews' exodus from Egypt was preceded by the Ten Plagues, whose miraculous nature revealed the greatness of Hashem and His ever-present Providence over this world, in particular with regard to His chosen people. Their actual departure from the land was in itself a miracle of incredible magnitude. As the *Midrash* relates, until that time no slave had ever escaped Egypt. Its borders were protected by vicious dogs, but the Jews were protected by Hashem's assurance that *to all the Children of Israel, no dog will sharpen its tongue (Sh'mos 11:7)*. As *Ramban* comments, this nation of more than one million souls left in a spirit of unparalleled joy, as a people clinging to the One Who had suspended the laws of nature again and again as He raised them from the depths of servitude and impurity to the heights of freedom and sanctity.

Yet, as the people continued their joyous exodus, at least some of them suffered a lapse of faith. When the Jews neared the Sea of Reeds, they were overtaken by Pharaoh and his army.

> *Pharaoh approached; the Children of Israel raised their eyes and behold! — Egypt was journeying after them; the Children of Israel cried out to Hashem. They said to Moshe, "Were there no graves in Egypt that you took us to die in the wilderness? What have you done to us to take us out of Egypt? Is this not the statement that we made to you in Egypt, saying, 'Let us be and we will serve in Egypt, for it is better for us to serve in Egypt than that we should die in the wilderness' ?"* (ibid. v. 10-12).

It is difficult to comprehend how a people that witnessed "signs and wonders in the land of the offspring of Cham"[1] could shortly thereafter demand of their redeemer, *What have you done to us?* *Ramban* comments that it seems unlikely that the same people who demonstrated faith in crying out in prayer to God (v. 10) could the next moment reject all the wonders that He had performed and declare, *It is better for us to serve in Egypt* (v. 12). *Ramban*, therefore, takes the approach that as the Jews stood facing the sea, they were divided in their faith. One group clung to Hashem and turned to Him in prayer, while another denied the wonders which they had seen and the prophecies they had been told. It is concerning this second group that Scripture states, *They rebelled by the sea, at the Sea of Reeds* (*Tehillim* 106:7). *Ramban's* explanation still leaves us with the fact that at least some of the Jews demonstrated an astounding lack of faith, when, only days before, after the slaying of the firstborn, the Egyptians themselves had *exerted themselves upon the people to send them out of the land hurriedly, for they said, "We are all dying!"* (*Sh'mos* 12:33).

---

1. From the *Maariv* prayer. *Mitzrayim* (Hebrew for Egypt) was a son of Cham (son of Noach).

ᵈ§ At the Sea of Reeds

Yet another puzzling negative episode occurred as the Jews miraculously passed through the split sea. The Torah relates:

וַיַּסַּע משֶׁה אֶת יִשְׂרָאֵל מִיַּם סוּף.

Moshe caused the Children of Israel to journey from the Sea of Reeds (ibid. 15:22).

He caused them to journey against their will, for the Egyptians adorned their horses with ornaments of gold, silver and precious stones, which the Jews found in the sea. Greater was the booty of the sea than the booty of Egypt, as it is written, "Wreaths of gold will we make for you, with points of silver" (Shir HaShirim 1:11).[2] Therefore, he [Moshe] had to make them travel on against their will (Rashi).

Chazal tell us that the revelation witnessed by a simple maidservant at the Splitting of the Sea was greater than that witnessed by Yechezkel *HaNavi*, who was shown the secrets of the Heavens![3] People who were in so exalted a spiritual state could, at the same moment, be so driven after earthly possessions that they had to be coerced into leaving the sea!

We must conclude that witnessing awesome miracles and attaining great spiritual heights is not a guarantee that one will not fall prey to his base desires and inclinations. Such is the power of the *yetzer hara*.

ᵈ§ Never-Ending Battle

Life is an endless series of *nisyonos*, spiritual tests. One requires constant vigilance to ensure that he be prepared at all times to face the tests that come his way. As stated in *Mesilas Yesharim*:

---

2. *Rashi* there explains that 'wreaths of gold' represents the booty of the sea which surpassed the 'points of silver,' the spoils taken in Egypt. The Jews left Egypt with an abundance of wealth given them by the Egyptians, in fulfillment of Hashem's promise to Avraham, *. . .and afterwards they will go out with abundant possessions* (Bereishis 15:14).

3. As described in the Book of *Yechezkel* ch. 1.

HaKadosh Baruch Hu has placed man in a world where there are many factors that can distance him from God, Blessed is He — these are the earthly desires. If man will become drawn after them, he will become ever more distant from the quintessential good. Thus, man truly finds himself in the midst of a powerful struggle, for all matters of this world, whether for bad or for good, are tests for him. On the one hand is poverty, on the other is wealth; the battle is being waged from all sides.

If he will struggle valiantly and be victorious on all fronts, then he will become the man of spiritual perfection, who will merit to attach himself to his Creator. He will depart the 'hallway' [that is this world] and enter the 'palace' [that is the World to Come] to bask in the light of life. To whatever degree he will conquer his inclination and lusts, distance himself from anything which would obstruct him from the ultimate good, and strive to become attached to Him, to that degree will he succeed in this regard and rejoice in Him...(ch. 1)

...He [the yetzer hara] is a man of war and is adept in the art of cunning. It is impossible to escape from him without great wisdom and forethought...(ch. 2).

Thus, life is essentially a never-ending battle to distinguish right from wrong and act accordingly. This battle is unlike any other, for in normal battle, when the enemy is knocked to the ground, he is likely to turn and flee, never to return. In the battle of life, however, the enemy is never totally defeated. Even after one has advanced spiritually and has begun to experience the sweetness of becoming close to his Creator, he cannot rest on his laurels. *...if you do not improve, sin rests at the door. Its desire is toward you, yet you can conquer it (Bereishis 4:7).* As *Rashi* comments on the word תְּשׁוּקָתוֹ, *its desire* — "[its refers to] sin, meaning, the *yetzer hara*, which forever desires to cause you to stumble."

৵§ The Strength to Persevere

The Torah's narrative of the Exodus teaches us another important lesson regarding the tests of life; namely, that the tests we face reflect our spiritual and emotional abilities and potential. Never are we presented with a test that we cannot overcome.

The opening of *Parashas Beshalach* reads:

> It happened when Pharaoh sent out the people that God did not lead them by way of the land of the Philistines because it was near, for God said: "Perhaps the people will have a change of heart when they see war, and they will return to Egypt." So God turned the people toward the way of the wilderness, to the Sea of Reeds (*Sh'mos* 13:17-18).

The Jews' ultimate destination was *Eretz Yisrael*. The most direct route there was through *the land of the Philistines*. But that apparent advantage was the very reason why Hashem did not lead them that way. Had the journey been direct, the people would have been tempted to return to the servitude of Egypt when attacked by hostile nations along the way.

This was a generation that had suffered countless trials and tribulations during its years of servitude and that was destined to face trying tests of faith during its sojourn in the Wilderness. Could a direct route back to the land of slavery and persecution really be too great a test to overcome? The *Ribono shel Olam*, Who sees into the heart of every man, knew that it might. Indeed, as *Rashi* notes, a call to return to Egypt was voiced even after the circuitous path had been taken![4] Hashem would not place the Jews in a situation where the enticements of their *yetzer hara* might be too much for them to withstand.

Contemplation of the above should be a great source of strength to us all. In life, one encounters situations which are extremely trying, which seem to drain one's emotional strength day by day. A person may come to a point where he finds himself on the brink of despair.

---

4. See *Bamidbar* 14:4.

To such a person we say: "Do not give up! Do not become broken! If you have been given this test, then surely your inner strength is sufficient to overcome it. Surely, you can subdue the urgings of your inclination, and act in accordance with the will of your Creator."

On the subject of *nisyonos*, it is worthwhile to cite the statement of *Shelah*, that it is forbidden for one to intentionally bring himself into a situation where his inclination will test him, "for who can be certain that he will gain the upper hand and that he will subdue his *yetzer hara*?" It is wrong to enter a situation that exposes a person to the *yetzer hara's* enticements, on the assumption that one has the strength to ward off such attacks.

◄§ The King and the Poor Wise Man

In *Koheles*, Shlomo *HaMelech* allegorically describes the workings of the *yetzer hara* upon the heart of man:

> There was a small town with only a few inhabitants; and a mighty king came upon it and surrounded it, and built great siege works over it. Present in the city was a poor wise man who by his wisdom saved the town. Yet no one remembered that poor man (*Koheles* 9:14-15).

Chazal (*Nedarim* 32b) explain that the *small town* refers to the human body; the *few inhabitants* are its limbs; the *mighty king* is the *yetzer hara*; and the *poor wise man* is the *yetzer tov*. The *yetzer hara* builds *great siege works* as he entices man to sin. The *yetzer tov* can save man through its wisdom, by steering him toward repentance and good deeds. *Yet no one remembered that poor man*, for "when the *yetzer hara* dominates, no one remembers the *yetzer tov*" (ibid.).

Iggeres HaRamban[5] opens with the following:

> *Accustom yourself to speak gently to all people at all*

5. *Letter of the Ramban* [R' Moshe ben Nachman, known as *Nachmanides* (1194-1270)]. In the final years of his life *Ramban* was forced to leave Spain, and he made the difficult journey to *Eretz Yisrael* where he lived until his death. It was during that time that he penned his famous letter to his son in Spain. Eloquently and pithily, the letter sets forth basic principles of ethics by which a Jew should conduct himself.

times. This will protect you from anger — a most serious character flaw which causes one to sin. Our Rabbis taught:[6] *"Whoever flares up in anger is subject to the discipline of all forms of Gehinnom, as it is written:*[7] *'Banish anger from your heart and remove evil from your flesh.' The evil mentioned here refers to Gehinnom, as it is written:*[8] *'And the wicked are destined for the day of evil.' "*

It is noteworthy that in impressing upon his son the dangers of anger, *Ramban* chose the above teaching, rather than the statements of *Chazal* which equate anger with idol worship (*Zohar* 1:27b; also cited in *Midrash*) and denial of the entire Torah (*Sifri, Shelach* 15:22). This can be explained based on another Aggadic statement regarding anger: "One who tears his clothes or smashes his vessels in anger should be considered in your eyes as an idol worshiper. This is the strategy of the *yetzer hara*: today it drives you toward one transgression, tomorrow it leads you to commit another, and ultimately it leads you to worship idols..." (*Shabbos* 105b). *Ramban* is emphasizing at the outset of his letter that uncontrolled anger can lead to transgression of the entire Torah. *Whoever flares up in anger is subject to the discipline of all forms of Gehinnom.* "All forms of Gehinnom" refers to the many forms of retribution one will incur for committing sin upon sin, the culmination of which is idol worship itself, ר"ל.

Ramban advises his son to avoid anger entirely. *Accustom yourself to speak gently to all people at all times.* In other words: Do not wait for anger to begin rising inside yourself and then face the test of self-restraint. Rather, avoid the test entirely, by conducting yourself in a manner that will not lend itself to anger at all. This advice reflects the words of *Mesilas Yesharim* cited above:

> *He [the yetzer hara] is a man of war and is adept in the art of cunning. It is impossible to escape him without great wisdom and forethought.*

---

6. *Nedarim* 22a.
7. *Koheles* 11:10.
8. *Mishlei* 16:4.

R' Yisrael Salanter wrote, "As everyone knows, *man was born to toil,*[9] to be a warrior in a spiritual struggle. Man is obligated to expend great effort in his service of Hashem; he is not to be content with merely doing that which his nature allows, while rejecting that which entails any sort of difficulty. With the latter, one is not really serving Hashem; rather, his nature is functioning on its own — and one can, Heaven forfend, be considered a פּוֹרֵק עוֹל, *one who removes from himself the yoke of Heaven,* when he places no efforts in his service, but merely does that which comes naturally.

"This is the fundament of man's service to his Creator, Blessed is His Name — to keep and to do even that which his heart does not desire. For if man will not set his heart and soul on doing that which is contrary to his own will, he is liable to commit every transgression in the Torah, ר"ל — even those which his nature and habits do not impel him to do" (*Ohr Yisrael* §17).

R' Yisrael's words should inspire us to realize our purpose in this world, which is but an anteroom before the World of Truth. No one can exonerate himself with the excuse that his innate nature was not conducive for proper service of Hashem — this is the purpose for which you were created! We are on this world to bring satisfaction to our Creator, through overcoming the negative traits that are a part of our nature and by withstanding the tests of life. While this task is not an easy one, we are assured by *Chazal* that "One who seeks to purify himself will be granted Heavenly assistance" (*Shabbos* 104a). We must take but the first step, and then Hashem will guide us along the path to success.

---

9. *Iyov* 5:7. See *Sanhedrin* 98b.

Pillars of Life

◆§ The Way of Hashem

כִּי יְדַעְתִּיו לְמַעַן אֲשֶׁר יְצַוֶּה אֶת בָּנָיו וְאֶת בֵּיתוֹ אַחֲרָיו וְשָׁמְרוּ דֶּרֶךְ
ה' . . .

*For I have loved him, because he commands his children
and his household after him that they keep the way of
Hashem . . . (Bereishis 18:19).*

In the above verse, *HaKadosh Baruch Hu* reveals that His reason
for informing Avraham of Sodom's impending destruction was His
love for Avraham. Further revealed is that the primary reason for this
love was not, as one might have thought, Avraham's unshakable
devotion to Hashem (as evidenced by his overcoming ten *nisyonos*,
trials). Rather, it was because Avraham would teach his descendants
the דֶּרֶךְ ה', *way of Hashem*.

What exactly is the דֶּרֶךְ ה'?

In *Yad HaChazakah* (*Hilchos Dei'os* ch. 1), *Rambam* discusses the
various *midos* that can be found in man and concludes that a Jew is
commanded to emulate the ways of his Creator, as it is written וְהָלַכְתָּ
בִּדְרָכָיו, *And you shall follow in His ways* (*Devarim* 28:90). *Rambam*
cites the well-known teaching of *Chazal*: "Just as He is called Compassionate, so should you be compassionate; just as He is called Merciful,
so should you be merciful" (*Shabbos* 133b).

Rambam ends his discussion with the following:

> *And how should one go about developing these atti-
> tudes so that they become a fixed part of himself? He*

should do those acts which reflect these attitudes, once, twice, thrice — repeating them on a steady basis until they become easy for him and are no longer burdensome ...

... These attitudes, which we are obligated to follow, are [collectively] called דֶּרֶךְ ה', *the way of Hashem. This is the path which our father Avraham taught his descendants, as it is written, "For I have loved him, because he will command his sons ..." One who follows this path brings goodness and blessing upon himself, as it is written (Bereishis 18:19), "... so that Hashem might then bring upon Avraham that which He had spoken of him."*

Thus, it was Avraham's *midos*, the superlative qualities which he bequeathed to his progeny, more than anything else, that endeared him to *HaKadosh Baruch Hu*.

In *Sha'arei Kedushah* (2:2), R' Chaim Vital writes that *midos* are the principles and fundamentals upon which the 613 *mitzvos* rest and are therefore not reckoned among the *mitzvos*.

Therefore, one must beware of bad character traits even more than he is zealous regarding the positive and negative commandments, for by being a virtuous person he will readily perform the commandments.

Thus, one can understand the astounding words of the Sages concerning virtues, that modesty and humility lead one to Ruach HaKodesh [Divine Inspiration] and the Shechinah [Divine Presence] rests upon him. They speak not of performance of mitzvos, but of midos! Understand this well — how the foundation of the performance of mitzvos is moral excellence — and vice versa.[1]

Of *midos ra'os*, destructive traits, R' Moshe Chaim Luzzato writes: "Arrogance, anger, jealousy and lust are all destructive traits whose evil is obvious and well known... Each one of them can bring a person to the most serious sins" (*Mesilas Yesharim* ch. 11).

---

1. This citation from *Sha'arei Kedushah* is discussed in greater length in Vol. I, discourse to *Parashas Chayei Sarah*.

~§ The Four Metzoraim

An incident in Scripture illustrates the kind of despicable behavior *midos ra'os* can evoke. During the First Temple era, the King of Aram mounted a siege of Shomron, capital of the Ten Tribes, which resulted in a calamitous famine. Meanwhile, four *metzoraim*[2] were outside the city gates, living apart from their brethren as the laws of *metzora* require. These men were debating what to do. They, too, were suffering from the famine. Whether they would remain or enter the famine-stricken city, they would die of hunger. They decided: *Let us now go and throw ourselves upon the camp of Aram. If they let us live, we will live, and if they kill us we will die* (II Melachim 7:4).

At night, they made their way to the Aramean camp — and found it deserted! Scripture relates the nature of that miracle. *Hashem had caused the Aramean camp to hear the sound of chariots and the sound of horses, the sound of a great army; so they said to one another, "Behold! — the King of Israel has hired the Hittite kings and the Egyptian kings to come upon us." They stood up and fled into the evening, abandoning their tents, their horses, and their donkeys — the camp just as it was — and they fled for their lives* (ibid. v. 6-7).

What happened next is astounding.

> These *metzoraim* arrived at the edge of the camp; they came to a tent and ate and drank. From it, they carried away silver, gold, and garments, and went and hid them; then they returned and went to another tent, carried away from there, and went and hid it (v. 8).

Scripture relates that the famine had reached a point where mothers had resorted to killing and eating their own children. Clearly, the *metzoraim* recognized that Hashem had wrought a great miracle for them and their people. Yet, after filling their stomachs with food and drink, their next act was to hoard treasures rather than

---

2. A *metzora* is one afflicted with *tzara'as*, a skin condition similar to leprosy which is a manifestation of the individual's guilt for specific sins. See the commentary of Rabbi Samson Raphael Hirsch to *Vayikra* 13:2.

concern themselves with their starving brethren.[3] Such is the warped behavior that materialistic desire can evoke.

Such *midos ra'os* can lie dormant within oneself for decades, until a situation causes them to become active and ultimately overcome the individual. R' Yisrael Salanter offers the example of a person who is a *masmid*, diligent student, by nature and dedicates his days and nights to the study of Torah. This person also has a natural desire for money — but this fact is for many years unbeknownst even to himself. For years, his needs are provided for by others while he remains a stranger to the world of business.

The day comes when he must provide for his family. The young man begins to do business and experiences the taste of profit making. Suddenly, the urge to make big money is upon him and he throws himself headlong into his work. Before long, he has all but forsaken the study of Torah, which had been his priority in life only a short while earlier.

Such is the power of *midos ra'os*.

Parashas Kedoshim (*Vayikra* ch. 19-20) begins with Hashem telling Moshe, דַּבֵּר אֶל כָּל עֲדַת בְּנֵי יִשְׂרָאֵל, *Speak to the entire assembly of the Children of Israel*. In contrast to standard procedure,[4] Moshe *Rabbeinu* assembled the entire nation and taught this *parashah* to everyone simultaneously. Why? שֶׁרוֹב גּוּפֵי תוֹרָה תְּלוּיִין בָּהּ, *Because most of the Torah's essential laws hinge upon it* (*Rashi* citing *Sifra*). *Parashas Kedoshim* contains an abundance of teachings related to human character. *Do not place a stumbling block before a blind man* (19:14);[5] *Do not be a gossipmonger among your people* (19:16); *Do not hate your brother in your heart* (19:17); *Do not take revenge and do not bear a grudge; Love your fellow as yourself* (19:18) . . .

---

3. Subsequently, the *metzoraim* experienced a change of heart. Motivated by fear of punishment for not informing the king of what had occurred, they went to the city gates and reported their discovery.

4. In the case of other commandments, it was not required that every Jew come and listen to Moshe's teaching. Rather, he taught it publicly and those who wanted to attend did so. Everyone was free to rely on the Elders and leaders to teach it to them later, or to answer their halachic queries whenever they came up. Here, however, because of the extreme importance of this *parashah*, everyone was required to attend (*Sefer HaZikaron*).

5. I.e., one should not give bad advice to an unsuspecting person, particularly if the adviser stands to benefit from the other's error (*Rashi, Sifra*).

Fulfillment of the above, as well as many other verses in this *parashah*, is contingent on the development of proper *midos*. Because *midos* are, as R' Chaim Vital puts it, the foundation of the entire Torah, *HaKadosh Baruch Hu* deemed it necessary for Moshe to teach this *parashah* to the entire nation — men, women and children.

◆§ Rabbi Akiva's Disciples

Each year, during *Sefiras HaOmer* (the Omer Counting), we observe mourning for the twenty-four thousand *talmidim* of Rabbi Akiva, who died during this period some two thousand years ago. The *Gemara* (*Yevamos* 62b) relates that they died מִפְּנֵי שֶׁלֹּא נָהֲגוּ כָּבוֹד זֶה בָּזֶה, *because they did not accord one another proper respect.*[6] After their death, "The world became [spiritually] desolate" [for the Torah became forgotten (*Rashi*)], until Rabbi Akiva became mentor to five new disciples who would be the leaders of the next generation.

While the identities of those twenty-four thousand *talmidim* are not known to us, we can assume that as disciples of Rabbi Akiva, they were men of great spiritual stature, as were his five later *talmidim*.[7] Yet, the *Ribono shel Olam* deemed it necessary to take their lives, leaving behind a desolate world.

Given our above discussion, we can understand why these *talmidim* died. Had the *talmidim* of Rabbi Akiva lived, *they* would have been the Torah disseminators of the next generation. However, to whatever degree their *midos* were deficient, to that degree would their Torah have been deficient. *Midos are the principles and fundamentals upon which the 613 mitzvos rest.* Because they were lacking in the prerequisites for Torah achievement, they died during the period of *Sefirah*, which is a time to ready oneself for the *Yom Tov* of *Shavuos* when the Torah was given.

---

6. The sin of Rabbi Akiva's disciples is the focus of the discourse to *Parashas Emor* in Volume I. HaRav Segal noted there that the spiritual level of R' Akiva's disciples was great and their sin must be understood in this context. They surely did accord one another proper respect *by our standards*. *Tzaddikim*, however, are judged according to their own exalted level of service; it was thus that the *talmidim* of R' Akiva were found guilty of sin.

7. They were: Rabbi Meir, Rabbi Yehudah, Rabbi Yosi, Rabbi Shimon and Rabbi Elazar ben Shamua.

It is absolutely imperative that *b'nei Torah* give attention to their own character development. One who has Torah without *midos* has nothing at all.

May we heed the words of R' Chaim Vital, who assures us, "Set these matters before you and without a doubt, your ways will meet with success."

The Revelation at Sinai

⊷ Its Purpose

M a'amad Har Sinai, the Revelation at Mount Sinai, was an awesome event, one without parallel. Amid thunder and lightning, the sound of the *shofar*, and flames that reached the very heavens, the word of the Living God was heard by an entire people. The men, women and children of the Jewish Nation stood together at the foot of the mountain and attained prophecy as Hashem uttered His commandments.

The Revelation left the people trembling with fear, and they requested that from then on Hashem's commands be communicated to them through an intermediary, namely, Moshe *Rabbeinu*....and *God shall no longer speak directly to us, lest we die (Sh'mos 20:16).*

Moshe responded:

אַל תִּירָאוּ כִּי לְבַעֲבוּר נַסּוֹת אֶתְכֶם בָּא הָאֱלֹהִים וּבַעֲבוּר תִּהְיֶה יִרְאָתוֹ עַל פְּנֵיכֶם לְבִלְתִּי תֶחֱטָאוּ.

Moshe said to the people: "Do not be afraid, for in order to raise you up did God appear, and so that His awe will be upon your faces so that you will not sin" (ibid. v. 17).

Our translation follows *Rashi*, who interprets נַסּוֹת to mean 'raise up': "[The purpose of the revelation was] to make you great in the world; your fame will spread among the nations, for God, in His glory, revealed Himself to you."

Ramban, however, cites *Rambam* in *Moreh Nevuchim*, who relates the term נַסּוֹת to נִסָּיוֹן, *test*:

> He [Moshe] told them, "Do not be afraid, for this that you have seen was so that when Hashem will test you to make known the level of your faith, and will send to you a false prophet who will attempt to contradict that which you have heard, you will never waver from the truth — for you have seen the truth with your own eyes."
>
> Thus, Moshe explained to them that it was in order to test them in the future that Hashem revealed Himself to them now, so that they would remain faithful to Him in every test.

Aside from the insight which *Rambam's* interpretation lends to the Revelation itself, a fundamental lesson can be gleaned from his words. Hashem does not subject a person to a test unless the person has the ability to pass that test. Hashem knew that at some future time the people would be tested when false prophets would attempt to sway them from their beliefs. To assure that all generations would have the spiritual wherewithal to reject the arguments of these wicked individuals, it was necessary for every member of the generation that received the Torah to become a true prophet and hear the word of Hashem directly, without any intermediaries. The truth of this revelation would be passed down from father to son, from mother to daughter, and would become the legacy of all future generations.[1]

◄§ The First Test

The Jews were faced with a difficult test only weeks after they received the Torah. Moshe ascended to Heaven the day after the Torah was given. Before ascending, he informed the people that he would return in forty days. The people counted the days until their leader would return. The Torah relates:

---

1. See *Ramban* to *Devarim* 4:9.

וַיַּרְא הָעָם כִּי בֹשֵׁשׁ מֹשֶׁה לָרֶדֶת מִן הָהָר.

The people saw that Moshe tarried in descending the mountain (Sh'mos 32:1).

For when Moshe ascended the mountain, he told them, "I shall return at the end of forty days, within the first six hours of the day." The people thought that the day of his ascension was included in the forty — but, in fact, he had said forty complete days. . .and the day of his ascension was missing its night [for the night had already passed before Moshe ascended]. He had ascended on the seventh of Sivan; thus, he was to descend on the seventeenth of Tammuz.

On the sixteenth of Tammuz, Satan came and brought chaos to the world. He created an atmosphere of intense darkness and confusion, to convey the impression that Moshe had surely died and that this was the source of the confusion which had come to the world (Rashi ibid.).

Rashi (citing *Shabbos* 89a) further relates that Satan showed the image of a deceased *Moshe Rabbeinu* being borne in the heavens.

The result of all this was the Sin of the Golden Calf, a sin so grievous that Hashem in His mercy spread its punishment throughout the generations, rather than exacting it in one devastating blow (see *Rashi* to *Sh'mos* 32:34). Given the above account of Satan's ruse, one may wonder why, indeed, the Jews were held accountable for this sin. They had been shown convincing evidence that Moshe was no longer alive. They found themselves in the Wilderness, certain that they had lost their great leader, who had led them out of Egypt and brought them to Sinai. In their desperation, they sought an alternative to his leadership, which is what the Golden Calf represented.[2] Why, then, were they faulted?

The answer to this lies in an understanding of the purpose of the Revelation at Sinai. *Hashem said to Moshe: "Behold, I am coming to you in a thickening of the cloud, so that the people may hear when I am speaking with you **and they will also believe in you forever.** . ."* (*Sh'mos* 19:9). In attaining prophecy at Sinai, the Jews of that

---

2. As explained by *Ramban* to 32:1.

generation personally acknowledged not only the authenticity of Torah, but also the authenticity of Moshe *Rabbeinu* as the prophet through whom the Torah was transmitted. That only truth could emanate from Moshe's mouth was a fact that had been proven for all time. *Rambam* formulates this belief in the Thirteen Principles of Faith:

> *I believe with complete faith that the prophecy of Moshe Rabbeinu, peace be upon him, was true, and that he was the father of the prophets — both those who preceded him and those who followed him* (Principle 7).

Moshe had told the people that he would be returning to them. They should not have doubted his words, despite having miscalculated the forty days of his ascent and despite Satan's efforts at misleading them. After having witnessed the Revelation as prophets, they should have understood that no amount of 'proof' could stand up against words that emanated from the mouth of Moshe. The entire episode was nothing more than a test — to determine whether or not their level of *emunah* was sufficient for them to maintain the lofty status they had achieved upon receiving the Torah. They failed.

◈§ 'It Is Not in the Heavens!'

More than a thousand years later, in the era of the *Mishnah*, the Sages were severely tested regarding a basic Torah principle — and they passed the test. The *Mishnah* (*Keilim* 5:10) records a dispute between a majority of the Sages and R' Eliezer regarding the halachic status of a type of oven. The Sages ruled that this oven could not contract *tumah*, ritual impurity, and R' Eliezer disagreed. The *Gemara* (*Bava Metzia* 59b) relates:

> *It was taught: On that day, R' Eliezer offered every possible response [to the Sages' position] but they would not accept his ruling. He [then] said to them: "If the halachah is as I contend, let this carob tree bear witness." The carob tree became uprooted from its spot to a place one hundred amos away. The Sages told him,*

"One does not bring proof from a carob tree." He then said, "If the halachah is as I contend, let this canal of water bear witness." The water rushed backwards. They told him, "One does not bring proof from a canal of water." He then said, "If the halachah is as I contend, let the walls of the beis midrash bear witness." The walls bent as if about to collapse. R' Yehoshua [one of the Sages] reprimanded them [the walls]: "If talmidei chachamim are besting one another in matters of halachah, what concern is it of yours?!"

The walls did not fall out of respect for R' Yehoshua, and they did not become erect out of respect for R' Eliezer; rather, they remained bent. R' Eliezer then said, "If the halachah is as I contend, let the Heavens bear witness!" A Heavenly voice announced "What have you [the Sages] with R' Eliezer, whose rulings are law in all instances?!" R' Yehoshua stood up and proclaimed, "It is not in the Heavens!"[3] What does this mean? R' Yirmiyah explained, "[It — the Torah — is not in the Heavens,] for the Torah has already been given at Mount Sinai. We pay no heed to a Heavenly voice, for it is written in the Torah, 'Follow the verdict of the majority.'"[4]

R' Nassan encountered Eliyahu HaNavi. He asked him, "What did HaKadosh Baruch Hu do at that moment [when R' Yehoshua proclaimed, 'It is not in the Heavens']?" Eliyahu told him, "He smiled and said, 'My son, you have bested Me, my son, you have bested Me.'"

Of this incident, R' Nissan Gaon (to Berachos 19b) writes, "The intent [of the Heavenly voice] was merely to test the Sages, to see whether or not hearing a Heavenly voice would induce them to put aside the traditions they had been taught. This is similar to that which is written, '...for HASHEM, your God, is testing you...' (Devarim 13:4). Through this test, the clarity of their tradition became

---

3. From Devarim 30:12.
4. Sh'mos 28:2

known. In declaring 'It is not in the Heavens,' R' Yehoshua intended to say: *The Torah of Hashem is perfect (Tehillim* 19:8) — it has already been given to us at Sinai, and it has been made known to us that not one word of it will ever be changed. Nothing is missing from our Torah and it contains no matters of doubt that would require a proof from Heaven."

Another of the Thirteen Principles of Faith is the following:

> *I believe with complete faith that this Torah will not be exchanged nor will there be another Torah from the Creator, Blessed is His name.*

As R' Yirmiyah explained, the Torah states that the *halachah* follows the majority opinion, and even a voice emanating from Heaven cannot supersede the Torah's words. The depth of the Sages' faith in this principle was determined through the test to which they were subjected when the Heavenly voice rang out.

◈ A World of Tests

The ultimate good that a human being can possibly attain is to bask in the splendor of the *Shechinah.* Man's purpose in this world is to attain spiritual perfection so that he can merit this great reward in the World to Come. Life in this world is an endless series of tests. With each test that he passes, one climbs a rung on the ladder to *dveikus,* attachment to Hashem, and earns himself eternal reward in the Next World.

> *Man finds himself [on this world] in the midst of a raging battle, for all matters in this world, whether for good or for bad, are, in fact, tests of man. . . If he will struggle valiantly and victoriously on all fronts, then he will become the man of perfection who will merit to attach himself to his Creator. He will depart the 'hallway' [that is this world] and enter the 'palace' [that is the World to Come] to bask in the light of life (Mesilas Yesharim ch. 1).*[5]

---

5. This passage from *Mesilas Yesharim* is quoted at greater length in the third discourse of this volume.

In facing the challenges of life, we must never forget that Hashem would not place us in a given situation were we unable to overcome whatever tests that situation presents.[6] It is for us to garner our spiritual abilities and scale the heights of *dveikus*.

Each person's life has its own set of trials and tribulations. At the same time, each generation as a whole is faced with communal tests, as were the Jews in the Wilderness. One of the most trying tests in all of Jewish history was the Holocaust. Can anyone conclusively explain the reason or reasons for the deaths of the Six Million? No, but this should not weaken our faith. We know that Hashem guides this world with absolute perfection. *The Rock — perfect in His work, for all His paths are justice; a God of faith without iniquity, righteous and fair is He (Devarim 32:4).* All that Hashem does is ultimately for the good. We may not understand, but our faith remains unshakable nonetheless.

Can one understand why the Soviet regime continues to thrive in all its glory[7] despite its incredible wickedness, particularly with regard to Jews and their religious observance? This question, too, must not weaken our faith.

Let us strive to overcome the tests of life and attach ourselves to the One Above. Through strengthening ourselves in matters of faith, we will merit the coming of *Mashiach*, when the veils of history will be pulled aside and past events will become perfectly clear for all the world to understand.

---

6. *Ramban (Bereishis* 22:1) comments that Hashem only tests righteous individuals who will survive a given challenge. Why does He test them if He knows in advance that they will pass the test? It is in order to grant them a kindness, to transform their hidden potential for great acts of faith into a reality.

A נִסָּיוֹן, *test*, which demonstrates the spiritual abilities of its performer, is akin to a נֵס, *banner*, which is unfurled and held aloft to identify its bearer. Thus did David *HaMelech* say: נָתַתָּ לִּירֵאֶיךָ נֵּס לְהִתְנוֹסֵס, *You gave those who fear You a banner to raise themselves (Psalms* 60:6), to which *Rashi* comments: "You have tested us in many trying and oppressive situations in order to provide us with the opportunity לְהִתְנוֹסֵס, *to be proven* faithful in all circumstances."

7. This discourse was delivered in the mid-1980's before the Gorbachov regime relaxed Soviet restrictions on Jewish observance.

Prerequisites for Torah

✑ Rephidim

בַּחֹדֶשׁ הַשְּׁלִישִׁי לְצֵאת בְּנֵי יִשְׂרָאֵל מֵאֶרֶץ מִצְרַיִם בַּיּוֹם הַזֶּה בָּאוּ
מִדְבַּר סִינָי. וַיִּסְעוּ מֵרְפִידִים וַיָּבֹאוּ מִדְבַּר סִינַי וַיַּחֲנוּ בַּמִּדְבָּר וַיִּחַן
שָׁם יִשְׂרָאֵל נֶגֶד הָהָר.

*In the third month from the exodus of the Children of
Israel from the land of Egypt, on this day, they arrived
at the wilderness of Sinai. They journeyed from
Rephidim and arrived at the Wilderness of Sinai and
encamped in the Wilderness; and Israel encamped there
opposite the mountain (Sh'mos 19:2).*

The above verses present an obvious difficulty, notes *Ohr
HaChaim.* Why does the Torah first mention the arrival of the
Jews at Sinai and then state that to get there, they had journeyed from
Rephidim? Ostensibly, the order should have been reversed. That
Rephidim is mentioned *after* Sinai indicates that in the word רְפִידִים
lay a key to what was soon to be accomplished — *kabbalas haTorah,*
receiving of the Torah.

Rephidim was where Amalek attacked *B'nei Yisrael* soon after they
had crossed the Sea of Reeds. How could such an attack have occurred
so soon after their miraculous exodus? *Chazal* find the answer to this
in the word רְפִידִים:

מַאי לָשׁוֹן רְפִידִים? . . . שֶׁרִפּוּ עַצְמָן מִדִּבְרֵי תוֹרָה.
What does the term רְפִידִים *imply? . . . That they became
lax [*שֶׁרִיפּוּ*] in their Torah study (Sanhedrin 106a).*

When the Jews arrived at Sinai, they *journeyed from Rephidim*, meaning, they left this laxity behind and arrived at Sinai ready to dedicate themselves to Torah study with renewed fervor and desire. As *Chazal* expound (*Berachos* 36b), "Torah can endure only in one who kills himself over it"; i.e., in one who studies with genuine self-sacrifice. *Ameilus*, relentless diligence, is the key to success in plumbing the depths of Torah.

Ohr HaChaim sees this verse as alluding to two other prime prerequisites for *kabbalas haTorah*.

וַיַּחֲנוּ בַּמִּדְבָּר, *And they camped in the Wilderness* — "This alludes to humility, for Torah can endure only in a person who considers himself lowly and humble like a wilderness upon whom all can tread."

וַיִּחַן שָׁם יִשְׂרָאֵל נֶגֶד הָהָר, *And Israel encamped there opposite the mountain* — "like one man with one heart" (*Rashi* from *Mechilta*). *Ohr HaChaim* cites the verse, *A sword upon those who are alone and they shall become fools* (*Yirmiyahu* 50:36), to which *Chazal* state, "A sword upon the enemies of Torah scholars[1] who engage in Torah study alone [without study partners], and not only that, but they become foolish as well" (*Taanis* 7a). In the words of *Ohr HaChaim*, "They [Torah scholars] must associate with one another, sharpen one another and show respect for each other's opinions. It is to this that the Torah alludes in writing וַיִּחַן, *and Israel encamped*, in the singular (literally, *and he camped*), for they became like one person, and thus became fit to receive the Torah."

⇜§ Hillel

The relationship between Torah scholarship and humility can be seen from the incident which led to the appointment of Hillel the Elder as *Nasi* (Prince) of the Jewish people. Hillel had studied in *Eretz Yisrael* under the leaders of his generation, Shemaya and Avtalyon. Upon their deaths, Hillel returned to Babylonia. When he returned to the Holy Land many years later, the B'nei (sons of) Beseira were the leading Sages. Then, a halachic question arose.

---

1. A euphemism for the scholars themselves. It is common in the writings of *Chazal* not to refer directly to Israel, Torah scholars or the like in a statement that implies punishment.

The Torah commands that the Pesach offering be slaughtered on the afternoon of *Erev* Pesach. That year, *Erev* Pesach fell on Shabbos. The people came to ask the B'nei Beseira whether or not the offering could be brought on Shabbos. The B'nei Beseira did not know the answer. Hillel was summoned and he showed through Scriptural exegesis that the Pesach offering is brought even on Shabbos.

> *Immediately, they [the B'nei Beseira] sat him [Hillel] at the head and appointed him Nasi over them. He spent the entire day expounding upon the laws of Pesach. Hillel then proceeded to criticize them. "What brought about that I should ascend from Babylonia and become a Nasi over you? It was your indolence, for you did not serve the two leaders of the generation, Shemaya and Avtalyon."*
>
> *The people then put forth the following question to Hillel. "What if the slaughtering knife was not brought on Erev Shabbos?" [I.e., can it be carried through the streets on Shabbos?] Hillel said to them, "I have heard this law [from my teachers], but I have forgotten it. But let Israel be; if they are not prophets, they are children of prophets." The next day, the Sages observed that those who had chosen a lamb as their offering had transported the slaughtering knife by placing it in the animal's wool, while those who had chosen a kid had placed the knife between the kid's horns . . .*
>
> *R' Yehudah said in the name of Rav: Whoever displays pride, if he is wise, his wisdom will leave him . . . We see this from Hillel. Initially, he criticized them, then later said, "I have heard this law but I have forgotten it"* (Pesachim 66a-b).

Chazal consider Hillel the epitome of humility: "One should always be humble like Hillel . . ." (*Shabbos* 35a). In criticizing the B'nei Beseira, Hillel acted purely *lesheim Shamayim*, for the sake of Heaven. It was precisely because his humility was of such an exalted level that Hillel was faulted for what he told the B'nei Beseira. His criticism of them conveyed a feeling of superiority, though this was not his intent. Because of this slight error in a pride-related matter, Heaven caused Hillel to subsequently forget a *halachah*.

In fact, in this very incident, Hillel's humility does come to the fore. His appointment as *Nasi* had come about as a result of the B'nei Beseira not knowing a *halachah*. Now, *he* did not know a *halachah*. Hillel surely realized that his admission of having forgotten what his teachers had taught him might cause the Sages to reconsider his appointment. At the very least, his having forgotten the *halachah* so soon after his rebuke of the B'nei Besira placed him in a very embarrassing situation. Would it not have been easier for Hillel to simply respond, "Let Israel be; if they are not prophets . . ." without admitting, "I have heard this law, but I have forgotten it"?

His response indicates more than a passion for truth. Had he been stricken with the malady of pride, he would have found sufficient rationalization to conceal the truth of his mental lapse. Hillel, however, was the classic עָנָיו, *man of humility*. His entire being was dedicated toward serving his Creator; nothing else mattered. Personal considerations did not exist; at the moment of trial, Hillel asked himself one question, "How does Hashem want me to respond?" The answer, he knew, was to respond with pure, unadulterated truth.[2]

◈ R' Yitzchak Elchanan

A more recent example of relentless diligence in study combined with deep humility was seen in the person of Rabbi Yitzchak Elchanan Spector, the great Kovno *Rav*. The following anecdotes illustrate these qualities.

A certain *talmid chacham* was in awe of R' Yitzchak Elchanan's fluency in the *Choshen Mishpat* section of *Shulchan Aruch*. This

---

2. *Iyun Yaakov* notes that Hillel did not reprimand the B'nei Beseira until after he was appointed *Nasi*. Until that point, Hillel had thought that perhaps the B'nei Beseira were guilty of pursuing honor, and that Heaven had punished them for this by causing them to forget the law regarding the slaughtering of the *Pesach* offering on Shabbos. However, when the B'nei Beseira asked Hillel to serve as *Nasi* in their stead, it became clear that they were men of deep humility. Hillel then reasoned that their not having known the *halachah* could only have occurred because of their not having gleaned sufficiently from the wisdom of Shemaya and Avtalyon. Therefore, he rebuked them.

scholar set his mind to equaling the Kovno *Rav's* mastery of this work. Some time elapsed before the two met. The man wasted no time in drawing R' Yitzchak Elchanan into a *Choshen Mishpat*-related discussion. The discussion ended with the man feeling quite frustrated.

"Tell me, please," he asked R' Yitzchak Elchanan, "how did you acquire such thorough knowledge?"

R' Yitzchak Elchanan replied, "I always kept count of how many times I had reviewed *Choshen Mishpat* — until I had reviewed it one hundred and one times. Then I stopped counting."[3]

Another story involving the Kovno *Rav* centers around a town some distance from Kovno where a storm had begun to brew. The *rav* of that town had issued a *p'sak* which clearly contradicted the opinion of the *Shach*, one of the primary commentators to *Choshen Mishpat*. It seems that in issuing his *p'sak*, the *rav* had simply overlooked the words of the *Shach*. R' Yitzchak Elchanan learned of what had happened and was quite concerned for the *rav's* prestige. The matter would surely cause the *rav* great embarrassment and might even cost him his position. R' Yitzchak Elchanan acted quickly. He immediately wrote a letter to the town's community leaders stating his concurrence with the *rav's* erroneous ruling. Later, R' Yitzchak Elchanan sent a telegram, which arrived ahead of the letter, in which he stated that he was retracting his original *p'sak* because it contradicted the opinion of the *Shach* which he had overlooked!

R' Yitzchak Elchanan was recognized as the *posek hador*, leading halachic authority, in all of Lithuania, White Russia and beyond. Yet, he was not concerned that such a glaring "omission" on his part might harm his own prestige. He *was* concerned, however, for the

---

3. HaRav Segal noted that success in Torah study cannot be achieved through diligence alone. One cannot succeed in his learning without a system of *chazarah*, review. As *Chazal* state, "Whoever learns but fails to review is like one who sows but fails to reap" (*Yalkut Shimoni, Yehoshua* 1:6). Human nature, however, is to pursue new knowledge rather than review what one has already learned. A *ben Torah* must overcome this natural tendency and accord *chazarah* its proper due.

Sefer Menuchah U'Kedushah writes, "I have heard that the pious one, the *Gra* [the *Vilna Gaon*] would submit a prospective *talmid* to the following test: He would instruct him to review a given matter many times. If the more he reviewed, the more its love grew in his heart, [inspiring him] to continue to review it without interruption — with this he found favor in his [the *Gaon's*] eyes to be accepted as his disciple."

other *rav's* prestige and went to great lengths to ensure that it remained untainted. What humility!

As *Ohr HaChaim* teaches, humility is a prime ingredient in successful Torah study. There is no doubt that R' Yitzchak Elchanan's incredible humility was a prime factor in his becoming a giant of his generation.

May we merit to becoming fitting receptacles to receive the Torah and together, like one man with one heart, diligently pursue its study.

The Torah Personality

Torah is even greater than priesthood or royalty; for royalty is acquired along with thirty prerogatives, and the priesthood with twenty-four gifts, but the Torah is acquired by means of forty-eight qualities. . .(Avos 6:6).

◈ The Camp in the Wilderness

The arrangement of the Jews' encampment in the Wilderness was Divinely ordained. *Every man shall encamp by his own banner with the sign [i.e. emblem] of their father's house (Bamidbar 2:2).* The *Midrash* relates that the encampment of the Jews according to their *degalim,* tribal banners, paralleled the arrangement of the Heavenly entourage which accompanied the *Shechinah* as it descended upon Mount Sinai when the Torah was given:

> *When HaKadosh Baruch Hu revealed Himself at Mount Sinai, tens of thousands of angels descended with Him, as it is written, "The entourage of God is twice ten thousand, thousands of angels; my Lord is among them, at Sinai in holiness" [Tehillim 68:18]. All the angels were grouped under degalim. . .When Israel saw this arrangement, it craved for the same: "If only we were grouped under degalim as they are!"*
>
> *. . .Said HaKadosh Baruch Hu, "You crave to be grouped under degalim? By your lives, I shall fulfill*

*your wish".. .HaKadosh Baruch Hu immediately in-
formed them through Moshe, "Go and group them
according to degalim as they desire" (Bamidbar Rabbah 2:3).*

Tiferes Tzion explains that with the level of prophecy which they
had been granted in order to receive the Torah, the Jews perceived the
deep spiritual significance which the angels' arrangement represented. The *degalim* were indicative of the Heavenly entourage's
sanctity and attachment to Hashem. It was this sanctity and
attachment for which the Jews yearned.

Klal Yisrael, in its heightened spiritual state at that moment in
history, was not satisfied with the incredible levels of sanctity and
dveikus, attachment to Hashem, that it had already attained. It
wanted more. It strove to reach the heights of the Heavenly angels.

In light of the above, the following *Midrash* requires explanation:

*When HaKadosh Baruch Hu instructed Moshe to
group the Jews according to degalim as they desired,
Moshe became concerned. He said, "Now, strife will be
found among the Tribes! If I will tell the tribe of
Yehudah to camp in the east, and they respond, 'This
does not suit me; I wish to camp in the south,' — and so
[may occur] with Reuven, Ephraim, or any other tribe
— .. .what will I do?"*

*HaKadosh Baruch Hu responded, "What is your
concern? They do not need you [to instruct them how to
camp], for they know on their own where to dwell. In
their hands is a document from their forefather
Yaakov, instructing them how to arrange the degalim; I
tell them nothing new... As they bore him [Yaakov,
after his death] and surrounded his bier, so will they
camp around the Mishkan" (ibid. §3).[1]*

1. The *Midrash* goes on to relate (see *Rashi* to *Bereishis* 50:13) that before his death,
Yaakov instructed his sons that only they, and not their sons, were to carry his bier
when it would be transported to *Eretz Yisrael* for interment in the Cave of
Machpelah. He further instructed them as to how they would be positioned around
his bier: Yehudah, Yissachar and Zevulun on the east; Reuven, Shimon and Gad on
the south; Ephraim, Menasheh and Binyamin on the west; and Dan, Asher and
Naftali on the north. Yaakov said, "Levi shall not carry my bier, since his

Ostensibly, Moshe's fears seem difficult to understand. Would a nation of prophets, who perceived the *Shechinah* and its entourage of angels *and aspired to the spiritual level of those angels,* lower themselves to bicker over where to set up camp? Would those whose hearts and souls were directed Heavenward engage in such strife?

We are forced to say that, yes, even prophets who aspire to ever loftier heights are capable of lowering themselves to the depths of strife. Otherwise, Moshe *Rabbeinu's* fears would have been unfounded. The lesson here is vital: A person can be soaring spiritually, involved in the most sacred endeavors, and yearning for further spiritual growth — while *midos ra'os,* destructive traits, lay dormant in his soul waiting for an opportunity to reveal themselves. No matter how great a person's spiritual achievements, he must forever be alert to the dangers inherent in such traits.

⋖ Yeravam ben Nevat

The case of Yeravam ben Nevat is a classic illustration of how *midos ra'os* can destroy the greatest of men. Yeravam was a great scholar who was appointed to office by Shlomo *HaMelech*, and became recognized as a leader when he daringly criticized the king for his wrongdoing.[2] The depths of Yeravam's scholarship is described in the following Aggadic teaching:

> And it was at that time that Yeravam left Jerusalem. The prophet Achiyah of Shiloh met him on the road; he [Achiyah] was wearing a new garment, and they were alone in the field (I Melachim 11:29).
>
> What is meant by "a new garment"? R' Nachman said: Like a new garment. Just as a new garment has no

---

descendants are destined to carry the holy Ark [and it is therefore not proper for him to carry a bier containing human remains]. Yosef shall not carry it because he is a ruler [and must be accorded special respect]. Menasheh and Ephraim [the sons of Yosef] shall take their places." The *Midrash* concludes that this is the intent of the verse (*Bamidbar* 2:2) which speaks of the Jews encamping according to their אתת, *signs;* i.e., the symbolic precedent which had been established at the time of Yaakov's death.

2. See below.

imperfection, so did the Torah of Yeravam have no imperfection. Alternatively: "A new garment" — that they [Achiyah and Yeravam] propounded new Torah insights, the likes of which no one had ever heard.

"And they were alone in the field" — R' Yehudah said in the name of Rav: That all Torah scholars were like blades of grass in comparison to them. Others say: That all Torah interpretations were revealed to them like an open field (Sanhedrin 102a).

During that encounter, Achiyah took hold of his garment and ripped it into twelve pieces. He then said to Yeravam, "Take for yourself ten pieces, for so says Hashem, the God of Israel: 'I shall tear the kingdom away from Shlomo and I shall give you ten of the Tribes' " (I Melachim 11:31).

It was after Shlomo's death that the kingdom was split between his son Rechavam and Yeravam, with Yeravam becoming king over all the Tribes except for Yehudah and Binyamin, as Achiyah had prophesied. Soon after ascending the throne, Yeravam became concerned regarding the forthcoming Succos pilgrimage to Jerusalem, when all Jewish males are required to offer sacrifices in the *Beis HaMikdash*, as required by the Torah. Yeravam said to himself:

Now the kingdom will return to the House of David...the hearts of the people will return to their master, to Rechavam, King of Yehudah. And they will kill me and return to Rechavam...(ibid. 12:26-27).

As the Gemara (*Sanhedrin* 102b) explains, it was forbidden for anyone to sit in the Temple courtyard, save for kings of the Davidic dynasty. This meant that only Rechavam and not Yeravam would be permitted to sit there before the multitudes on Succos. Yeravam reasoned, "If they see Rechavam sitting while I am standing, they will say, 'This one [Rechavam] is the king and this one [Yeravam] is his servant'; and if I sit, then I will be considered a rebel against the monarchy and they will kill me..."(*ibid.*).

After conferring with his advisors, Yeravam decided upon the following solution: At opposite extremities of his kingdom, he would set up places of worship as substitutes for the House of Hashem in

Jerusalem. At each of these sites, a golden calf would be placed.[3] No longer would the Ten Tribes have to enter the land of the other kingdom, which, Yeravam claimed, had been rejected by Hashem. Yeravam went so far as to declare a festival on the fifteenth of the eighth month, in place of Succos, which falls on the fifteenth of the seventh month!

The presence of the golden calves eventually led to the proliferation of various forms of idolatry among the Tribes. Until their exile by King Sancheriv of Assyria, the Ten Tribes never succeeded in ridding their land of idolatry. Thus does the prophet write: "And Yeravam led Israel astray from the ways of Hashem and caused them to sin grievously" (II Melachim 17:21). To the verse (Mishlei 28:24), He is a comrade of the man of corruption, Chazal comment, "He is a comrade to Yeravam ben Nevat who corrupted Israel so that they strayed from Hashem and sinned grievously" (Berachos 35b).

In informing Yeravam that he would ascend the throne, Achiyah had told him that the Ten Tribes would be torn from the Davidic monarchy because of the sins of Shlomo's wives, who turned to idol worship in Shlomo's old age. Yet this lesson did not prevent Yeravam from leading his entire kingdom into the quagmire of idol worship. Moreover, the Gemara relates that Yeravam earned the throne for his having dared to rebuke the king when Shlomo closed the wide breaches in the walls of Jerusalem which his father, David, had made. The purpose of these breaches was to allow the Jews easy access to the Holy City during Festival pilgrimages (see I Melachim 11:27). Yet Yeravam himself perpetrated the most heinous acts to prevent his people from making such pilgrimages.

This was a man whose Torah scholarship was virtually incomparable, a man who had been promised by Hashem, And it will come to pass, that if you will heed all that I command you, and you will go in My ways, and you will do that which is just in My eyes. . .then I will

---

3. Yeravam convinced the people that just as Jerusalem was no longer their capital, so had the Beis HaMikdash ceased to be their sanctuary. It was, therefore, necessary to build sanctuaries in the land of the Ten Tribes. In his grand plan, the golden calves would serve as intermediaries in bringing the Shechinah to rest at these sites (Radak). [This was the original purpose of the Golden Calf in the Wilderness — see Ramban to Sh'mos 32:4.]

be with you and I will build for you an enduring house, as I built for David, and I shall give Israel to you (ibid. v. 38).

Where did Yeravam go wrong?

∽§ The Source

R' Nachman said: Yeravam's arrogance drove him from this world (Sanhedrin 101b).

Maharsha (ibid.) explains how arrogance caused Yeravam to err time and again. Earlier, the Gemara related: R' Yochanan said, In what merit did Yeravam accede to the throne? For he rebuked Shlomo [for the sake of Heaven]. And why was he punished? Because he rebuked him in public.

Maharsha questions this, for, as cited above, Scripture states clearly that Yeravam was punished for having caused his brethren to embrace heathen gods. Maharsha then explains:

It is as the Sages have stated, "One sin leads to another sin." Were it not for Yeravam's arrogance which caused him to rebel against the House of David [by publicly rebuking the king], he would not have come to lead Israel astray through idol worship.

Maharsha offers another compelling insight. As mentioned above, Yeravam set up two golden calves in his territory to provide his people with 'alternatives' to the Beis HaMikdash in Jerusalem. As mentioned above, Yeravam feared that his appearance in the Temple courtyard would place him in a tenuous position. "They will say, 'This is the king and this is his servant...' " Fear of being killed prevented him from attempting to sit in the Temple courtyard in the way of a Davidic king. This is astounding, for should not another factor — namely, the Torah — have prevented Yeravam from attempting this?! As mentioned above, the Halachah as transmitted to Moshe Rabbeinu at Sinai forbids anyone but kings of the Davidic dynasty from sitting in the courtyard. Why did Yeravam, the talmid chacham par excellence, not base his decision on Halachah rather than fear of incurring the people's wrath? Maharsha explains: "Due to his arrogance, he was not concerned with this sin; rather, he was concerned only that they might kill him."

And ultimately, it was Yeravam's arrogance that caused him to reject the greatest opportunity of all — to dwell eternally in the company of the *Shechinah*:

> *The Holy One, Blessed is He, seized Yeravam by his cloak and told him, "Repent, and then I and you and [David] the son of Yishai will stroll together in the Garden of Eden."*
>
> *Yeravam asked, "Who will be first [i.e. who will be the more prominent one]?"*
>
> *Hashem responded, "The son of Yishai."*
>
> *Said Yeravam, "If so, I do not want it." (Sanhedrin 102a).*

The above dialogue is incredible. After having sinned and caused others to sin, Yeravam is urged by Hashem to mend his ways and reclaim his share in the World to Come. How eternally grateful he should have been! How could he dare to ask, "Who will be first?" and how could he reject Hashem's offer when the answer he received was not to his liking?

> *R' Elazar HaKapar says: Jealousy, lust and a desire for honor remove a man from the world (Avos 4:28).*

A person can know the entire Torah in all its breadth and depth. He can perform awesome deeds of righteousness for the sake of Heaven. He can aspire to attain lofty heights of spiritual attachment. He can attain all of the above — and still sink into the abyss of sin and self-destruction if he will not cleanse his soul of *midos ra'os*. A thirst for honor, a lust for wealth, or any other negative yearning, can destroy even the greatest of men.[4]

Let no one delude himself into thinking that Yeravam's case was one of a kind and is not relevant to us. It is. We are all descendants of

---

4. R' Chaim Shmulevitz (*Sichos Mussar*) is of the opinion that originally Yeravam, not David, was to be the more prominent one. This is implied by the words, "I *and you* and the son of Yishai will stroll together." However, so obsessed was Yeravam with a desire for honor that he wanted his preeminence spelled out more clearly. Because of this incredible display of arrogance, Yeravam's place was switched with David's.

Adam who was created from the dust of the earth. We are human and have human failings — and unless we seek to refine those failings, we risk falling prey to them.

There is only one sure method for subduing one's *yetzer hara* — the study of *mussar*. We are not speaking here of works which offer lengthy expositions and novellae on the subject of ethics. These works serve a purpose, but their study falls in the realm of general Torah study, not *mussar* study. True *mussar* study must be with feeling; it must touch the far recesses of one's soul so that he will be spiritually ready when the moment of trial arrives. Classic works such as *Mesilas Yesharim* and *Sha'arei Teshuvah* are excellent *mussar* texts. When studying *mussar*, one should employ the proven method of repeating to himself many times Scriptural verses and Talmudic maxims which apply to a given character trait. For example, one who wishes to quell a desire for honor should repeat to himself many times the verse, תּוֹעֲבַת ה' כָּל גְּבַהּ לֵב, *Hashem despises all those of arrogant heart* (*Mishlei* 16:5). This will make a lasting impression on the soul of the student, so that he will flee from honor rather than foolishly pursue it.

As with everything in life, one needs *siyata diShmaya*, Heavenly assistance, to perfect his character. One should *daven* that he be granted such help and it will surely be forthcoming. The same applies to other areas of service to Hashem. If one has difficulty concentrating during *tefillah*, then he should pray with sincerity, "Ribono shel Olam! I find it hard to *daven* with proper *kavanah*. Please help me have *kavanah*."

Hashem calls out to each and every one of us, "Open for Me [in your heart] an opening like the eye of a needle and I will open for you an opening like that of a huge hall." Let us strive to do our share and, with *siyata diShmaya*, we will succeed.

Day of Reflection

⊷§ Cause and Effect

Rambam (*Hilchos Ta'anios* 5:1-4, based on *Mishnah Ta'anis* 4:6) writes:

> There are days when all Israel fasts because of the misfortunes that occurred then, in order to awaken the hearts and to open the ways of repentance. Let this be a reminder of our evil deeds and our forefathers' deeds that were like our present deeds until they caused those misfortunes for them and for us. For through the recollection of these matters, we will repent to improve, as Scripture states (*Vayikra* 26:40): "And they shall confess their transgression and the transgression of their fathers."

Rambam goes on to list the Four Fasts and the events which occurred on those days.[1]

---

1. *Rambam* continues:

"These days are:

"The third of Tishrei, on which Gedaliah ben Achikam was killed and [therefore] the remaining ember of Israel [in their land] was extinguished, thus bringing about the completion of their exile.

"The tenth of Teves, when the wicked King Nebuchadnezzar laid siege to Jerusalem, bringing it to dire straits and distress.

"Five [tragic] events occurred on the Seventeenth of Tammuz: The Tablets were broken; the *Tamid* offering was discontinued in the days of the First Temple; the walls of Jerusalem were breached in the days of the Second Temple; the wicked

At the very opening of *Hilchos Ta'anios, Rambam* writes: "It is a positive Scriptural commandment to cry out and to sound trumpets[2] for any misfortune that comes upon the community ... This is the way of *teshuvah*, that when a misfortune comes and the people cry out over it and sound the trumpets, they come to the realization that it is because of their wicked deeds that this has happened to them, as it is written, *Your sins have turned these [blessings] away [from you], your iniquities have withheld the good from you* " (*Yirmiyahu* 5:25).

When one is confronted with adversity, it is natural to seek to remove its cause. When the Jewish people find themselves in dire straits, they dare not attribute their troubles to ordinary cause and effect. Everything that happens to us is through *Hashgachas Hashem*, Divine Providence; a specific chain of cause and effect is merely one of countless methods at Heaven's disposal for bringing about a desired result. The true cause of communal troubles is sin and the way to rid ourselves of such troubles is *teshuvah*.

It would seem that a person who attributes misfortune to natural causes, rather than Divine Providence, is lacking belief in a most fundamental principle of Judaism. As *Ramban* writes (*Sh'mos* 12:16), "... And from the great and well-known miracles, one comes to recognize the hidden miracles, which are the foundation of the entire Torah. For a man has no share in the Torah of Moshe *Rabbeinu* until he believes that all our happenings and occurrences are miraculous — there is nothing natural in them at all."

Rambam, however, seems to take a different view of the man who attributes events and occurrences to natural factors. In his opening to *Hilchos Ta'anios* (part of which was cited above), he writes:

Apostumos burned the Torah, and placed an idolatrous image in the Temple.

"Five [tragic] events occurred on Tishah B'Av: It was decreed upon Israel in the Wilderness that it [i.e. that generation] should not enter the Land [of Israel]; the First and Second Temples were destroyed; and a great city named Betar was conquered. In that city were tens of thousands of Jews with a great king whom all of Israel and its Sages thought was the Messianic king. The city fell to the Romans and all its inhabitants were killed; it was a catastrophe akin to the Temple's destruction.

"And on this day that was destined for punishment, the wicked Turnus Rufus plowed the [Second] Temple site and its environs, in fulfillment of the verse, *Zion will be plowed like a field* (Jeremiah 26:18)."

2. See *Bamidbar* 10:9.

> *But if they do not cry out and do not sound the shofar,*
> *but say, "This happened to us because of natural causes,*
> *and this distress occurred coincidentally," this is the*
> *way of cruelty and causes them to adhere to their evil*
> *deeds, and this will cause the accumulation of further*
> *distress . . .*

Rambam does not describe such an attitude as heretical, or foolish. He calls it *cruel.* Why?

Surely, *Rambam* does not dispute *Ramban's* words that "a man has no share in the Torah of Moshe *Rabbeinu* until he believes that all our happenings and occurrences are miraculous . . ." This, as we have already stated, is a fundamental principle of Judaism. *Rambam*, however, is teaching us that the *primary* sin of one who denies this principle is one of *bein adam l'chaveiro*, between man and his fellow. For such an attitude can only lead to further retribution, as *Rambam* goes on to demonstrate from a passage in the Torah:

> *"Yet you [still] behave casually with Me! Then I will*
> *behave toward you with a fury of casualness" (Vayikra*
> *26:23-24). This means: When I bring upon you distress*
> *in order to induce you to repent, if you say that it is*
> *casual [i.e., coincidental], I will multiply upon you a fury*
> *because of that casualness of yours (Hilchos Ta'anios*
> *1:3).*

A Jew must realize that his attitude towards life does not affect only himself; the actions and attitudes of every Jew have a great bearing on the fortunes and future of the entire Jewish people. As the *Gemara* (*Kiddushin* 40b) states:

> *A person should always perceive himself as though he*
> *were half guilty and half meritorious. If he performs one*
> *mitzvah, he has tipped the balance for himself toward*
> *the side of merit. If he commits a single trans-*
> *gression, woe to him — for he has tipped the balance for*
> *himself toward the side of guilt, as it is written, "And one*
> *sin forfeits much good" (Koheles 9:18).*
> *. . . R' Elazar ben R' Shimon says: . . . The world is*
> *judged on the basis of the majority of its inhabitants, and*

*the individual is based on the majority of his deeds. If he
performed a single mitzvah, he is fortunate — for he has
tipped the balance for himself and for the entire world
toward the side of merit. But if he committed a single
transgression, woe to him — for he has tipped the balance for himself and for the entire world toward the side
of guilt . . .*

Thus does *Rambam* define a complacent attitude toward distress
and misfortune as *cruel.*

◄§ Measure for Measure

The *Midrash* (*Bereishis Rabbah* 60:2) writes that Divine *chesed*,
kindness, is shown to the world in merit of Avraham *Avinu*, the
paragon of *chesed*. One man's actions initiated a flow of Divine kindness that continues uninterrupted to this day. A Jew must be ever
cognizant of the weight that his actions carry in Heaven. In the words
of the *Chofetz Chaim* (*Sha'ar HaZechirah* Ch. 2), "It is well known
that the way in which a person conducts himself in this world awakens a corresponding conduct from Above, each attribute as it applies.
If one overlooks the hurt caused him by others [מַעֲבִיר עַל מִידוֹתָיו] and
he acts toward others with kindness and compassion, then he awakens
the attribute of compassion in Heaven and *HaKadosh Baruch Hu* will
show the entire world compassion in his
merit. *The fruits of man's mouth will satiate his soul*[3] — he will merit
that Hashem will have mercy upon him as well and remove his sins,
as they [*Chazal*] have stated, 'Whoever is compassionate towards
others, Heaven will be compassionate towards him' (*Shabbos* 151b);
'Whoever refrains from exacting his measure [of retribution for the
wrong caused him], will have all his sins removed' " (*Yoma* 23a).

"Jerusalem was destroyed only because its inhabitants decided
matters exactly according to Torah law" (*Bava Metzia* 30b). The
Gemara goes on to explain: "They limited their decisions to the letter
of the law of the Torah and did not go beyond the letter of the law."
The generation of the Destruction was unforgiving; there was no

---

3. Paraphrased from *Mishlei* 18:20.

room for understanding or compromise. Each man sought to extract from his fellow whatever the law allowed. *HaKadosh Baruch Hu* judged them accordingly. There was no room for leniency; strict justice was their fate.

If we sincerely desire to bring this *galus* to an end, we must strive to acquire the sterling quality of being מַעֲבִיר עַל מִידוֹתָיו, *refraining from exacting one's [rightful] measure*. And let us act stringently with regard to the commandment of וְאָהַבְתָּ לְרֵעֲךָ כָּמוֹךָ, *love your neighbor as yourself* (*Vayikra* 19:18). Heaven will surely respond accordingly.

◈§ The Key

I n the first blessing of *Shemoneh Esrei*, we say:

וְזוֹכֵר חַסְדֵי אָבוֹת, וּמֵבִיא גוֹאֵל לִבְנֵי בְנֵיהֶם לְמַעַן שְׁמוֹ בְּאַהֲבָה.
[Blessed are You, Hashem . . .]Who recalls the kindness of the Patriarchs and brings a Redeemer to their children's children, for His Name's sake, with love.

The Patriarchs were men of extraordinary faith, who overcame trial upon trial with love and devotion. Yet, it is their kindness that we mention in this blessing, for it is their *bein adam l'chaveiro*, interaction with their fellow men, that will ultimately bring about the Redemption.

The importance of *bein adam l'chaveiro* in the scheme of Jewry's fate and fortunes need not be elaborated upon. The armies of the wicked King Achav were victorious in battle in merit of the brotherhood which existed among them, while the armies of the righteous King Shaul suffered defeat because they lacked true brotherhood (*Devarim Rabbah* 4:5).

The *Haftarah* of Yom Kippur morning focuses on the purpose of fasting and the proper manner of *teshuvah*.

> [The people ask,] "Why did You not see when we fasted? We afflicted ourselves but You ignored it!"
> [And Hashem answers,] "Because on your fast day you sought out personal desires and you oppressed all

whom you *aggrieved! Because you fast with grievance and strife, and strike with a wicked fist; you do not fast as befits this day, to make your voice heard above. Can such be the fast I choose, a day when man merely afflicts himself? Can it be bowing his head like a bulrush and making a mattress of sackcloth and ashes? Do you call this a fast and a day of favor to Hashem?*

"Surely, this is the fast I choose: open the bonds of wickedness, dissolve the groups that pervert [justice], let the oppressed go free and annul all perverted [justice]. Surely you should divide your bread with the hungry, and bring the moaning poor to your home; when you see the naked, cover him; and do not ignore your kin.

"Then your light will burst forth like the dawn and your healing will speedily sprout; then your righteous deed will precede you and the glory of Hashem will gather you in. Then you will call and Hashem will respond, you will cry out and He will say, 'Here I am!' — if you remove from your midst perversion, finger-pointing and evil speech" (Yeshayahu 58:3-9).

Tishah B'Av, the day on which both the First and Second *Batei Mikash* were destroyed, is a day for reflection and introspection. It is imperative that on this day we embark on the path of *teshuvah*, and at the same time, involve ourselves in the needs of our fellow Jews, so that Hashem will hearken to our cries and restore us to our land.

The Call of the Shofar

⋄§ A Time to Improve

Imagine yourself looking out the window of an airplane high above the ground below. The buildings, trees, cars — everything that you see — seem so small and insignificant.

As we sit in *shul* prior to the blowing of the *shofar* on Rosh Hashanah, every one of us rises high above the vanities of everyday life and finds himself in a totally different world. We sense the spirituality of the moment and this impels us to focus on our purpose in this world. The earthly desires which are so enticing at the moment of trial are now perceived as trivial and lacking substance — which, indeed, they are.

On this day, we ponder our spiritual successes and failures of the past year. Hashem has tested each of us in a variety of ways. One can rest assured that every effort he expended in his struggles with his *yetzer hara* is an immeasurable source of merit. And what of our failures? This awesome Day of Judgment is a time when we can and must strive for improvement. The *shofar* blasts themselves inspire us toward this end. As *Rambam* writes:

> Although the blowing of the shofar on Rosh Hashanah is a Scriptural decree [and must therefore be observed whether or not one knows the reason for it], there is an allusion to it: "Awake, O sleepers, from your sleep! Arouse yourselves, O slumberers, from your slumber! Scrutinize your deeds! Return with contrition! Remember your Creator! Those of you who forget the truth in

the futilities of the times and let your years elapse in futility and emptiness...peer into your souls, improve your ways and your deeds. Each of you should abandon his evil way and his bad thoughts" (Hilchos Teshuvah 3:4).

On Rosh Hashanah, one should be forever cognizant of what is transpiring Above ... As *Rambam* writes in that same chapter:

Just as a person's merits and sins are weighed at the time of his death, so, too, are the merits and sins of all who enter this world weighed each year on Rosh Hashanah. One who is found to be righteous is sealed for life. One who is deemed wicked is sealed for death. As for one who is evenly balanced [between good and bad deeds], his fate is suspended until Yom Kippur. If he repents he is sealed for life and if not he is sealed for death (§3).

⋖§ The Essentials of Teshuvah

As is evident from the texts of the Rosh Hashanah *tefillos*, we do not enumerate our sins on this day. Nevertheless, to experience this awesome day without contemplating *teshuvah* is to overlook the very essence of the Days of Awe. As we say in *Mussaf*, "*Teshuvah, tefillah* and *tzedakah* remove the evil of the decree."

True *teshuvah* is comprised of two essential components: חֲרָטָה, *remorse over the past* and עֲזִיבַת הַחֵטְא, *giving up the sin [for the future]*.[1] With חֲרָטָה, one totally rejects the sinful deeds that he has committed. As *Rabbeinu Yonah* puts it (*Sha'arei Teshuvah* 1:10), the penitent should reflect, "What have I done? How did it happen that the fear of God was not before my eyes and that I did not fear the [Torah's] reproofs against sin and [its warnings of] terrible punishments? I did not have mercy on my own body, my eyes did not take pity to avoid bringing destruction upon it — all for a moment of earthly pleasure.

---

1. The commentators agree that וִדּוּי, *confession*, falls under the category of חֲרָטָה. In fact, וִדּוּי is the only aspect of *teshuvah* that is specifically mentioned in the Torah.

". . .An ox knows its owner, a donkey its trough,[2] but I did not know [my Creator], I did not perceive; rather, I acted as if I had freed my soul from its Master. I tasted [what I perceived as] my honey, thereby ignoring my end; I robbed and extorted, I trampled upon the poor, and I did not remember the day of death when my soul will leave behind nothing but my corpse and its earth."

Regarding עֲזִיבַת הַחֵטְא, *giving up the sin [for the future], Rabbeinu Yonah* (ibid. §11) writes that one "abandons his wicked ways and resolves with all his heart that he will never again return to this path." *Rambam* writes the following: "And how does one repent? A sinner should abandon his sinfulness, banish it from his thoughts and conclude in his heart that he will never commit such acts again, as it says, *Let the wicked man abandon his way . . . (Yeshayahu* 55:7) . . . [Let him do all this to such a degree that] the Knower of Secrets will bear witness that he will never repeat the sin in question, as it says: *Take with you words and return to Hashem. Say unto Him . . . [Bear witness for us that] we shall no longer refer to our handiwork as our god (Hoshea* 14:3-4). And he must also confess with his lips and declare those things that he has concluded in his heart" *(Hilchos Teshuvah* 2:2).

❧ Three Resolutions

Our ultimate goal should be to fulfill the Torah in its entirety. However, this cannot be accomplished overnight. Moreover, if we set our goals too high, we are likely to fail. The proper way of self-improvement is step by step. I suggest that all of us accept upon ourselves the following three *kabbalos*, resolutions (בְּלִי נֶדֶר) as a first step:

1) To strive to strengthen our Torah study both qualitatively and quantitatively.

Let us begin by increasing our daily Torah study by five minutes.[3] One cannot imagine the impact that is made in Heaven when one sits down to study for five additional minutes in order to fulfill a

---

2. From *Yeshayahu* 1:3.
3. HaRav Segal was addressing the students of his yeshivah, who are engaged in the full-time study of Torah.

resolution that he undertook on Rosh Hashanah. This seemingly insignificant act is a demonstration that one is translating his thoughts of self-improvement into action. And of course this is only a beginning.

2) Our *kabbalos* must include matters of *bein adam l'chaveiro*, between man and his fellow. *Baruch Hashem*, our generation is one in which *chesed* abounds, but we cannot be content with this alone. It is imperative that each of us strives to improve his *midos*, particularly that of being מַעֲבִיר עַל מִידוֹתָיו, *refraining from exacting one's [rightful] measure* (i.e., *one who overlooks the hurt caused him*). *Chazal* (*Rosh Hashanah* 17a) have taught that one who acquires this trait will have all his sins forgiven. *Rashi* explains the term מַעֲבִיר עַל מִידוֹתָיו to mean that one refrains from 'measuring out' (מִדָּה = measure) a corresponding response to those who have caused him hurt. For this, says *Rashi*, "the Attribute of Justice [responds in kind] by not scrutinizing this person's deeds; rather, it lets him be." Regarding development of this attribute, *Rabbeinu Yonah* (*Sha'arei Teshuvah* 1:28) comments: "This is an extremely noteworthy pathway of hope [for gaining atonement], as it is written, *Let him put his mouth to the dust — there may be hope. Let one offer his cheek to the one who smites him, let him be filled with disgrace*" (*Eichah* 3:29-30).

Someone related to me that he once visited the *Chofetz Chaim* and found him crying. When asked what was wrong, the *Chofetz Chaim* replied, "*Chazal* have taught that one who is מַעֲבִיר עַל מִידוֹתָיו will have all his sins forgiven. I, however, do not even have the opportunity to be worthy of this reward, for no one ever causes me the slightest bit of hurt!"

It is unfortunate that many do not share the *Chofetz Chaim's* attitude. How often do minor infractions or slights erupt into full-scale disputes! Using the *Chofetz Chaim's* approach, one should view every personal slight as an opportunity to acquire the precious attribute of מַעֲבִיר עַל מִידוֹתָיו and its reward. Then, he will grow spiritually through such occurrences, rather than becoming ensnared in the net of hatred and strife.

3) Our final *kabbalah* for the present should be to increase our zealousness in *shemiras halashon*, guarding one's tongue. Let us all accept upon ourselves to follow the worldwide calendar schedule

which calls for daily study of two *halachos* in *Sefer Chofetz Chaim* and one page in *Sefer Shemiras HaLashon*. Such daily study will make us knowledgeable in this all-important area of *Halachah* and will leave us with the necessary awareness to refrain from forbidden speech. Once *shemiras halashon* becomes a matter of habit, the battle has been won.

Ask yourself: Why is it that Jews the world over refrain from talking during the entire *Mussaf* of Rosh Hashanah — a period of some two hours or more? The answer is training. Children are taught from their early youth than one does not speak from the time the blessings on the *shofar* are said until after the last *shofar* blast has been sounded. It is this training that makes refraining from speech so easy during *Mussaf*. Similarly, if we will train ourselves not to speak that which is halachically forbidden, then the matter of *shemiras halashon* will not be difficult.

৵§ The Guarantee

The *kabbalos* that we have accepted are certainly a great source of merit in this season of judgment. However, there is another matter that must be addressed, upon which all our *kabbalos* hinge.

A loan often requires one or more guarantors who ensure that, one way or another, the loan will be repaid. In a similar sense, when we stand before the *Ribono shel Olam* on Rosh Hashanah, hopeful that our *kabbalos* will tip the scale in our favor, we must provide some sort of guarantee that we will follow through on our resolutions. That guarantee is the study of *mussar*. Only through daily *mussar* study can one truly refine himself and climb the ladder of spiritual improvement. With *mussar* study, we can rest assured that our *kabbalos* are only a portent of greater things to come.

In merit of our *teshuvah*, may all the ill be granted a speedy recovery, may the childless be blessed with children, may those who seek to marry find their predestined match, and may everyone merit the particular salvation that he or she needs. May the Jewish Nation merit its collective salvation with the coming of *Mashiach*, speedily and in our time.

"Call Him When He is Near"

⋗ The Power of Our Deeds

"**D**uring the *Aseres Yemei Teshuvah* (Ten Days of Repentance), the heart of one who fears Hashem should tremble, when he realizes that his every deed is being recorded" (*Sha'arei Teshuvah* 2:14).

When a person is preparing to stand trial before an earthly court, he is totally preoccupied with the impending judgment. His daily routine is altered, his work is interrupted or put aside entirely as he seeks ways to achieve a favorable verdict. Surely, then, when a person is on trial before the King of kings, and his fate for the year to come hangs in the balance, he should interrupt his normal routine and set aside time each day to ponder his ways. Moreover, the prophet's words (*Yeshayahu* 58:6), *Seek Hashem when He can be found; call Him when He is near*, refer to the *Aseres Yemei Teshuvah* when Hashem is most favorably disposed toward His people and awaits our return through the *teshuvah* process (*Rosh Hashanah* 18a).

As we engage in introspection, it is important that we have a proper understanding of the power inherent in a Jew's every deed.

The *Mishnah* states (*Avos* 2:1):

דַּע מַה לְמַעְלָה מִמְּךְ — עַיִן רוֹאָה, וְאוֹזֶן שׁוֹמַעַת, וְכָל מַעֲשֶׂיךְ בַּסֵּפֶר נִכְתָּבִים.

Know what is above you — a watchful Eye, an attentive Ear and all your deeds are recorded in a book.

R' Chaim of Volozhin offers an original interpretation of this dictum: דע — *Know*, מה לְמַעְלָה — *that whatever occurs Above*, מִמְּךָ — *is your doing*. The words and deeds of every Jew have a profound impact in the Upper Spheres. Each *mitzvah* that a Jew performs achieves a degree of תִּקוּן, *perfection*, Above, while each sin effects a פְּגַם, *blemish*, in the Upper Worlds. Thus, the effect of a Jew's deeds reach far beyond the limits of his soul. The fate of all that exists is in our hands in a very real sense.

כִּי אֶת כָּל מַעֲשֶׂה הָאֱלֹהִים יָבָא בְמִשְׁפָּט עַל כָּל נֶעְלָם אִם טוֹב וְאִם רָע.

For God will judge every deed — even everything hidden — whether good or evil (Koheles 12: 14).

R' Yochanan understands the term נֶעְלָם, *hidden*, as a reference to שְׁגָגוֹת, *unwillful transgressions*. He wept and exclaimed, "A servant whose master considers unwillful transgressions as willful transgressions — what recourse can he have?" (*Chagigah* 5a).

R' Yochanan's question begs an answer. Why should a person be held accountable for שְׁגָגוֹת? Is one really to blame if, for example, he forgets that it is Shabbos and turns on a light? The same question can be asked regarding the Yom Kippur confession, "For the sin that we have sinned against You under duress and willfully." Why should an act committed under duress require atonement?

The *haftarah* of Shabbos *Shuvah* begins, *Return Israel, to Hashem, your God, for you have stumbled through your sins* (*Hoshea* 14:2). The *Vilna Gaon* explains that just as each *mitzvah* infuses the soul with *kedushah*, sanctity,[1] so does each sin committed willfully sully the soul with a degree of *tumah*, impurity. Once the soul has been tarnished it is more apt to stumble unintentionally and commit sins without thinking or under duress. The prophet Hoshea exhorts Israel to return to Hashem, for it has *stumbled* unintentionally *because of the sins* which it committed willfully.

R' Yochanan did not mean to imply that Hashem equates שְׁגָגוֹת, *unintentional transgressions* with זְדוֹנוֹת, *willful transgressions*. R'

---

1. HaRav Segal often notes that the performance of most *mitzvos* is preceded by a blessing in which we praise Hashem, אֲשֶׁר קִדְּשָׁנוּ בְּמִצְוֹתָיו, "Who has sanctified us through His *mitzvos*."

Yochanan merely taught that there is a degree of culpability even for שְׁגָגוֹת, since they come about as a result of זְדוֹנוֹת.

Thus, *teshuvah* is far more than a process through which one avoids retribution. It is truly a cleansing process, as it purifies one's soul from the effects of sin and removes the barriers between oneself and Heaven that sin creates. To quote *Rambam* (*Hilchos Teshuvah* 7:6):

> Great is teshuvah, for it brings one close to the Divine Presence, as it is written, "Return, Israel, unto Hashem, your God" ... Yesterday, this man was contemptible, distant from God — but today, he is loved and desired, close and beloved...Yesterday, he was separated from Hashem, God of Israel — but today, he cleaves to the Divine Presence, as it is written, "You who cling to Hashem, your God — you are all alive today" (Devarim 4:4).

◄§ "Everything Hidden"

In expounding upon the phrase עַל כָּל נֶעְלָם, *even everything hidden*, in the above-cited verse, the *Gemara* understands the term כָּל, *everything [hidden]*, to include culpability for even seemingly insignificant acts. "Shmuel said: This refers to someone who spits in the presence of a neighbor who finds this repulsive." Shmuel's teaching illustrates to what extent the Torah obligates us in matters בֵּין אָדָם לַחֲבֵירוֹ, *between man and his fellow*. Even an act that is not directly *between* ourselves and others is considered a sin if it causes others any sort of discomfort or unpleasantness.

With regard to the judgment of Rosh Hashanah, *Rambam* writes (*Hilchos Teshuvah* 3:3) that one who is found to be righteous is sealed for life, one who is deemed wicked is sealed for death, and one who is evenly balanced between good and bad has his fate suspended until Yom Kippur. Shmuel's teaching means that one can, Heaven forfend, tip the Heavenly scales against himself by neglecting to clean up after he eats, leaving the table a repulsive mess for the next person. If we have been guilty of such inconsiderate behavior, then we should include it in our Yom Kippur confession and resolve to correct it in the future.

On the phrase אִם טוֹב וְאִם רָע, *whether good or evil*, the *Gemara* says, quoting the academy of R' Yanai: "This refers to one who gives a coin to a poor man in public. R' Yanai once saw a certain person giving a coin to a poor man in public, and told him, 'It would have been better had you not given it to him, for now that you have given it to him you have shamed him.' " In this interpretation, אִם טוֹב וְאִם רָע, *whether good or evil*, refers to an act that is basically good, but contains within it a measure of evil — and for this, too, one must face judgment.

How instructive, then, is this verse from *Koheles* for those who seek to make full use of the golden opportunity that is the *Aseres Yemei Teshuvah*. The verse teaches that: 1) One's deeds have a profound effect on his soul and, as such, may determine the course of his future actions as well. 2) When satisfying one's own needs, one may never cause discomfort — no matter how indirect or insignificant — to another. 3) One must strive to insure that his deeds are entirely positive, without any sort of blemish.

≈§ Tzom Gedaliah

T*zom* (*The Fast of*) *Gedaliah* commemorates the murder of Gedaliah ben Achikam which brought to an end the remaining Jewish settlement in *Eretz Yisrael* following the destruction of the First *Beis HaMikdash*. Gedaliah was a *tzaddik* and the leader of that settlement. From the fact that *Chazal* chose to mark this final phase of the Destruction by establishing a fast on the day of his murder,[2] we learn that the death of a *tzaddik* is as tragic as the destruction of the *Beis HaMikdash* (*Rosh Hashanah* 18b).

However, *Chazal* also inform us that an error on Gedaliah's part led to his own death. He was informed that Yishmael ben Nesanyah, with the backing of the king of Aram, was intent on killing him. Gedaliah refused to accept this wicked report about another Jew. The

---

2. According to one opinion, the murder actually took place on Rosh Hashanah. *Chazal* therefore established the closest weekday, i.e. the third of *Tishrei*, as a fast.

report proved accurate, as Yishmael ben Nesanyah did murder him. While the *Halachah* forbids one to believe as fact a bad report concerning another Jew, one should take the necessary precautions when harm could result should the report prove accurate.

Gedaliah is severely faulted for having totally rejected the report and not having taken such precautions. The prophet states: "And the pit into which Yishmael cast the corpses of the men that he slew *by the hand of Gedaliah*" (*Yirmiyahu* 41:9). *Radak* explains that the corpses referred to are those of the men whom Yishmael slew along with Gedaliah. Because Gedaliah's passive behavior led to their deaths, Scripture considers it as if he had killed them (*Niddah* 61a).

There is an important lesson in this. Gedaliah's rejection of the report was a *chumrah*, stringency, that was contrary to *Halachah*. The ramifications of his mistake were awesome and he is blamed for them.

B'nei Torah who strive for spiritual heights often adopt voluntary stringencies in their personal habits and conduct. It is imperative that *b'nei Torah* distinguish clearly between *chumros* and *Halachah*. Before adopting *chumros*, one must be certain that they are halachically sound and that they will not ultimately prove harmful to oneself or one's family.

Chumros which in themselves seem exemplary may actually lead to serious transgression. If a husband adopts a *chumrah* that places unnecessary hardship on his wife, or if a *bachur* adopts a *chumrah* which his parents oppose and which causes strife and aggravation in the home, then he has acted contrary to Torah.

A *bachur* should not return home during *bein hazmanim*, intercession, and spend his time lecturing his family with words of *mussar*. He should rather lecture himself — this certainly has a basis in *Halachah*! As for his parents, he should inquire of them as to how he can be of help. Being *machmir*, stringent, regarding *kibud av v'eim* is certainly praiseworthy! Note that aside from the *mitzvah* to honor one's parents, one can also fulfill the *mitzvah* of וְאָהַבְתָּ לְרֵעֲךָ כָּמוֹךָ, *love your fellow as yourself* (*Vayikra* 19:18), by being sensitive and responsive to one's parents' needs. וְאָהַבְתָּ לְרֵעֲךָ כָּמוֹךָ is another *mitzvah* in which one should seek stringencies.

May we make proper use of this day of fasting and come to Yom Kippur as sincere and complete *ba'alei teshuvah*.

Proper Perspectives

ᴇᴤ The Collective Soul of Israel

Forty days after receiving the Torah at Sinai, Israel fell from its awesome spiritual level with the sin of the Golden Calf. Only the prayers of Moshe *Rabbeinu* could save the people from annihilation. The climax of the pardon achieved by Moshe came in a prophecy where *HaKadosh Baruch Hu* revealed to Moshe the שְׁלֹש עֶשְׂרֵה מִדּוֹת שֶׁל רַחֲמִים, *Thirteen Attributes of Mercy.*

The *Zohar* (*Parashas Naso* 131) teaches that there are actually two series of Divine attributes. The second series was pronounced by the prophet Michah and forms the core of the *Tashlich* service.[1] It reads:

> מִי אֵל כָּמוֹךָ נֹשֵׂא עָוֹן וְעֹבֵר עַל פֶּשַׁע, לִשְׁאֵרִית נַחֲלָתוֹ. לֹא הֶחֱזִיק לָעַד אַפּוֹ כִּי חָפֵץ חֶסֶד הוּא. יָשׁוּב יְרַחֲמֵנוּ יִכְבֹּשׁ עֲוֹנֹתֵינוּ וְתַשְׁלִיךְ בִּמְצֻלוֹת יָם כָּל חַטֹּאתָם. תִּתֵּן אֱמֶת לְיַעֲקֹב חֶסֶד לְאַבְרָהָם אֲשֶׁר נִשְׁבַּעְתָּ לַאֲבֹתֵינוּ מִימֵי קֶדֶם.
>
> *Who, O God, is like You, Who pardons iniquity and overlooks transgression for the remnant of His heritage? Who has not retained His wrath eternally, for He desires kindness! He will again be merciful to us; He will suppress our iniquities and cast into the depths of the sea all their sins. Grant truth to Yaakov, kindness to*

---

1. *Zohar* refers to the attributes revealed to Moshe as לְתַתָּא, *lower ones,* and those of Michah as תְּלֵיסַר מְכִילִין דְּרַחֲמֵי עִילָאִין, *Thirteen Tiaras of Supreme Mercy.* The Thirteen Attributes enumerated by Michah parallel the original, lower ones and loosely correspond to them. The precise relationship of the two series is discussed in *sifrei Kabbalah.*

Avraham, as You swore to our fathers from ancient times (Michah 7:18-20).

An interpretation of this second series of attributes is the theme of the classical work *Tomer Devorah* by the *Ramak*.[2] The Thirteen Attributes are meant to be emulated by man and the *Ramak* takes pains to show how man can, indeed, pattern his own behavior after them. Let us examine two of these attributes.

וְעֹבֵר עַל פֶּשַׁע, *Who pardons iniquity* — Hashem Himself, and not any agent or deputy, grants man forgiveness for his sins. As David *HaMelech* expressed it: כִּי עִמְּךָ הַסְּלִיחָה, *for with You is the forgiveness* (*Tehillim* 130:4). Hashem Himself pours water, as it were, to wash away the stains of sin from man's soul. Should the sinner not feel shamed that the King of kings must come to wash *his* filthy garments?!

Tomer Devorah concludes: "This is exactly how every person should be. One should never say, 'Must I correct someone else's sin or perversion?' One should not think this way, for *HaKadosh Baruch Hu* Himself corrects man's sins and cleanses the filth of his iniquity."

לִשְׁאֵרִית נַחֲלָתוֹ, *For the remnant of His heritage* — the word שְׁאָר means both *remnant* and *relative*.[3] Hashem loves *Klal Yisrael* as if the Jewish people were a close relative. Scripture states: *In all their sorrows He is afflicted* (*Yeshayahu* 63:9). Hashem cannot bear His people's pain or disgrace, for the Jewish nation is His שְׁאָר.

From Hashem's love for us, we should learn how to love one another. In essence, all Jews are one. Our souls are united and in each soul there is a portion of all the others. This concept is the basis of the principle that כָּל יִשְׂרָאֵל עֲרֵבִים זֶה לָזֶה, *all Jews are responsible for one another* (*Shavuos* 39a). Since each Jewish soul possesses a portion of all the others, when a Jew sins, his wrong affects not only his own soul, but also the collective soul of Israel.

In pondering the above, one begins to view sin from an entirely new perspective. People tend to view sin as a private matter between Hashem and themselves. As we have seen, this is a gross

---

2. R' Moshe Kordevero, one of the most profound and systematic teachers of the *Zohar*, and a leading figure among the Kabbalists of sixteenth century Safed. The *Arizal* referred to the *Ramak* as his teacher and master.

3. See *Vayikra* 21:2.

misconception. Every sin one commits affects the entire Jewish people. Awareness of this truth should inspire us to approach our actions with added responsibility.

Perhaps this was Rabbi Akiva's intent in saying: וְאָהַבְתָּ לְרֵעֲךָ כָּמוֹךָ זֶה כְּלָל גָּדוֹל בַּתּוֹרָה, *Love your neighbor as yourself — this is the primary rule of the Torah (Rashi* to *Vayikra* 19:18 citing *Sifra*). Every Jew should love his neighbor as himself, for he and his neighbor are truly one. And because they are truly one, each should strive to observe all of Torah to the best of his ability, for if not, his neighbor will be adversely affected.

The above also lends insight to an interpretation of *Chazal* regarding the episode of the Golden Calf. The Jews had committed that sin while Moshe was in Heaven, receiving the First *Luchos* (Tablets) from Hashem. Hashem told Moshe: *Descend, for your nation has become corrupt (Sh'mos* 32:7). *Chazal* (cited by *Rashi*) interpret: [Hashem told Moshe,] "Descend from your greatness; I granted greatness to you only because of them." The exalted spiritual level which Moshe *Rabbeinu* had attained was reflective not only of his own spiritual greatness, but also of the greatness of the collective Jewish soul which he represented. Once that collective soul had plummeted from its previous status, Moshe's status fell as well.

◆§ David's Path

For there is no man who will not sin (II Divrei HaYamim 6:36). While a proper perception can serve as a deterrent against sin, it will not prevent us from sinning at all. However, it should inspire us to undertake a process of *teshuvah* which can undo the harm that our deeds have caused.

In his *Sha'arei Teshuvah*, *Rabbeinu Yonah* devotes the entire first section to a comprehensive discussion of the twenty principles of repentance. He quotes frequently from Psalm 51, in which David *HaMelech* beseeches *HaKadosh Baruch Hu* to forgive him for the sin involving Bas Sheva (II *Shmuel* ch.11-12). *Rabbeinu Yonah* refers to that psalm as פֶּרֶק הַתְּשׁוּבָה, *the Chapter of Repentance*, because it is יְסוֹד מוּסָד לְעִקְּרֵי תְּשׁוּבָה, *the basic foundation of all the principles of repentance (Sha'arei Teshuvah* 1:23). In the chapter's beginning, David pleads: הֶרֶב כַּבְּסֵנִי מֵעֲוֹנִי וּמֵחַטָּאתִי טַהֲרֵנִי, *Abundantly cleanse me from my iniquity, and from my sin purify me* (v. 4), for, as we have explained, *HaKadosh Baruch Hu* Himself cleanses us from sin. Further on in the chapter, David beseeches:

לֵב טָהוֹר בְּרָא לִי אֱלֹהִים וְרוּחַ נָכוֹן חַדֵּשׁ בְּקִרְבִּי. אַל תַּשְׁלִיכֵנִי מִלְּפָנֶיךָ וְרוּחַ קָדְשְׁךָ אַל תִּקַּח מִמֶּנִּי. הָשִׁיבָה לִי שְׂשׂוֹן יִשְׁעֶךָ וְרוּחַ נְדִיבָה תִסְמְכֵנִי.

A pure heart create for me, O God, and a steadfast spirit renew within me. Cast me not away from Your Presence, and Your Holy Spirit take not from me. Restore to me the joy of Your salvation, and with a generous spirit sustain me (v 12-14).

Rabbeinu Yonah elaborates:

The penitent should pray to Hashem that He wipe away his willful sins like a cloud and his errors like a mist,[4] that He desire him, show him favor and accept his entreaties as if he had not sinned . . . For it is possible that the sin should be forgiven and he should be redeemed from any retribution or decree, but Hashem will still have no desire for him and will not look favorably upon his offerings [i.e., his service of Him]. Therefore, as one will note in David's prayer of repentance, after he requested, "Abundantly cleanse me from my iniquity and from my sin purify me," he prayed further regarding Divine favor, that Hashem's favor toward him be as it was prior to the sin. Thus, he prayed, "Cast me not away from Your Presence, and Your Holy Spirit take not from me." He then prayed, "Restore to me the joy of Your salvation," that Hashem's miracles and salvation be with him and that the spirit of God rest upon him as it did previously. He continued, "With a generous spirit sustain me," as if to say, "I have been diminished by iniquities and I am not worthy of Your miracles or that You reveal Your sacred power on my behalf. Though You have forgiven my sin, I am not worthy of being loved and finding favor as in

---

4. From *Yeshayahu* 44:22.

earlier times. Nevertheless, 'With a generous spirit sustain me,' for there is no limit to Your generosity and goodness" (Sha'arei Teshuvah 1:42).

For our *teshuvah* to be considered complete, we must emulate the way of David, whom *Chazal* describe as "the man who made the yoke of repentance sublime" (*Moed Katan* 16b). Our efforts at improving our actions must be accompanied by sincere prayer that Hashem remove the barriers which our sins brought about and that we find favor with Him as before.

৵§ The Power of the Community

The *Gemara* (*Rosh Hashanah* 18a) raises the following contradiction. One verse states, *For what nation is so great that God is close to it, like Hashem our God is whenever we call to Him?* (*Devarim* 4:7), while a second verse states, *Seek Hashem when He is close, call to Him when He is near* (*Yeshayahu* 55:6) — implying that there is a specific time when Hashem is close to us and readily accessible. The *Gemara* answers that the first verse refers to the *tzibur*, community. The *tzibur's* power is such that its prayers at any given time can cause a Divine decree to be rescinded. The second verse refers to the individual, who can bring about the annulment of Divine decrees only when Hashem is especially close to His people — during the *Aseres Yemei Teshuvah*, Ten Days of Repentance.

What is the definition of *tzibur*, community? Earlier, the *Gemara* (17a) cited a *Baraisa* which dwells on a passage in *Tehillim* ch. 107. *Those who go down to the sea in ships, who do their work in many waters — they have seen the deeds of Hashem and His wonders in the watery deep* (v. 23) . . . *They cried out to Hashem in their distress, from their woes He removed them* . . . (v. 28). The *Baraisa* notes the unusual נו"ן הֲפוּכָה, *reversed nun*, which precedes verse 23 and each of the five succeeding verses and is a sign of exclusion or diminution; i.e., that not all who cry out when in peril are answered. This teaches us, says the *Baraisa*, that only those who cry out *before* the Divine decree has been issued will be delivered.

Now, the passage speaks not of an individual, but of a group at sea — *those who go down to the sea in ships* . . . But does not the community always have the power to effect the annulment of a Divine decree through prayer? The *Gemara* answers, "They [of whom Psalm 107 speaks], too, are considered individuals."

The *Rosh Yeshivah*, Harav Meir Tzvi,[5] שליט״א, explains that a group is considered a community only if its members are concerned for one another, as reflected in the plural form of their prayers. In the case of the typical seafarer caught in a tempest at sea, the terror of the moment does not allow him to think of anyone other than himself. He cries out for his life, oblivious to the fact that other lives are threatened as well. Therefore, "they are considered individuals."

It is of utmost importance that one always include the *tzibur* in his prayers. This is why the entire text of the *Shemoneh Esrei* is in the plural. When one beseeches the *Ribono shel Olam* to accept his efforts toward *teshuvah*, he should ask that the efforts of his fellow Jews be accepted as well. In this way, the merit of the community will accompany his entreaties.

One should note that the *Arizal* advised that immediately preceding *Shemoneh Esrei* one contemplate the *mitzvah* of וְאָהַבְתָּ לְרֵעֲךָ כָּמוֹךָ, *Love your neighbor as yourself.*

⇜ The Spark in Every Jew

R' Aharon Kotler writes that even one who is categorized as a *rasha*, wicked man, by the Heavenly Court on Rosh Hashanah can still effect a change in his verdict through repentance during the *Aseres Yemei Teshuvah* (*Mishnas R' Aharon*, Vol II p. 179). Sincere *teshuvah* always accomplishes; no one should ever consider himself beyond the point of return. Even one who has sunk to the lowest levels of spiritual decadence can be born anew through *teshuvah*. This truth is illustrated in two incidents recorded in the *Midrash* (*Bereishis Rabbah* 65:22).

At the time of the Destruction, when the Romans prepared to enter the *Beis HaMikdash*, they declared, "Let a Jew enter first." They turned to a Jew named Yosef of Shisa and told him, "Enter! Whatever you take is yours to keep." Yosef entered and came out

---

5. Rabbi Meir Tzvi Ehrentrau, *Rosh Yeshivah* of the Manchester Yeshivah and son-in-law of HaRav Segal.

carrying a menorah of gold. The Romans said, "It is not fitting for a commoner to use this. Enter again and take something for yourself." This time, Yosef refused, saying, "Enough that I have angered my Creator once, must I anger Him again?" The Romans, however, were insistent that he obey their order. When he persisted in his refusal, they tortured him to death by putting him in a carpenter's vise and dragging him over it. He cried out again and again, "Woe unto me that I have angered my Creator."

The second incident involves Yakum of Tzroros, the nephew of the Tanna, R' Yosei ben Yoezer of Tzereidah. Yakum had forsaken the Torah. Once, he was riding on a horse on Shabbos when he came upon Roman soldiers escorting his revered uncle, who was being carried on a horse, to the gallows. Yakum exclaimed, "Look at the horse that my master let me ride and look at the horse that your Master has made you ride." R' Yosei replied, "If this [i.e., the earthly pleasures which Yakum was enjoying] is the lot of those who anger Hashem, how much more the reward of those who do His will!" Yakum responded, "Has anyone done His will more than you?" R' Yosei responded, "If this is how Hashem acts toward those who do His will, how much more with those who anger Him."

These words cut through Yakum like a knife. He subjected himself to the four methods of execution (stoning, burning, beheading and strangling). R' Yosei fell asleep and saw Yakum's bed being borne aloft. He exclaimed, "In a brief moment, he has preceded me to *Gan Eden.*"

Yosef of Shisa and Yakum of Tzroros had sunk to unimaginable levels of depravity. One defiantly entered the House of Hashem to take its sacred treasures for himself, while the other mocked the leader of his generation,[6] his own uncle, as he was being taken to die *al kiddush Hashem*. Yet, even when they had sunk so low, a spark of holiness still burned within them. Suddenly, each was overcome by the enormity of his sins and the spark within him burst into a huge flame. In a moment, each had become a *ba'al teshuvah*.

May we and all of *Klal Yisrael* merit to be inscribed and sealed in the Book of *Tzaddikim*, as we return to Hashem with all our hearts and souls.

_____

6. See *Chagigah* 16a.

Season of Our Gladness

◈ Uplift of Spirit

In the *Shemoneh Esrei* of *Yom Tov*, we say, "And You, Hashem, our God, have lovingly given us appointed times for gladness, festivals and seasons for joy..." Every *yom tov* is a time of שִׂמְחָה, *gladness*. However, only Succos is called זְמַן שִׂמְחָתֵנוּ, *the season of our gladness*. The source of this appellation is the verse (*Devarim* 16:14) where the term שִׂמְחָה is used specifically in connection with Succos (though it applies to the other *Yamim Tovim* as well). Why, indeed, is שִׂמְחָה associated with Succos more than with Pesach and Shavuos?

The giving of the Torah at Sinai was followed, less than two months later, by the Sin of the Golden Calf (*Sh'mos* ch. 32-33). After descending the mountain and being made aware of the sin, Moshe *Rabbeinu* prayed on behalf of his people and they were granted a reprieve. On the tenth of Tishrei (the date of Yom Kippur), Moshe descended with the second *Luchos* (Tablets), and the next day informed the people that they were to begin preparations for the construction of the *Mishkan*. *Chazal* inform us of the relationship between the *Mishkan* and the Sin of the Golden Calf:

אֵלֶּה פְקוּדֵי הַמִּשְׁכָּן מִשְׁכַּן הָעֵדֻת. . .

These are the accounts of the Mishkan (Tabernacle), the Mishkan of testimony. . .(38:21)

The Mishkan of testimony — A testimony for Israel that HaKadosh Baruch Hu forgave them for the Sin of the Golden Calf, for He manifested His Presence among them (Rashi citing Midrash).

The "testimony" to which *Rashi* refers was not directed toward the nations of the world; it was for the Jews themselves. After Moshe returned from Heaven, broke the first *Luchos*, destroyed the Golden Calf and made clear the severity of the sin that had been committed, the people were left broken in spirit. *And they mourned ... and the Children of Israel removed [from themselves] their ornaments [which they had received] from Horeb[1] (Sh'mos* 33:4,6). They felt broken spiritually, for they felt it impossible to attain forgiveness after having strayed so grievously. The fact that Hashem would manifest His Presence upon the *Mishkan* proved that they *had* been forgiven. This awareness revitalized their spirit and they approached their Divine service with renewed vigor.[2]

The joy of Succos can be explained in a similar sense. The season of soul-searching and introspection which commences with Rosh Chodesh Elul becomes more intense with the advent of Rosh Hashanah and reaches its climax with Yom Kippur, when we enumerate our sins in confession upon confession and beg forgiveness. Those who approach this season with the seriousness that it demands might well become dispirited after having spent so much time pondering their spiritual failings. R' Yisrael Salanter writes in a letter that in days past "every man was seized with dread by the voice which proclaimed the blessing of the month of Elul" (*Ohr Yisrael* §14). Forty days and countless tears later, such a man might find it hard to mend his broken heart.

Yom Tov is a time of special closeness between Hashem and His people; this closeness is the source of the joy that permeates the *Yom Tov* experience. The *mitzvah* of *succah* symbolizes this closeness in a most unique way. The *Gemara* states that the *succah* represents the עַנְנֵי הַכָּבוֹד, *Clouds of Glory*, through which Hashem's Presence was manifest during the Jews' sojourn in the Wilderness and which sheltered them from harm.[3] Succos is the *season of our gladness*

---

1. I.e., Mount Sinai. *Sforno* explains the term 'ornaments' as a reference to the spiritual gifts which they had been granted at Sinai.

2. See Vol. I, discourse to *Parashas Tetzaveh*.

3. The *Vilna Gaon* (*Shir HaShirim* 1:2) showed how the very date on which Succos commences is related to the Clouds of Glory.

After the Sin of the Golden Calf, the Clouds withdrew from the people. Moshe returned from Heaven with the second *Luchos* on the tenth day of Tishrei (the date of Yom Kippur) at which time Hashem forgave the nation for its sin and renewed because its arrival revives our broken spirit and infuses us with joy, both because it is *Yom Tov* and because its primary *mitzvah*[4] represents the special bond that exists between *HaKadosh Baruch Hu* and *Klal Yisrael*.

Five *mitzvos* are uniquely associated with Succos: 1) *succah* 2) *arba minim* (the four species) 3) to rejoice 4) *nisuch hamayim*, the libation of water upon the altar in the *Beis HaMikdash* and 5) the holding of the *aravah* (willow) on *Hoshanah Rabbah*.[5] The abundance of *mitzvos* during this *Yom Tov* also serves to uplift our spirits and add to our joy.

☙ "Go, Eat Your Bread in Joy"

In truth, the completion of the repentance process that begins in Elul and concludes with Yom Kippur is also cause for joy. Thus does *Rama* state at the close of the laws of Yom Kippur (624:5), "We eat and are joyous on the night on which Yom Kippur ends, for it partakes somewhat of the quality of *yom tov*." The source for this law is a *Midrash* (cited by *Tur*): Upon the conclusion of Yom Kippur a בַּת קוֹל, *Heavenly voice*, is heard declaring, "Go, eat your bread in joy and drink your wine with a good heart, for your deeds have already found favor with Hashem!" (*Koheles* 9:7).

In the Book of *Tehillim*, David *HaMelech* describes the holy city of Jerusalem: *Fairest of sites, joy of all the earth, Mount Zion by the northern sides, city of the great king (Tehillim 48:3)*. In what sense was the holy city *joy of all the earth? Rabbeinu Yonah (Sha'arei Teshuvah 4:15)* cites the *Midrash*:

His covenant with them. On the next day, Moshe instructed the people to begin bringing contributions for the *Mishkan*. The contributions poured in for the next two days until, on the fourteenth of Tishrei, they were weighed and measured and handed over to those who would construct the *Mishkan* and its vessels. The next morning, the fifteenth of Tishrei, construction began — and the Clouds of Glory returned.

4. Primary in the sense that it becomes one's dwelling throughout the festival.

5. The first three are of Scriptural origin; *nisuch hamayim* was transmitted to Moshe at Sinai and is alluded to in the Torah (see *Taanis* 2b); and the holding of the *aravah* is of prophetic origin (מִנְהָג נְבִיאִים).

*When a man would commit a sin unintentionally, he
would become worried, fearful and gripped by trembling over his sin — until he would go up to Jerusalem
and offer his sacrifice. Then he would be entirely joyful.
Regarding this it is written, "Fairest of sites, joy of all
the earth."*

Chazal teach, "The [spiritual] status of *ba'alei teshuvah* cannot be
attained [even] by perfect *tzaddikim*" (*Berachos* 34b). *Teshuvah*
reaches to the Heavenly Throne (*Yoma* 86b); one who engages in
sincere soul-searching can achieve a closeness with Hashem that he
might never have dreamed attainable.

Sefer Sha'arei Teshuvah opens with the following:

*Among the kindnesses which the Blessed One has done
for His creations [i.e., mankind] is that He prepared for
them the way to ascend from within the snare of their
deeds and to escape the trap of their sins; to save their
souls from destruction and to remove His wrath from
upon them.*

We may suggest that the phrase לַעֲלוֹת מִתּוֹךְ פַּחַת מַעֲשֵׂיהֶם, *to **ascend**
from within the snare of their deeds*, alludes to the potential for
spiritual growth that is inherent in *teshuvah*. Through *teshuvah*, one
can *rise* to limitless heights, far above the spiritual level he had
maintained prior to having sinned. *The [spiritual] status of ba'alei
teshuvah cannot be attained even by perfect tzaddikim.* Is it any
wonder, then, that the *yom tov* which immediately follows Yom
Kippur is referred to as זְמַן שִׂמְחָתֵנוּ, *the season of our gladness?*

⤳ Song of the Ba'al Teshuvah

In the era of the *Beis HaMikdash*, the height of the Succos
festivities was the *Simchas Beis HaSho'eivah*, the joyous celebration in the Temple court which preceded the water drawing on each
night of *Chol HaMoed*. As *Rambam* (*Hilchos Lulav* 8:14) notes,
though all of Israel was welcome at the event, not everyone was
permitted to participate in the singing and dancing. The *Mishnah*
(*Succah* 5:4) states, "Devout men and men of good deeds would

dance before them with flaming torches that were in their hands and would utter before them words of song and praise." The *Gemara* (*Succah* 53a) cites a *Baraisa*:

> Some of those [who offered praise] would exclaim, "Praiseworthy was our youth, in that it did not shame our old age" — these were the חֲסִידִים וְאַנְשֵׁי מַעֲשֶׂה, *pious men and men of good deeds*. Others would exclaim, "Praiseworthy is our old age, in that it atoned for our youth" — these were the ba'alei teshuvah. Both these and those exclaimed, "Praiseworthy is the one that did not sin. As for one that sinned — let him repent and he shall be forgiven."

Rabbeinu Yonah (*Sha'arei Teshuvah* 4:8) writes that the joy of the *ba'al teshuvah* is an integral part of the *teshuvah* process. "Therefore our Sages stated that one who holds a *seudah* (festive meal) on *Erev Yom Kippur* is considered as if he has fulfilled a command to fast on [both] the ninth and tenth of Tishrei, for he has demonstrated joy over the arrival of the day of his atonement — and this bears witness to his [previous] worry over his sins and sorrow over his transgressions." To whatever degree one has returned to Hashem through *teshuvah*, to that degree he is joyous over having attained atonement.

Rambam discusses the nature of the joy that permeated the *Simchas Beis HaSho'eivah*: "The celebration of a *mitzvah* and the joy one expresses as a result of his love of God — such celebration is an extraordinary form of Divine service." The *ba'al teshuvah*, perhaps more than anyone else, can experience this joy in its fullest sense. As *Rambam* writes in *Hilchos Teshuvah* (7:6):

> Great is teshuvah, for it brings one close to the Divine Presence, as it is written, "Return, Israel, unto Hashem, your God" (Hoshea 14:2)...Yesterday, this man was contemptible, distant from God — but today, he is loved and desired, close and beloved...Yesterday, he was separated from Hashem, God of Israel — but today, he cleaves to the Divine Presence, as it is written, "You who cling to Hashem, your God — you are all alive today" (Deuteronomy 4:4).

⚜ A Lesson For All Seasons

The quality of שִׂמְחָה, *gladness*, is crucial to one's service of Hashem all year round. *Serve Hashem with gladness, come before Him with joyous song* (Tehillim 100:2). What is the source of this gladness? The psalm continues, *Know that Hashem, He is God, it is He Who made us and we are His, His nation and the sheep of His pasture.* The power of *teshuvah* is, in itself, cause for joy and love of Hashem. *Chazal* (Yerushalmi Makkos 2:6) relate that neither wisdom nor prophecy nor Torah could accept the possibility of cleansing one's soul through *teshuvah*. Wisdom decreed that the sinner should be pursued by his own evil. Prophecy declared that sin must result in death. The Torah indicated that atonement could be achieved only through the bringing of guilt-offerings. It was *HaKadosh Baruch Hu* Who decreed, "Let him [the sinner] repent and gain atonement," as it is written, *Good and upright is Hashem, therefore, He guides sinners on the way* (Tehillim 25:8).

Contemplation of one's sins should not be cause for despondency. In discussing the path of repentance for one who has sinned by chance (as opposed to a habitual sinner), *Rabbeinu Yonah* writes: "The beginning of this man's repentance is regret, to experience sorrow in his heart and bitterness in his soul over his sin. After this, he should instill within himself, with each passing day, ever more awe of Hashem" (Sha'arei Teshuvah 1:1). The term אַחֲרֵי כֵן, *after this*, implies that one's sorrow should be with a limit; חֲרָטָה, *regret*, is but a first step. Having accomplished this, one must not allow himself to be consumed by feelings of guilt, for this can lead to יֵאוּשׁ, *despair*. Instead, one should seek to develop greater *yiras Hashem*, so that he will be more zealous in his observance of *mitzvos* and more removed from the possibility of sin. As for past sins, it is sufficient to set aside time each day to ponder such matters.

It is worthwhile to cite the well-known statement of R' Aharon Karliner: "עַצְבוּת, *despondency*, is not a sin in and of itself — but the sins to which עַצְבוּת can lead, no sin can cause."

In *Maariv*, we pray: וְהָסֵר שָׂטָן מִלְּפָנֵינוּ וּמֵאַחֲרֵינוּ, *And remove from spiritual impediment from before us and from behind us.* We may suggest that the term מִלְּפָנֵינוּ, *from before us*, refers to the *yetzer hara*'s efforts at enticing us to sin. Having succeeded, the *yetzer hara* then attacks מֵאַחֲרֵינוּ, *from behind us*, as he attempts to convince us that our spiritual decline has brought us beyond the point of return. In reciting this *tefillah* each night, we pray that we be granted Heavenly assistance to be saved from such harmful thoughts. Rather than despair, we should rejoice in the opportunity to renew our closeness with the One Above and use our past experiences as a springboard for reaching new heights in *avodas Hashem*.

Great is *teshuvah*, for through it, intentional sins (זְדוֹנוֹת) are considered as merits (זְכֻיּוֹת). This refers to תְּשׁוּבָה מֵאַהֲבָה, *repentance out of love* (*Yoma* 86a).

In his *Yesod HaTeshuvah*, *Rabbeinu Yonah* writes that one should take stock of his deeds on a regular basis. If his findings are positive "and he has not found abominations, then let him thank and give praise before his Creator for having helped him against his enemies, and for his having been privileged to spend an hour of repentance in this world." An important aspect of spiritual growth is the recognition of one's accomplishments in correcting past faults and in other aspects of *avodas Hashem*.

May the joy of Succos inspire us to serve Hashem throughout the year in a spirit of love, repentance and joy.

The Light That is Torah

כִּי נֵר מִצְוָה וְתוֹרָה אוֹר.

For a mitzvah is a lamp, and the Torah is light (Mishlei 6:23).

◄§ Victory of the Spirit

Tur (*Hilchos Chanukah*, ch. 670), citing *Maharam of Rothenburg*, states: "The customary indulging in feasts on Chanukah is not obligatory, for they [*Chazal*] established these days as a time of הַלֵּל and הוֹדָאָה (praise and thanksgiving) and not מִשְׁתֶּה and שִׂמְחָה (feasting and joy)."[1]

In commenting on the above, *Bach* differentiates between Chanukah and Purim, when there is a specific obligation of מִשְׁתֶּה and שִׂמְחָה. The miracle of Purim centered around the decree to annihilate the entire Jewish nation. Hashem brought about the issuance of this decree as punishment for the Jews having indulged in the feast of King Achashverosh. In celebration of the miracle which granted them new life, the Jewish people celebrate each year with a *seudas mitzvah*. The miracle of Chanukah, however, centered around the decrees of King Antiochus against Jewish observance. The Greeks wanted the Jewish people to forsake their Torah way of life in favor of their own culture, which glorified the physical and extolled indulgence in temporal pleasures. The Greeks were quite

---

1. See *Shulchan Aruch, Orach Chaim* 670:2.

content to allow the Jews to remain alive — as long as they abandoned those *mitzvos* which are at the core of Jewish belief. This decree, writes *Bach* (based on a *Baraisa*) was, in fact, a Divine retribution for the Jews having become lax in their *mitzvah* observance. The *mesiras nefesh*, self-sacrifice, of the *Chashmonaim* to preserve Torah life and restore the service to the *Beis HaMikdash* brought about the great miracle of their victory over the Greeks and the discovery of the flask of oil which miraculously burned for eight days. Thus, Chanukah is a celebration of the spirit, a *yom tov* which commemorates a victory of the spirit led by warriors of the spirit, the *Chashmonaim*.

Bach concludes, "Thus was the festival established only to offer *hallel* and *hoda'ah*, a service of the heart."

In the *Al HaNisim* prayer, we speak of the Greek plan לְהַשְׁכִּיחָם תּוֹרָתֶךְ וּלְהַעֲבִירָם מֵחֻקֵּי רְצוֹנֶךְ, *to make them forget Your Torah and to compel them to stray from the statutes of Your will*. Torah, when studied with true diligence and dedication, permeates one's soul with *kedushah*, sanctity, and one's mind with שֵׂכֶל הַיָּשָׁר, *an objective intellect*. Torah study, more than any other *mitzvah*, quells the desires that entice a person toward sin. "I have created the *yetzer hara* and I have created the Torah as its antidote" (*Kiddushin* 30b). It was the *kedushah* of Torah and all that it represents which the Greeks sought to destroy and it was the *Chashmonaim* — the עוֹסְקֵי תוֹרָתֶךְ, *diligent students of Your Torah* — who prevailed and caused the light of Torah to dispel the darkness of Greece.

◆§ The Only Weapon

The Torah (*Bereishis* 32:25-33) tells of the struggle between Yaakov *Avinu* and the Angel of Eisav, who is Satan. Why did Satan choose to do battle with Yaakov and not with Avraham and Yitzchak who preceded him? R' Elchonon Wasserman (*Kovetz Ma'amarim*) cites the prophet's cry, *Why was the land destroyed? Because they forsook My Torah* (*Yirmiyahu* 9:11-12), to which the Sages (*Yerushalmi, Chagigah* 1:7) commented, "HaKadosh Baruch Hu was relenting regarding the sins of idolatry, adultery and murder, but He was not relenting regarding the sin of *bitul Torah* (disruption of Torah study)."

R' Elchonon explained this by way of a parable: In war, even a great victory cannot be considered decisive as long as the losing army still retains its arms. However, when one side has been disarmed, then the war is surely over. In the struggle with one's *yetzer hara*, there is only one weapon that can achieve victory: "*I have created the yetzer hara and I have created the Torah as its antidote.*"

As long as the Jewish people hold steadfast to the study of Torah, then even when they sin grievously, there is hope that they may repent. "If only they had forsaken Me but still observed [the study of] My Torah, for its light would have returned them to the good" (*Yerushalmi,* ad loc.). However, when the diligent study of Torah has been abandoned, the sole weapon against the *yetzer hara* has been lost. Faith without toil in Torah is fragile, because man's passions will dominate his heart and distort his way of thinking. The battle is lost.

R' Elchonon concludes with a quote from the holy tongue of his teacher, the *Chofetz Chaim*, זצ"ל:

דעם יֵצֶר הָרַע אַרְט נִיט אַ אִיד זָאל פַאסְטְעָן, אוּן וויינֶען, אוּן דאוונֶען אַ גאנצען טָאג, אַבִּי נִישְׁט לֶערְנֶען!

The yetzer hara does not mind if a Jew fasts, cries and prays all day — as long as he does not study Torah!

Avraham *Avinu* was the "pillar of *chesed*" in this world; Yitzchak was the "pillar of service to Hashem"; Yaakov was "the pillar of Torah." Following the rule that the happenings of the Patriarchs are a portent for their descendants (מַעֲשֶׂה אָבוֹת סִימָן לַבָּנִים),[2] the struggle between Yaakov and Satan foretold that Satan's primary efforts against the Jewish people would always be directed at weakening their study of Torah.

Chanukah, when we celebrate the victory of זֵדִים בְּיַד עוֹסְקֵי תוֹרָתֶךְ, *sinners [being delivered] into the hands of the diligent students of Your Torah,* is a most opportune time to strengthen our Torah study and thereby persevere over the darkness in which Satan seeks to envelop us.

---

2. See *Ramban* to *Bereishis* 12:6.

⋗ Act Intelligently

A s mentioned above, the diligent study of Torah endows the student with שֵׂכֶל הַיָּשָׁר, *an objective intellect.* One who is imbued with the wisdom of Torah examines a given situation through the prism of Torah truth. His reasoning is free of personal interest and prejudice and reflects the timeless teachings that his mind has absorbed. "Whoever engages in Torah study for its own sake [לִשְׁמָהּ] . . . from him people enjoy counsel and wisdom, understanding and strength. . ." (*Avos* 6:1).

There is another aspect of שֵׂכֶל הַיָּשָׁר that is an outgrowth of diligent Torah study and upon which one's success as a servant of Hashem may hinge. *Parashas Ki Savo* contains the *berachos u'kelalos,* the blessings with which the Jewish people will be rewarded for proper *mitzvah* observance and the punishments which they will incur should they stray from the Torah's path. The concluding verse of that *parashah* reads:

וּשְׁמַרְתֶּם אֶת דִּבְרֵי הַבְּרִית הַזֹּאת וַעֲשִׂיתֶם אֹתָם, לְמַעַן תַּשְׂכִּילוּ
אֵת כָּל אֲשֶׁר תַּעֲשׂוּן.
And you shall safeguard the words of this covenant and you shall execute them, so that you will act intelligently in all that you do (Devarim 29:8).

Awareness of man's purpose in this world should impel us to *act intelligently,* that is, to have a proper sense of priorities and understanding of right and wrong, and to act accordingly.

R' Moshe Chaim Luzzato's *Mesilas Yesharim* (ch. 2) explains the quality of זְהִירוּת, *alertness,* as follows:

> *That a person be alert with regard to all his actions and endeavors, meaning, that he ponder and keep watch over his deeds and ways in order to determine whether or not they can be considered good ... since man possesses knowledge and intellect to save himself and to escape the ruination of his soul, how can he possibly ignore that which is his salvation?*

It is sad, but true, that people can consider themselves to be meticulous in their religious observance while, in fact, their actions indicate a distorted sense of priorities and values.

An illustration of grossly distorted values is found in the *Gemara* (*Chullin* 122a) regarding the laws of *tumas meis*, ritual defilement through contact with a corpse. The *Mishnah* states that the skin of a human corpse conveys *tumas meis*. According to one opinion, this is not a Biblical law. Rather, *Chazal* decreed *tumah* upon the skin of a human corpse so that people will not make spreads out of the skins of their deceased parents! As *Tosafos* (*Niddah* 55a) explains, this decree accomplished its purpose because people tend to treat *tumah* restrictions more seriously than they do other prohibitions.

We are speaking here of a person who is so corrupt that he is ready to perform the ultimate disgrace and use the skins of his father or mother for spreads. The *mitzvah* to honor one's parents, one of the Ten Commandments, does not exist, as far as he is concerned. Yet, this same individual would desist from such behavior lest he become *tamei* through Rabbinic decree![3] It is clear that people can go through life with a totally distorted view of things, treating matters of utmost gravity as unimportant and vice-versa.

We consider ourselves far removed from such behavior. Nevertheless, we must ask ourselves honestly whether our dealings in matters *bein adam l'chaveiro*, between man and his fellow, are not contrary to the שֵׂכֶל הַיָּשָׁר approach that one would expect from a *ben Torah*. For example, one may accept upon himself personal *chumros*, stringencies, that may in themselves be quite admirable, but which may cause difficulty to others. If such is the case, then any reward that such *chumros* might bring is surely nullified by one's having ignored the Torah commandment to love one's neighbor as oneself.[4]

---

3. A similar illustration can be found in Vol. I, discourse to *Parashas Bo*.

4. When invited to the home of an affluent *talmid* for the Friday night meal, R' Yisrael Salanter asked how the man usually conducted his Shabbos *seudah*. Hearing that it was filled with *zemiros* and lengthy *divrei Torah*, and usually stretched far into the night, R' Yisrael said that he would accept the invitation on the condition that the meal be shortened by two hours; additional *zemiros* and *divrei Torah* could be recited after the table was cleared. Of course the *talmid* agreed, though R' Yisrael's stipulation left him perplexed.

Friday night, after the table was cleared, R' Yisrael asked that the cook, a poor Jewish woman, be asked to come to the table.

With regard to Torah study, let us take the example of a student who rushes out of the *beis midrash* to wash his hands so that he can study Torah in purity — and spends the next half hour in idle conversation before returning to the *beis midrash*. He has been zealous with regard to a Rabbinic decree (which, at times, may be fulfilled by wiping one's hands on a clean surface), while transgressing the severe sin of *bitul Torah*, disruption of Torah study. Moreover, he has lost worlds — literally! — for, as the *Vilna Gaon* writes, every word of Torah study is a *mitzvah* for itself.

Chanukah is a time for the student of Torah to renew his studies with added diligence, to give thought to the importance of studying without interruption and to examine his ways to see whether or not they are reflective of the wisdom to which he has dedicated himself.

"Thus was the festival established only to offer hallel and hoda'ah, a service of the heart." May the light of Chanukah inspire us to serve Hashem with *seichel hayashar* and a pure heart.

"I apologize," he told her, "if you found yourself rushed in serving the food tonight. I am to blame for the relatively short intervals between courses."

"Apologize?!" the woman responded. "A thousand blessings upon you! You see, I am always thoroughly exhausted by the time Shabbos arrives. The long Friday night meals are sheer torture for me. Tonight, however, I can go home early."

It was then that R' Yisrael's *talmid* understood his *rebbi*'s request.

Food For the Soul

✑ The Custom

The fifteenth of *Shevat*, commonly referred to as *Tu Bi'Shevat* (ט״ו = 15) is the New Year for trees (*Mishnah Rosh Hashanah* 1:1).[1] *Magen Avraham* (*Orach Chaim* 131:16) cites the custom of eating a variety of fruits on *Tu Bi'Shevat* in honor of the day. *Magen Avraham* also cites *Talmud Yerushalmi* which makes note of the concept of partaking of food for the specific purpose of expressing praise and thanks to Hashem.[2]

Thus, the purpose of the *Tu Bi'Shevat* custom is primarily the praise and thanks that are inherent in the blessing recited over the fruits.

✑ The Gain is Our Own

In offering such praise and thanks, we are actually heightening our own *yiras shamayim*, awe of Heaven. This concept is expressed in the following Talmudic passage:

---

1. Trees that blossom before the fifteenth of Shevat cannot be combined for tithing purposes with trees that blossom afterwards. Also, trees that blossom in the third year of the *Shemittah* cycle before the fifteenth of Shevat are treated as fruits that grew in the second year and require the separation of *maaser sheni* rather than *maaser ani*.

The *Gemara* (*Rosh Hashanah* 14a) explains that the year of trees is reckoned from Shevat since by that time most of the year's rainfall — from which the trees grow — has ended.

2. See *Yerushalmi Kiddushin* 4:12 with *P'nei Moshe* commentary.

R' Meir said: One is obligated to recite one hundred blessings each day, as it is written (Devarim 10:12): וְעַתָּה יִשְׂרָאֵל מָה ה' אֱלֹקֶיךָ שֹׁאֵל מֵעִמָּךְ [כִּי אִם לְיִרְאָה אֶת ה'…], *"And now, Israel, what does Hashem, your God, ask of you? [Only that you fear Hashem…] (Menachos 43b).*

Rashi (ibid.) explains that R' Meir derives his teaching from the word מָה, *what*, which is homiletically read as מֵאָה, *one hundred*. In R' Meir's interpretation, the verse is telling us: "One hundred blessings is what Hashem, your God, asks of you, so that you will fear Hashem…"

Rambam (*Hilchos Berachos* 1:1) writes that *Chazal* instituted the recitation of *berachos*, "so that one be ever cognizant of his Creator and be in awe of Him."

However, this goal can be attained only if our *berachos* are recited in the manner in which *Chazal* intended. *Rosh*, in his classic *Orchos Chaim*,[3] states:

> *Regarding all foods and drinks of which one partakes, do not omit a blessing both before and after — and recite them with the fullest concentration of which you are capable…for when speaking of Him, do not be like those of whom it is said (Yeshayahu 29:13), "With his mouth and lips he honors Me, but his heart is distant from Me"* (Orchos Chaim §38).[4]

Unfortunately, the matter of reciting *berachos* falls under the category of מִצְוֹת קַלּוֹת שֶׁאָדָם דָּשׁ בַּעֲקֵבָיו, *minor mitzvos which one tramples upon with his heel*. The term קַל, *minor*, refers not to the *mitzvah*'s actual status, but to the status which the average person accords it. For example, בִּטּוּל תּוֹרָה, *disruption of Torah study*, is in fact a very serious sin, for the study of Torah is equivalent to all other

---

3. *Rabbeinu Asher*, known as the *Rosh* (רא"ש), was a leading thirteenth-century Halachist and Talmudist. His *Orchos Chaim* is a collection of short ethical and *mitzvah*-related directives divided into seven sections, one for each day of the week. Many yeshivos customarily recite the appropriate section at the conclusion of *Shacharis* during the month of Elul.

HaRav Segal has suggested that his *talmidim* accept upon themselves to study and review each day of the year two or three statements in *Orchos Chaim*.

4. The verse continues, *and their fear of Me was by force of habit.*

mitzvos combined (*Mishnah Peah* 1:1) and *bitul Torah* is equivalent to all transgressions combined. Yet, one can find devout Jews who will not hesitate to interrupt someone in the midst of study for some trivial reason. This, unfortunately, is their habit and they give nary a thought to what they are doing. They have taken a *mitzvah* which is paramount and accorded it secondary status. Even worse, by disrupting others, one is in the category of חוֹטֵא וּמַחֲטִיא אֶת הָרַבִּים, *a sinner who causes others to sin.*

And so it is with *berachos.* In *Sha'arei Teshuvah* (1:8), *Rabbeinu Yonah* lists a number of sins which people do not view as sins at all. Among this list is הַזְכָּרַת שֵׁם שָׁמַיִם לְבַטָּלָה, *mentioning the Name of God in vain.* This sin involves transgression of the negative commandment *You shall not use the Name of Hashem, Your God, in vain* (*Sh'mos* 20:7) and the positive commandment *Fear Hashem your God* (*Devarim* 10:20). Contrary to common assumption, transgression of this sin is not limited to instances where the Name of Hashem is expressed needlessly. As stated in *Yesod V'Shoresh HaAvodah* (2:2), it is also transgressed when one pronounces His Name without proper *kavanah*, concentration.[5] Thus, if one's lips move in recitation of a *berachah* while his mind is elsewhere, he has transgressed a most serious sin. Yet, a person can go through his entire lifetime without giving the matter even a moment's thought.

৵ Accomplishing It

Recognizing that reciting a *berachah* is a serious matter is only half the battle. One can be truly God-fearing and sincerely strive to perfect every aspect of his service to Hashem, yet find himself incapable of maintaining concentration during *davening* or when reciting a *berachah*. How, indeed, does one master this all-important ability?

---

5. HaRav Segal further noted that one who slurs his words when reciting a *berachah* is likewise guilty of pronouncing the Name of God in vain. Two common errors in the pronunciation of *berachos* are the slurring of מֶלֶךְ הָעוֹלָם so that the words sound like מֶל כָּעוֹלָם and the pronunciation of אֲדֹנָי as אֲדֹנָי.

HaRav Segal encouraged his *talmidim* to always *daven* from a *siddur*, for this, he said, is a great aid toward having proper *kavanah*.

In *Ruach Chaim* (3:1), R' Chaim of Volozhin offers a parable of a king who orders his servant to find his way to a rooftop. It is logical for the servant to accomplish this by way of a ladder, climbing it rung by rung. The king will not be upset in the least if he sees his servant doing just this. However, the king *will* be upset if he sees his servant wasting his time by remaining on the bottom rung without making any attempt to climb higher.

Similarly, one who strives to grow in his service of Hashem need not feel that he must 'reach the top' in a single leap. Such attempts usually end in failure and frustration. However, one can and should strive for gradual improvement, climbing the spiritual ladder rung by rung.[6]

With regard to *berachos*, it is difficult for one who has been accustomed all his life to reciting *berachos* without proper *kavanah* to suddenly make a complete turnabout and recite every *berachah* properly. Therefore, one should begin by selecting a certain time each week when he will make an extra effort to recite *berachos* with proper *kavanah*. It seems to me that the ideal time for this is Shabbos, for the *kedushah*, sanctity, inherent in the day makes it a most opportune time for spiritual growth. Initially, one should direct his efforts toward the proper recitation of three *berachos*. Having succeeded, he can set five *berachos* as his next week's goal. Having mastered this ability when reciting *berachos* on Shabbos, he can then proceed to mastering it during weekdays as well. Having mastered it with regard to *berachos*, he can then set his goal toward reciting the daily *tefillos* with proper *kavanah*. In *Shemoneh Esrei*, one should begin his efforts with the opening blessing[7] and then attempt to master the remaining blessings, one at a time.

One should note that the *Rambam*, in a letter to his son, mentioned the importance of reciting the opening blessing of *Bircas HaMazon* with proper *kavanah*. Surely, the *Rambam's* intent was that *initially* his son should strive to recite the opening blessing with proper *kavanah*; then he should proceed to master the remaining *berachos* as well.

---

6. R' Chaim of Volozhin uses this parable to explain the teaching that one should study Torah even *shelo lishmah*, not for its own sake, for such study will eventually lead to the desired study that is *lishmah*.

7. Reciting this *berachah* of *Shemoneh Esrei* with proper *kavanah* is most crucial. See *Shulchan Aruch* 101:1.

When reciting a *berachah* before partaking of food or drink, it is good to ponder for a moment the *berachah's* significance. When, for example, one is about to eat an apple and recite a *berachah* in praise of the One Who 'creates the fruits of trees,' one should ponder the wonders of Hashem in causing the apple to be what it is — a delicious, healthy food whose appearance is pleasing to the eye, a food that grew from a tree that is itself the product of a tiny seed. At the very least one should take a moment to ponder the fact that he is about to express praise of the One Above.

Before reciting the *berachah* שֶׁהַכֹּל נִהְיֶה בִּדְבָרוֹ, *through Whose word everything came to be*, one should ponder the fact that everything in this vast universe exists only because such is the will of the One and Only God.

Every morsel that we eat, every beverage that we drink, affords us a new opportunity to recognize and thank Hashem. If we will utilize these opportunities in the desired manner, then each *berachah* that we recite will bring us to yet a higher level of *yiras shamayim*.

Purim Insights

◆§ Unusual Importance

C hazal attach unusual importance to the *mitzvah* of reading the *Megillah*.

> *The Kohanim engaged in their sacrificial service, and the Levi'im on their platform [providing musical accompaniment to the service] and the Israelites at their station [attending the service] must all abandon their service and go to hear the Megillah reading. The scholars of the school of Rebbi [R' Yehudah HaNasi] relied on the above in ruling that one must interrupt one's study of Torah and go to hear the Megillah reading (Megillah 3a).*

The *Gemara* even entertains the possibility that פַּרְסוּמֵי נִיסָא, *publicizing the miracle*, supersedes the concept of כְּבוֹד הַבְּרִיוֹת, *human dignity*. According to this reasoning, reading the *Megillah* would take precedence over attending to a מֵת מִצְוָה, *unattended corpse*. Though the *Gemara* concludes that this is not so, its hypothesis underscores the importance of קְרִיאַת הַמְגִילָה, *reading the Megillah*.

This point is borne out yet further by the laws regarding the *Megillah* reading. Women are obligated in this *mitzvah* (*Orach Chaim* 687:1) and parents are to bring even young children to hear the reading (689:1).[1] All are required to hear the reading both by night and by day and one must hear every word of the reading in order to fulfill his or her obligation.

In publicizing the Purim miracle through the reading of the *Megillah*, we make known a number of fundamental lessons which, if understood and absorbed, can elevate our service of Hashem. Let us study a few of them.

◄§ Danger's True Cause

After learning of Haman's plan to exterminate the Jews, Mordechai rent his clothes, donned sackcloth and placed ashes upon himself. He went into the midst of the city and cried out in anguish.

Learning of this, Queen Esther sent garments to Mordechai so that he could clothe himself and enter the palace to speak with her. He refused this, for he did not want to interrupt his *tefillos* for even an instant. Esther then summoned Hasach, one of the king's chamberlains:

> וַתְּצַוֵּהוּ עַל מָרְדֳּכָי לָדַעַת מַה זֶּה וְעַל מַה זֶּה.
>
> *She ordered him to go to Mordechai, to learn what this was and why it was (Esther 4:5).*
>
> *R' Yitzchak said: Esther sent the following message to Mordechai: "Perhaps Israel has transgressed the Five Books of the Torah of which it is written (Sh'mos 32:15),* מִזֶּה וּמִזֶּה הֵם כְּתוּבִים, '*on this side and on this side they [the Ten Commandments] are written'?"* (Megillah 15a).[2]

Esther understood that Mordechai's donning of sackcloth meant that the Jews were in danger, but she did not know the nature of the danger or its source. In inquiring of Mordechai, she was not interested in hearing of a possible political happening or other event that may have precipitated the danger. Her first concern was to learn the

---

1. As long as they will not cause disturbance.
2. *Maharsha* explains this in light of *R' Saadiah Gaon's* teaching that all 613 *mitzvos* are encompassed within the Ten Commandments.

danger's *spiritual cause*. Esther understood that whatever happens to the Jewish people, both as a nation and on an individual level, occurs through *hashgachah pratis*, Divine Providence. If a decree against the Jews had been issued, then its root cause *must* be sin.

Chazal teach that one does not bang his finger in this world unless it has been so decreed Above (*Chullin* 7b). When travail strikes, ר״ל, one should look beyond the apparent cause and take stock of his deeds and ways — not in a spirit of gloom and depression, but with the realization that *as a man disciplines his son, so does Hashem, your God, discipline you* (*Devarim* 8:5).

◆§ Hidden Miracles

In discussing the Torah's stress on remembering the Exodus from Egypt, *Ramban* (*Sh'mos* 16:13) states a basic principle of Torah outlook:

> ... And from the great and well-known miracles, one comes to recognize the hidden miracles, which are the foundation of the entire Torah. For a man has no share in the Torah of Moshe Rabbeinu until he believes that all our happenings and occurrences are miraculous — there is nothing natural in them at all.

The Purim story, as recorded in *Megillas Esther*, is a classic illustration of this principle. It contains no open miracles. When examined individually, each episode in the *Megillah* seems to be a completely natural event; some, in fact, could have occurred in any royal court of that era. A new king celebrates his rise to power with a lavish feast; the queen slights him and is killed for her crime; two of the king's chamberlains plot to kill him, but their plot is discovered and they are killed. Were these not fairly common occurrences in the monarchies of old?

However, when taken in totality, the events of *Megillas Esther* cannot be explained as anything but an intricate and wondrous Heavenly plan designed to bring about the salvation of the Jewish people. Moreover, upon careful study, one can see the *hashgachah pratis* in the individual events themselves. The removal of Vashti made way for a new queen and from among the thousands of candidates for this position, Esther was chosen.[3] Bigsan and Seresh discussed their plot to kill Achashverosh precisely at a time when Mordechai was nearby and could overhear their plot. It would have been logical for the king to reward Mordechai immediately, but Hashem wanted Achashverosh to put the matter aside until the fateful night when sleep eluded him and he ordered that his record book be read to him. At precisely the moment when Mordechai's deed was being discussed, Haman arrived at the palace — to ask that Mordechai be hung!

Earlier, when Haman, upon leaving the first feast of Esther, had met a defiant Mordechai, the *Megillah* states, *Haman restrained himself and returned home ... and Haman recounted to them the glory of his wealth and his many sons ...* (5:10). The *Vilna Gaon* explains that Haman was at the height of his glory when he left the private feast which Esther had tended for only the king and himself. Mordechai's defiance at precisely that moment cast Haman into a trauma which endangered his life. He recounted the glory of his wealth and honor to his cohorts in order to drive away his anguish and restore his spirit. That very night, Haman returned to the palace to ask that Mordechai be hung. When the king asked him, *What shall be done for the man whom the king wants especially to honor?* (6:6) Haman was certain that the king was referring to none other than himself. He learned of his error when Achashverosh told him, *Hurry, then, get the robe and the horse as you have said and do all this for Mordechai the Jew, who sits at the king's gate. Do not omit a single detail from all that you have spoken!* (6:10)

Should not the trauma of that moment, or the hours that followed when Haman led Mordechai through the streets of Shushan, have

---

3. It has been noted that Achashverosh's favoring Esther even though she refused to divulge her nationality and kindred is one of the *Megillah's* great hidden miracles. Achashverosh had killed his first queen for refusing to obey his orders and appear at his feast. Vashti had good reason not to appear, for she had become stricken with *tzara'as* (a condition similar to leprosy). Yet, in his fury, Achashverosh was unforgiving. On the other hand, in seeking to know Esther's background, the king was merely asking her to reveal that which any husband has a right to know. Moreover, he went to great lengths to induce her to tell her secret, tending a feast in her honor, remitting taxes and sending gifts in her name (*Megillah* 13a). Yet, her steadfast refusal did not cause her to lose favor in his eyes.

been sufficient to kill Haman? How did this arrogant, glory-hungry man survive being disgraced as his arch-enemy was accorded the glorious honor for which he so lusted? That he *did* survive was, indeed, a great miracle. *HaKadosh Baruch Hu* kept Haman alive so that he would be unmasked by Esther at her second feast, receive the punishment that was due him and see his evil designs thwarted.

ᴐᖆ Light From the Darkness

The salvation of the Jews in *Megillas Esther* involved people and events that, ostensibly, spelled trouble for the Jews. It was Haman who advised Achashverosh to kill Vashti (*Megillah* 12b). Vashti's removal paved the way for Esther, who brought about Haman's downfall. Esther's inviting Haman to the feast made the Jews fearful that she was becoming friendly with their enemy and would not come to the defense of her brethren.[4] Haman, on the other hand, viewed the invitation as a sign of his incomparable greatness. Of course, both feelings were wrong. The feast's purpose was to bring about Haman's end and the Jews' salvation.

In our personal lives, as well, the end of a matter is often not the way we would have imagined it to be at first. Occurrences that seem advantageous often bring about problems, while that which appears to be bad is often the source of improvement of our lot. We must always bear in mind that Hashem's ways are beyond human comprehension. As wise as we may be, we can never be absolutely certain of a matter's end result. All that we can and must do is ensure that our actions are in full consonance with Torah. Having acted in this way, we can place our full trust in the One Above, with the confidence that He will guide matters toward a conclusion which, ultimately, is in our very best interests.

---

4. The *Gemara* relates: What was Esther's reason for inviting Haman to the banquet? ... Rabbi Nechemiah said: So that the Jews would not say, "We have a sister in the royal palace," and neglect to pray for Divine mercy (*Megillah* 15b).

੶ Turning Point

After informing Esther of Haman's plan to exterminate the Jews, Mordechai instructed her to go before the king and plead for her people. Esther responded that, as was well known, anyone that came before the king without being summoned risked being put to death. Therefore, to go before the king on her own initiative would be endangering herself and jeopardizing her mission. She had not been seen by the king for thirty days and in all likelihood would soon be summoned. It seemed logical, she reasoned, to wait for the king to summon her.

Mordechai responded:

> Do not imagine that you will be able to escape in the king's palace any more than the rest of the Jews. For if you persist in keeping silent at a time like this, relief and deliverance will come to the Jews from some other place, while you and your father's house will perish. And who knows whether it was just for such a time as this that you attained your royal position! (Esther 4:13-14).

Esther accepted Mordechai's words and asked that he proclaim a three-day fast; on the third day, she went before the king. She found favor with Achashverosh, who accepted her invitation that he and Haman join her for a feast. Thus began the salvation of the Jewish people.

Without a doubt, the moment when Esther submitted herself to heeding Mordechai's words is a major turning point in the *Megillah*. Though her feelings on the matter were logical and seemed correct, she submitted herself totally to Mordechai's Torah wisdom. It may well be that this submission, more than anything else, is what earned Esther the inestimable merit of having the miracle occur through her. It may also be that this act is what merited that the story be recorded as a book of כִּתְבֵי קוֹדֶשׁ (Holy Scriptures) bearing Esther's name and that it be read year after year for all generations.

The ability to accept criticism and act upon it is most critical for anyone who desires to be a true servant of Hashem. Accepting criticism often involves a great test of will. Esther passed the test and thereby gained boundless reward for herself and salvation for her people.

Following the Sin of the Golden Calf, Moshe *Rabbeinu* describes the Children of Israel as an עַם קְשֵׁה עוֹרֶף, *stiff-necked people* (*Sh'mos* 34:9). In the Book of *Devarim* (ch. 9), where this episode is repeated, *HaKadosh Baruch Hu* tells Moshe, "I have observed this people, and behold, it is a stiff-necked people. Let Me be and I will eradicate them, and erase their name from beneath the heavens..." (*Devarim* 9:13-14).

It would seem that such punishment was justified by the mere fact that the people had committed the heinous sin of idolatry. Why did Hashem indicate their being stiff-necked as justification?

Sforno comments:

> *It is impossible to be righteous and have an upright heart if one is stiff-necked, for such a person follows the stubbornness of his heart and mind — even when a teacher demonstrates with clear proof that his thoughts are improper and will lead to no good. This is because he does not pay heed to the teacher, as if his neck was hard like an iron sinew, in a manner that does not allow him to turn any which way. Therefore, he follows the stubbornness of his heart as is his way (ibid. v. 6).*

Where the episode is first recounted, *Sforno* comments that when people are *stiff-necked* "there is no hope that they will repent" (*Sh'mos* 32:9).

The Purim miracle occurred through Esther because she was not at all stiff-necked when it came to accepting rebuke. One who is stiff-necked can experience the day of Purim and come away with very little, because he lacks the attribute that made this day a reality.

The key to spiritual growth is *mussar* study. However, *mussar* study cannot inspire unless the student approaches it with a sincere desire to take its words to heart and effect a change within himself. If, after studying *mussar* or listening to a *mussar shmuess* (discourse), one can walk away impassively, then there is little hope that he will ever improve. If, however, one walks away with resolve to act upon what he has studied or heard, then he has already set himself apart from those who are קְשֵׁה עוֹרֶף, *stiff-necked*. He has embarked on the road of *teshuvah*.

PART II

General Themes

Obligations of a Torah Jew

◆§ Glorifying Hashem

Mesilas Yesharim (ch. 11) discusses at length the various levels of falsehood that exist among mankind. After delineating these levels in descending order of destructiveness, the author writes:

> The Sage [Shlomo HaMelech] has informed us that all this is contrary to the will of the Creator, Blessed is He, and His pious ones, as it is written (Mishlei 13:5), "A righteous one hates falsehood." It is regarding this that the admonishment "distance yourself from falsehood" is written. Note that it does not say, "guard yourself against falsehood"; rather, "distance yourself." This is meant to alert us to the great extent to which we must distance ourselves and flee from falsehood . . .
>
> Our Sages have taught, "The seal of HaKadosh Baruch Hu is truth" (Shabbos 55a). Now, if truth is what Hashem has chosen as His seal, then how despicable must its opposite be before Him! . . . Truth is one of the pillars upon which the world exists (Avos 1:18); it follows, then, that one who speaks falsehood is considered as if he has destroyed the world's foundation.

All of us consider ourselves men of truth, whose spoken word is in consonance with the Torah's requirements in this area. Let us, however, examine a brief phrase of the daily tefillah and see whether or not we utter it each day as a statement of truth.

In *Baruch She'amar*,[1] the blessing which opens the *Pesukei D'Zimrah* portion of *Shacharis*, we say:

נְגַדֶּלְךָ וּנְשַׁבֵּחֲךָ וּנְפָאֶרְךָ וְנַזְכִּיר שִׁמְךָ וְנַמְלִיכְךָ. . .
We shall exalt You, praise You, glorify You, mention Your Name and proclaim Your reign . . .

Each morning, then, we declare our intention to glorify Hashem's Name anew. וּנְפָאֶרְךָ, *We shall glorify You!* How does one truly glorify His Name? *Chazal*, citing a Scriptural verse, provide the answer:

> A Jew should study Scripture and Mishnah, serve Torah scholars and deal graciously with his fellow man. Then others will say of him, "Fortunate is his father who taught him Torah! Fortunate is his teacher who taught him Torah! Woe to those who do not study Torah! He who studies Torah — how pleasant is his behavior and how proper are his deeds." To him may the verse be applied: "And He said to me: עַבְדִּי אָתָּה יִשְׂרָאֵל אֲשֶׁר בְּךָ אֶתְפָּאָר 'You are My servant, Israel, in whom I will be glorified' " (Yeshayahu 49:3).

Thus, for one's declaration of וּנְפָאֶרְךָ to be true, his deeds and speech must be of a type that serves to enhance Hashem's glory. In succinct terms, his behavior must be one of *kiddush Hashem*.

✑ Chilul Hashem

Mesilas Yesharim (ch. 11) discusses the concept of *chilul Hashem* at great length:

> The various aspects of chilul Hashem are numerous and significant, for man must be exceedingly concerned for the honor of his Master. One must carefully scrutinize and ponder all that he does so that there not

---

1. The commentators record an ancient tradition that this prayer was transcribed by the *Anshei Knesses HaGedolah* (Men of the Great Assembly) some 2400 years ago from a script that fell from Heaven.

result a disgrace to the honor of Heaven, God forbid. We have been taught: [R' Yochanan ben Beroka said: "Whoever desecrates the Name of Heaven in secret, they will exact punishment from him in public;] unintentional or intentional, both are alike regarding chilul Hashem."

... Each man, in accordance with his own spiritual level and his standing in the eyes of his generation, must exercise forethought so that he does not do something unbefitting a person of his stature. For man's alertness and meticulousness in service of Heaven must reflect his stature and wisdom; if not, then the Name of Hashem is desecrated through him, God forbid. It is an honor to the Torah when one who devotes himself exceedingly to its study is likewise devoted to correcting and refining his midos. To the extent that such refinement is lacking, the study of Torah is disparaged — and this is a disgrace, Heaven forfend, to the Name of Hashem, Who gave us His holy Torah and commanded us to toil in its study so that we attain spiritual perfection.

Thus, whether or not one has committed a *chilul Hashem* may depend on his station in life. The greater one's spiritual level and his standing in the eyes of others, the greater is his obligation to be the kind of person whose ways reflect the Torah's teachings.

Chazal teach that when a *ben Torah's* ways do not serve to glorify Hashem's Name, the opposite is achieved:

However, if one studies Scripture and Mishnah and serves Torah scholars, but is not honest in his dealings, and does not converse pleasantly with people — what do others say of him? "Woe to he who studies Torah! Woe to his father who taught him Torah! Woe to his teacher who taught him Torah! He who studies Torah — how corrupt are his deeds and how ugly is his behavior!" To him may the verse be applied: "In that men said of them: 'These are Hashem's people but they are departed from His land' " (Yechezkel 36:20).

One should not underestimate the severity of *chilul Hashem*. *Chazal* state: "For a person who has been guilty of *chilul Hashem*, there is no power in *teshuvah* to suspend his judgment, nor in Yom Kippur to atone, nor in affliction to cleanse; rather, all of these suspend the judgment and death cleanses" (*Yoma* 86a).[2]

◆§ The Key

What can one do to ensure that his daily proclamation, "וּנְפָאֶרְךָ, *and we shall glorify You*," be a true one? He must study *mussar*. For if one studies *mussar* properly, he is at least *striving* to become the sort of person whose actions bring glory to Hashem.

Rabbeinu Yonah writes in *Sefer HaYirah*:

> Passages of *yiras Hashem* should forever be upon your lips, such as, הֱוֵי עַז כַּנָּמֵר, "*Be bold like a leopard* ... [to carry out the will of your Father in Heaven]" (*Avos* 5:23); [...] סוֹף דָּבָר הַכֹּל נִשְׁמָע [אֶת הָאֱלֹהִים יְרָא., "*The sum of the matter, when all has been considered: [Fear Hashem ...]*" (*Koheles* 12:13); וְעַתָּה יִשְׂרָאֵל מָה ה' אֱלֹהֶיךָ שֹׁאֵל מֵעִמָּךְ [כִּי אִם לְיִרְאָה אֶת ה'., "*And now, Israel, what does Hashem, your God, ask of you? [Only that you fear Hashem ...]*" (*Devarim* 10:12); מְאֹד מְאֹד הֱוֵי שְׁפַל רוּחַ, "*Be exceedingly humble*" (*Avos* 4:4). Accustom yourself to this practice and you will not stumble.

Rabbeinu Yonah's words provide the key to successful *mussar* study. When, in the course of *mussar* study, one comes upon a classic verse or statement of *Chazal* related to self-improvement, he should review it many items with intensity, so that its message can permeate his being and bring about a change within himself.

---

2. One should note that there *is* an alternative to death in cases of *chilul Hashem*. *Sha'arei Teshuvah* (4:16) states: "... For one who has been guilty of *chilul Hashem* ... there is a restorative cure for his wound, namely, that he constantly sanctify the name of Hashem." *Kiddush Hashem* through speech and deed is an atonement, measure for measure, for *chilul Hashem*.

Chazal state: "Man's *yetzer hara* seeks to overpower him every day; if not that *HaKadosh Baruch Hu* aids him, he could not withstand it" (*Kiddushin* 30b). Citing the verse, "Hashem despises all who are arrogant of heart" (*Mishlei* 16:5), *Rabbeinu Yonah* comments that an arrogant person cannot hope for Hashem's assistance in overcoming his *yetzer hara*. It is inevitable, then, that the *yetzer hara* will subdue him.

Can one who ponders this thought fail to seek to rid himself of this despicable trait? Sincere *mussar* study such as the type that we have described must ultimately effect a change within the student.

✑ The Chofetz Chaim's Works

Only a short while ago, Heaven granted our people a great gift, the *Chofetz Chaim*, of blessed memory. The *Chofetz Chaim's* many *sefarim* should be studied by every *ben Torah*. It is imperative that his works on the topic of *shemiras halashon* be studied again and again. The *Chofetz Chaim's sefarim* cover the full gamut of Torah outlook: faith and trust in Hashem, awe of Him, diligence in Torah study — every wonderful attribute to which a Jew should aspire is discussed between the covers of the *Chofetz Chaim's* works. Moreover, *Chazal* tell us that words that flow from the heart enter the heart of the one to whom they are spoken. Words that flowed from the holy and pure heart of the *Chofetz Chaim* will surely make a profound impression upon the hearts of all who study them.

In the *Chofetz Chaim's* halachic classic *Mishnah Berurah* and its secondary commentaries is to be found scores of thoughts related to spiritual refinement. In the opening passage of *Be'ur Halachah*, the *Chofetz Chaim* cites the six constant *mitzvos* enumerated by *Sefer HaChinuch* which one can fulfill at every available moment. The fifth *mitzah* relates to our discussion:

> *Fear of Hashem should always be upon him so that he will not sin. Regarding this the Torah writes, "Hashem, your God, you shall fear" (Devarim 6:13). One who is faced with the temptation to sin is obligated to arouse his spirit and take to heart at that moment that*

HaKadosh Baruch Hu takes note of all man's actions even when they are committed in utter darkness, and that He will visit retribution upon man in accordance with his sinful ways, as it is written, " 'If a person will hide himself in a hidden place will I not then see him?' says Hashem" (Yirmiyahu 23:24).

๏ Practical Advice

We have already mentioned that continuous review of the classic *mussar* teachings has a telling effect upon one's *neshamah*. May I suggest that every *ben Torah* begin his day by strengthening himself in matters of faith and fear of Hashem. After washing *negel vasser*, one should recite the two paragraphs of *Ani Maamin* in which we acknowledge belief in Hashem's system of reward and punishment, and that He knows our every deed and thought.

After reciting *Bircas HaTorah* and the appropriate passages, one should say the following Mishnaic teaching: דַּע מַה לְמַעְלָה מִמְּךָ — עַיִן רוֹאָה, וְאוֹזֶן שׁוֹמַעַת, וְכָל מַעֲשֶׂיךָ בַּסֵּפֶר נִכְתָּבִים, *Known what is above you — a watchful Eye, an attentive Ear and all your deeds are recorded in a Book (Avos 2:1).*

The *Halachah* requires that one review the weekly *parashah* twice and its *Targum* once (*Shulchan Aruch* 285:1). Ideally, one should review *Rashi's* commentary as well. Such study is a prime means for strengthening one's *emunah*, faith.

It is related that once a disciple of R' Itze'le Peterberger was experiencing inner doubts regarding matters of *emunah*. R' Itze'le advised him to study the weekly *parashah* with *Rashi* each week. The disciple heeded this advice and his doubts disappeared. He grew to become a distinguished Torah personality.

One's waking hours[3] should be filled primarily with Torah study — a study that is marked by *uninterrupted diligence*. There is no comparison between Torah study that is uninterrupted and Torah study that is interrupted. Worse still, is Torah study interrupted by frivolous conversation or *lashon hara*. In the Chofetz Chaim's words:

---

3. HaRav Segal added that after reciting the bedtime *Shema*, one should ponder thoughts of Torah until sleep overtakes him.

If one's learning is marked by interruptions, then a spirit of sanctity will not come to rest upon him [while he is studying]. Conversely, if his learning is consistent, then a great and awesome sanctity will come to rest upon him each time he studies (Shemiras HaLashon, Sha'ar HaTorah §3).

Avoiding *bitul Torah*, disruption of Torah study, is of paramount importance — and it is not nearly as difficult as some might imagine. As R' Chaim of Volozhin writes, service of Hashem is like climbing a tall ladder; it can be done, but it must be accomplished with steady determination, one rung at a time. One who is plagued by the temptation to converse with his friends during learning sessions should first attempt to avoid such talk for one learning period each day. Once this has been accomplished, the time frame should be extended every so often, until one's study sessions are filled with nothing but the study of Torah.

Each night during *Maariv*, we say, "Therefore, Hashem, our God, upon our retiring and upon our arising, we will discuss Your decrees and we will rejoice with the words of Your Torah and with Your commandments for all eternity. For they are our life and the length of our days and about them we will meditate day and night." Here, too, let us not be guilty of uttering an untruth. If one does not yet experience true joy and sweetness in Torah study, then let him study with added diligence and without interruption, so that the sanctity of Torah will permeate his heart and fill it with an indescribable joy.

May we merit to glorify Hashem through deed and word until the time when all the world will acknowledge Him as the One and Only King.

At the Pinnacle of the Universe

There are commandments which stand at the pinnacle of the universe and yet people treat them with levity (Berachos 6b).

[Which stand] at the pinnacle of the universe — such as tefillah (Rashi).

◄§ Proper Perception

The *Gemara* states: "Whoever designates a מָקוֹם קָבוּעַ, *permanent place*, for his prayer service, the God of Avraham will surely come to his assistance. And when this person departs the world they will mourn for him and say, Woe, where is the humble one?! Woe, where is the pious one, disciple of Avraham?!" (*Berachos* 6b).

The above praise was said of one of the great sages of the Mishnaic period. Rabban Gamliel addressed the sages and asked (*Berachos* 28b), "Is there anyone who knows how to compose a benediction against the heretics?" Shmuel *HaKattan* came forth and composed the *VeLamalshinim* (And for slanderers . . .) blessing for the weekday *Shemoneh Esrei*. Of Shmuel *HaKattan*, the *Gemara* (*Sanhedrin* 11a) states: "He was deserving that the *Shechinah* come to rest upon him, but his generation was not deserving of this. And when he died they said of him, Woe, where is the pious one! Woe, where is the humble one . . .?!"

How can it be, asks *Rabbeinu Yonah* (*Berachos* 6b), that the praise said of Shmuel *HaKattan* can be applied to any individual by mere merit of his having designated a permanent place for his prayer service?!

Rabbeinu Yonah explains:

> They [Chazal] did not mean that because of designating a permanent place alone [one is deserving of such praise]. Rather, [they meant] that this person is so exacting with regard to prayer that he is also meticulous in this, to designate a permanent place for prayer. Since he loves prayer to such an extent, surely he possesses the trait of humility, so that his tefillos will find acceptance before the Omnipresent, as it is written, "A heart broken and crushed, O God, You despise not" (*Tehillim* 51:19).[1] For if he will not possess the trait of humility, he will never be able to pray with proper concentration and his tefillos will never be accepted before the Omnipresent, Blessed is He. Now, since he has acquired the trait of humility, he will likewise acquire the even greater quality of חֲסִידוּת, piety, for one trait leads to yet another, as it is stated, "Humility leads to piety. . ." (*Avodah Zarah* 20b).
>
> Thus, through exactness in prayer, one merits all these qualities and the above praise will be said of him when he departs this world.

We may suggest another explanation for the praise of one who designates a place for prayer. A person sets aside a place for a specific service when he attaches great importance to that service. Because it is something special, he will perform it only in a particular spot designated for it. It is not the designation of a place for prayer that merits praise, but the perception which motivates the act.

To be considered what *Rabbeinu Yonah* describes as an אוֹהֵב הַתְּפִילָה, *one who loves prayer*, one must have a proper understanding of the purpose of praying to the One Above. Prayer is not intended merely as a means of requesting our needs. As *Maharal* explains, the *primary* purpose of prayer is to draw us closer to Hashem. When one prays, he becomes conscious of how dependent he is on Hashem for his every need, for his very existence. He becomes cognizant of his real station in life, that of a servant whose constant striving should be to serve his Master with total dedication.

---

1. See *Sotah* 5b.

This is prayer's primary function. We now understand why *Shacharis* opens with *Baruch She'amar* in which we praise the God *Who spoke and the world came into being . . . Who maintains creation . . . decrees and fulfills . . . has mercy upon His creatures . . . lives forever and endures to eternity . . .* Similarly, *Bircas HaMazon* opens with a blessing in which we acknowledge that all sustenance comes from Hashem and that He sustains us *with grace, kindness and mercy.* Recognition of these concepts is the very essence of prayer.

When one prays in the proper manner, he becomes more keenly aware of his true mission on this world, and thereby becomes worthy of Hashem's infinite blessings.

Chazal (based on *Devarim* 11:13) refer to prayer as עֲבוֹדָה שֶׁבַּלֵּב, *service of the heart.* In its plain meaning, עֲבוֹדָה שֶׁבַּלֵּב describes prayer as something which, by definition, requires feeling and concentration, not mere lip service. The term has another connotation as well. Prayer, when approached properly, is a service which *refines the heart*, as it draws the supplicant closer to his Creator and deepens his understanding of the purpose of life.[2]

⇜§ How to Pray

Chovos HaLevavos (*Sha'ar Cheshbon HaNefesh* ch. 3) writes of the importance of proper *kavanah*, concentration, when praying:

> *When involving yourself with duties which require both body and heart, such as when praying before God, Blessed is He . . . remove from your heart any thought which might distract you from your prayers. Then, you must contemplate to Whom your tefillos are being directed, what it is you hope to derive from them, and the words and concepts that you will express.*
>
> *Know that the words of tefillos which man utters with his mouth are like the skin of a fruit, while the*

---

2. The root of תְּפִילָה is פלל, to *judge*, to *differentiate*, to *clarify*, to *decide*. Related to פלל is the root פלה, meaning a clear separation between two things. Prayer is the soul's yearning to define what truly matters and to ignore the trivialities that are sometimes mistaken as essential (*Siddur Avodas HaLev*).

*thoughts that accompany them are the fruit itself. The
words of prayer which one verbalizes are like the
physical body, while concentration on thei meaning is
prayer's soul. Therefore, when a person prays with his
tongue alone, while his mind drifts off to other matters,
his prayer is like a body without the soul, a skin without
the fruit . . . Regarding such a person, Scripture states:
"Because this nation has approached Me, honoring Me
with their mouths and lips, but their heart was far from
Me, and their fear of Me was by force of habit"*
(Yeshayahu 29:13).

*This can be likened to a servant whose home is
being graced by the presence of his master. The servant instructs his wife and children to honor the
master and attend to his every need — while the
servant himself goes off to engage in some matter
of levity! Of course, the master, upon seeing
this, becomes incensed. Instead of accepting the
honor and comfort offered him by the wife and
children, the master throws everything in the servant's
face.*

*So it is with prayer. If one's heart and inner self do not
participate in the tefillah process, then God does not
accept the prayer of his limbs and tongue.*

We conclude the *Shemoneh Esrei* with David *HaMelech's* entreaty:
יִהְיוּ לְרָצוֹן אִמְרֵי פִי וְהֶגְיוֹן לִבִּי לְפָנֶיךָ, ה׳ צוּרִי וְגֹאֲלִי, *May the expressions
of my mouth and the thoughts of my heart find favor before You,
Hashem, my Rock and my Redeemer* (Tehillim 19:15). Says *Chovos
HaLevavos*: "This is in itself a great disgrace, that one should claim
to have spoken before God with his heart while his heart was
actually somewhere else — and he beseeches God to accept his
heart's meditation and that it should cause him to find favor before
Him!"

It is not for us to pray with the Kabbalistic intents revealed by the
Arizal. Simple concentration on *peirush hamilos*, the plain meaning
of the text, is both required and sufficient. One should begin by
striving for proper *kavanah* when reciting the opening blessing of

Shemoneh Esrei[3] and gradually improve the remainder of his *davening* as well.[4]

One should not underestimate the power with which one invests his *tefillos* when concentrating on their plain meaning. R' Chaim of Volozhin writes:

> *The Anshei Knesses HaGedolah (Men of the Great Assembly) who composed the text of the Shemoneh Esrei numbered one hundred and twenty scholars. Some of these were prophets as well as Sages. What they achieved can never be duplicated. They invested each word of the liturgy with a power to affect all of creation, from the smallest atomic particle to the most enormous galactic mass. Moreover, the effect of each word leaves a different impression on the cosmos. The impact of the evening tefillah is not the same as the impact of the prayer offered on the previous morning. All this is possible because a spirit of Divine holiness guided the authors: Through them the Almighty Himself implanted within each word infinite power and unlimited effect.*
>
> *Since no human being can possibly fathom the awesome depth of each word of prayer, one should rather pray with pure and simple intent. As he pronounces each word, he should picture in his mind's eye a mental image of the actual word as it is written. He should concentrate on raising the words heavenward to their celestial source ... One who prays in this fashion will make an impact with every word.*
>
> *Therefore, the Gemara describes the words of prayer as "matters which stand at the pinnacle of the universe," because every phrase of prayer actually rises up to heaven in its shape of letters and words, and impacts on the entire universe (Nefesh HaChaim 2:13).*

May we merit that our *tefillos* be uttered with true concentration and from the depths of our hearts.

---

3. See *Shulchan Aruch* 101:1.
4. This is discussed at greater length in the discourse to *Tu Bi'Shevat*.

Chinuch

ᵉᵍ Lifelong Education

Educate a youth according to his way, [so that] even when he will grow old he will not stray from it (Mishlei 22:6).

In this verse, Shlomo *HaMelech* defines the kind of *chinuch*, religious education and upbringing, we are required to provide our children. It must be a *chinuch* whose impressions and fine points will remain with the child all his life, up to and including old age. *Chinuch*, by definition, must stand the test of time.

R' Simchah Zissel Ziv (*'Der Alter'*) of Kelm sees another timely message in this verse. He interprets its latter half to mean that though one's years of formal education have ended, his *chinuch* should not end. Rather, from then on he should continue with *self-chinuch*, always seeking to learn, always striving to refine his ways. *Even when he will grow old*, he should not cease from this. In this light, R' Simchah Zissel explains why the Hebrew term for "Torah scholars" is *talmidei chachamim*. A true *chacham*, scholar, always sees himself as a *talmid*, student, for he is forever engaged in the process of self-education and improvement (*Chachmah U'Mussar* §130).

In his famous *Iggeres*, the *Vilna Gaon* writes that until the day of death, one should "afflict" himself — not through physical affliction, but by harnessing his physical desires and restraining his tongue from forbidden speech. This is included in the lifelong *chinuch* to which R' Simchah Zissel referred.

✑ A Classic Example

A dear friend of mine, who passed away not long ago, was a classic example of one forever engaged in self-*chinuch*. His primary concern in life was Torah and *mitzvos*; his business endeavors were of secondary concern.

I recall the time I showed him the *Sefer Erech Apayim*, which focuses on the trait of anger. He told me that he personally would have great benefit from studying such a work. When we met again some time later, my friend informed me that he had purchased the *sefer* and that he deeply appreciated my having told him of it. He mentioned that he had instructed his children to study the work as well.

It is common for businessmen to study the financial section of the newspaper during breakfast each morning. My friend also studied business-related material during his morning meal, but his text was different. He chose *Sefer Mitzvas HaBitachon*, the classic collection of verses and comments on the subject of *bitachon* (trust in Hashem), by R' Shmuel Hominer. When I visited him at the hospital when he was already seriously ill, I saw this *sefer* lying on his night table. I commented that it was truly an awesome work. He was not able to speak, but he nodded his head in agreement.

Until his very last moments, he continued to strengthen himself in these matters. *Even when he grew old, he did not cease from educating himself.*

Concurrently, he did not cease from guiding his children along the path of Torah and *yiras Hashem*. When his children were growing up, he would arise early to study *Mishnayos* with them before *Shacharis* and would also study works of *mussar* with them. His wonderful children are a credit to him and to the exceptional *chinuch* which they received.

✑ Proper Parenting

The story is told of a *talmid chacham* who arrived in a town where he was a total stranger. Someone approached him and said, "I am looking for someone to slaughter an animal for me. Are you, perhaps, a *shochet*?" The scholar replied that he was not. A few moments later, the visitor turned to the other man and asked, "Perhaps you could loan me some money?" The man was taken aback. "I don't even know you and you expect me to lend you money?!" Replied the scholar, "You were willing to trust me with the *kashrus* of your meat, yet you are not willing to trust me with your money!"

Warped attitudes like the one illustrated above are, unfortunately, not uncommon. People are extremely zealous when a potential profit is involved; they will leave no stone unturned when it comes to determining whether or not a given venture is viable. Yet, when their children's *chinuch* is at stake, many are content to rely entirely on the yeshivos to produce a finished product that will be a credit to Hashem and His Torah. This is a mistake. No matter how outstanding a given yeshivah staff is, it cannot be expected to do the *entire* job — there must be major input as well from the child's father and mother. Testing a child in his weekly studies is not sufficient. A parent must maintain careful watch over his child's behavior, and know who his friends are, how he spends his free time, what sort of literature he reads, etc.

A *talmid chacham* related to me that his wife was a childhood friend of a daughter of the Brisker *Rav*. When the two girls would do schoolwork together in the *Rav's* home, the *Rav* would pass by the room they were in from time to time in order to listen to their conversation as they studied. This was a *gadol* to whom every minute was *kodesh kadashim*, a precious jewel that was not to be wasted! Obviously, he considered this time well spent, for he was fulfilling his obligation as a parent.

One area where parental supervision is an absolute imperative is that of literature. To our misfortune, there exists many a religious home where publications that are totally contrary to Torah can be found. Some of these works contain teachings that contradict the very tenets of our faith, while others are filled with thoughts and/or illustrations that are immoral and which awaken the reader's sinful desires. Such thoughts can remain with a person all his life and lead to sin each time they are conjured in his mind, ר"ל.

Rashi states that Hashem associated His name with Yitzchak *Avinu* even during the latter's lifetime, because by that time Yitzchak was "blind, confined to his home. . .and the *yetzer hara* had ceased to dwell within him" (*Bereishis* 28:13). We, however, who *can* see and are not confined to our homes, must be ever vigilant that our sanctity as Jews not be diminished by exposing our eyes to forbidden sights.

It is the obligation of parents to ensure that their sons utilize the years immediately following their completion of secular high school for total immersion in the study of Torah. No one is guaranteed that a post-high school education will result in his finding a good source of livelihood. Unfortunately, I have seen all too many students embark on career studies immediately after high school and later struggle to make ends meet. Conversely, one who dedicates himself to Torah study and character development in these very crucial years so that he can develop into a genuine *ben Torah* will, in that merit, earn himself *siyata diShmaya*, Heavenly assistance, in his endeavors.

May we merit to raise our offspring in the way of Torah and derive true *nachas* from them in this world and the next.

Reaching Out

‿§ The Time is Now

The *Midrash* (*Bereishis Rabbah* 25:3) lists ten famines that are mentioned in Scripture. "The first occurred in the days of Adam...the tenth will occur in the future, as it is written, *Behold, days are coming, says Hashem Elohim, when I shall send a famine in the land — not a hunger for bread, nor a thirst for water, but to hear the word of Hashem*" (*Amos* 8:11). This verse seems to foretell a most wonderful happening at the End of Days. However, if this is the case, then why does the *Midrash* list this hunger with nine others that clearly brought mankind great difficulty and distress?

The answer to this is found in the very next verse. *And they shall wander from sea to sea and from north to south, they shall scatter to seek the word of Hashem, but they will not find it.*

We are living in such a time. *HaKadosh Baruch Hu* has performed great wonders before our eyes in bringing about the fall of the oppressive, atheistic Soviet regime. A government which, for seventy years caused untold suffering to millions of Jews and tried to sever them completely from their heritage, has crumbled from within, without a war being fought. Clearly, this event must be seen as a prelude to yet greater happenings, may they occur speedily and in our time.

The gates of Russia are now open, and thankfully, many of our brethren are begging to be circumcised, begging to know the Torah whose truth they have been denied all these years. Their thirst for the word of Hashem, after decades of exposure to a philosophy that ridiculed religion as "the opium of the masses," is testimony to the spark of *kedushah*, sanctity, that is present in every Jewish *neshamah* and which can never be extinguished.

Many are thirsting, but sadly, their thirst is not being quenched. *And they shall wander from sea to sea and from north to south, they shall scatter to seek the word of Hashem, but they will not find it.* All the work that is being accomplished for the sake of Russian Jewry is but a fraction of what could be done! Many more must come forward to offer their time, talents and/or financial support, if we are to truly rise to the challenge which now confronts us.

Thrice daily, in the *Aleinu* prayer, we say, "Therefore, we put our hope in You, Hashem our God, that we may soon see Your mighty splendor, to remove detestable idolatry from the earth, and false gods will be utterly cut off...Then all humanity will call upon Your Name, to turn all the earth's wicked toward You." Today's situation tests our sincerity in uttering this *tefillah*. We now have the opportunity to bring back scores of Jews who for decades have been indoctrinated with the falsehoods of "detestable idols," but whose souls now yearn to "call upon His Name." Have we truly hoped all these years to see the day when "detestable idolatry" will be removed from the earth and all humanity will call Hashem's Name? Are we doing all we can to help our Russian brethren discover the beauty and truth of Torah? Are we doing *anything at all* to help them realize this desire? Let us ponder these questions truthfully and resolve to do whatever is in our power to bring Torah and *mitzvos* to those still living in the former Soviet Union as well as those who have emigrated to other lands.

❧ The Reward of Reaching Out

Tana D'Vei Eliyahu (ch. 8) states:

> Elkanah [father of the prophet Shmuel] would go up to [the Mishkan in] Shiloh four times a year. Three of these visits were mandated by the Torah,[1] while the fourth was a voluntary visit which Elkanah accepted upon himself...

---

1. The Torah requires that all Jewish adult males journey to "the place that He will choose" (*Devarim* 16:16) in advent of Pesach, Shavuos and Succos and offer sacrifices there. The "place" to which the Torah refers was the site where a permanent dwelling had been erected as an abode for the *Shechinah*. This place was first the *Mishkan* of Shiloh (see *Chagigah* 6a) and later the *Beis HaMikdash* in Jerusalem.

Elkanah, his wives, children, brothers, sisters and other relatives would join him in his pilgrimage...On the way, they would stop to spend the night in the midst of a town, the women congregating in one place, the men in another place. The men would converse with the local men, the women with the local women, the old with the young. The entire city would become aware of their presence and ask, "Where are these people going?" They would be told, "To the house of Hashem in Shiloh, for from there Torah and good deeds go forth. Why not come along and we will go there together?" Immediately, the eyes of the local citizens would well up with tears and they would say, "We shall go with you."

...The next year, the scene would be repeated and five entire families would join...the following year, ten entire families...until finally, the entire town was inspired and everyone — sixty families in all — would go up. The path which they took one year was not the one which they took the following year [so that new people would be inspired to join]...until all of Israel joined in the pilgrimage.

Thus, Elkanah caused that the people of Israel were deemed meritorious; he inspired them regarding mitzvos and multitudes gained merit through him. HaKadosh Baruch Hu, Who sees into the heart of every man, said to him, "...By your life, a son shall come forth from you who will cause Israel to be deemed meritorious, will inspire them regarding mitzvos and through whom multitudes will gain merit."

R' Chaim Vital (Sha'arei Kedushah 2:7) cites the above teaching and adds, "Avraham merited his lofty spiritual levels only because of the souls which they [Avraham and Sarah] made in Charan (Bereishis 12:5)[2] ... and the leaders of all generations are either rewarded or punished because of this matter." He then cites the Zohar (Sh'mos 128b):

---

2. I.e., the souls which they inspired toward belief in Hashem.

The righteous must pursue the sinners [and return
them to the proper path] ... and it is this praise more
than any other in which HaKadosh Baruch Hu takes
pride ... Thus does it say regarding Aharon, "And
many he returned from sin" (Malachi 2:6) ... Take
note, that one who grabs hold of a sinner and succeeds
in causing him to abandon the path of sin, merits three
praises which no other person merits. He merits to
subdue the forces of impurity; that HaKadosh Baruch
Hu takes pride in him; and to maintain both the upper
and lower worlds...He will merit to see children from
his children, and will earn reward in this world and in
the next...

Were people to realize how much benefit and merit is
brought to the righteous [i.e., the ba'alei teshuvah] and
how much they themselves [i.e., those who bring them
back] merit because of them, they would pursue them
as one who pursues life itself.[3]

When engaging in outreach, our primary goal should, of course, be
to educate others in *mitzvah* observance and introduce them to the
study of Torah. At the same time, however, it is important that they
come to recognize and appreciate the Torah's stress on ethics and
character development. Study material should include works of
mussar. Moreover, the instructor should, through his own behavior
and attitudes, serve as an example of the Torah's lofty standards. In
the words of *Chazal*:

A Jew should study Scripture and Mishnah, serve
Torah scholars and deal graciously with his fellow
man. Then others will say of him, "Fortunate is his
father who taught him Torah! Fortunate is his teacher
who taught him Torah! Woe to those who do not
study Torah! He who studies Torah — how pleasant is
his behavior and how proper are his deeds." To him
may the verse be applied: "And He said to me: 'You are
My servant, Israel, in whom I will be glorified'"
(Yeshayahu 49:3).

---

3. This last paragraph, cited by R' Chaim Vital, is not found in the standard edition
of *Zohar*.

◆§ Learning as We Teach

When working with ba'alei teshuvah, the committed Jew should learn as he guides and instructs, for there is much to learn from those who have willingly broken with their past to embrace Torah and its way of life.

Earlier, we referred to the *Aleinu* prayer. That prayer begins:

עָלֵינוּ לְשַׁבֵּחַ לַאֲדוֹן הַכֹּל, לָתֵת גְּדֻלָּה לְיוֹצֵר בְּרֵאשִׁית, שֶׁלֹּא עָשָׂנוּ
כְּגוֹיֵי הָאֲרָצוֹת, וְלֹא שָׂמָנוּ כְּמִשְׁפְּחוֹת הָאֲדָמָה.

It is our duty to praise the Master of all, to ascribe greatness to the Molder of primeval creation, for He has not made us like the nations of the lands and has not emplaced us like the families of the earth.

The thousands of ba'alei teshuvah in our midst sing this praise by way of their very essence. They have come to recognize the emptiness and falsehoods of secular life as opposed to the truth and beauty of Torah. Their observance of Torah and mitzvos is with a vibrancy, an excitement and exhilaration at having discovered Hashem's word after years of living in darkness.

We, to whom Torah has been a way of life since birth, tend to lose sight of our purpose in this world. "Man was created only to delight in Hashem, to bask in the splendor of His Presence. . .In truth, the place of this pleasure is the World to Come . . . however, the way to reach the destination of our desire is this world . . . and the means which bring man to this goal are the mitzvos" (Mesilas Yesharim ch.1).

Each morning, we recite the blessing of שֶׁלֹּא עָשַׂנִי גּוֹי, *[Blessed are You, Hashem. . .] for not having made me a gentile.* Why, then, do some find it necessary to dress according to the whims of today's fashion designers, the immoral trendsetters of secular society? Is this not a contradiction to שֶׁלֹּא עָשַׂנִי גּוֹי and to our thrice-daily thanks שֶׁלֹּא עָשָׂנוּ כְּגוֹיֵי הָאֲרָצוֹת, *for He has not made us like the nations of the lands?* Today's styles breach the barriers of tznius that are so crucial to the sanctity of our people.

On the subject of styles, I have been informed that certain women have taken to purchasing wigs which allow for some of their own hair to be seen. Regarding this matter, it is sufficient to quote the *Chofetz Chaim:*

The Zohar [Parashas Naso] is very stringent, that no hair at all should be seen [protruding from beneath a woman's head covering], for this brings poverty to the home, brings about that one's children should not become men of stature in their generation, and allows forces of impurity [סִטְרָא אַחֲרָא] to come to dwell in one's home. This surely applies to one who goes out in public in such a manner (Mishnah Berurah 75:14).

◆§ Lifelong Impressions

It is heartbreaking, indeed, when one hears that a boy or girl from an Orthodox home, educated in the finest yeshivah or Bais Yaakov, has abandoned the ways of his or her parents and is no longer religious. Most heartbreaking of all is that sometimes it is the parents themselves who are to blame, for they have allowed immorality and heresy to become a part of their home. I am referring, of course, to homes where secular periodicals are commonplace and where television is viewed.

How can anyone honestly say that they and their children will not be adversely affected by such things?

The following was related to me by a doctor, who heard it from the surgeon involved:

Once, this surgeon performed brain surgery on a certain woman. While the surgery was in progress, the woman began to sing an aria from an Italian opera. After the surgery, when the woman was fully alert, the surgeon asked her where she had learned the piece. At first, the woman was dumbfounded. She had no interest in opera and certainly knew nothing of Italian opera. She thought and thought until she remembered that as a little girl, her school teacher had once taken the class to an Italian opera. Though the incident had meant nothing to her and decades had passed since it had occurred, the opera remained embedded in her memory. The surgical procedure had touched a part of her brain which caused her to recall this childhood event while she was in surgery and under the influence of anesthesia.

What we see and hear even once can leave a lifelong impression in our minds. What a child sees once can cause him or her spiritual harm many years later. A child subjected to the decadence of television or today's periodicals is a child whose mind and heart have been tainted by immorality and other forms of sin.[4]

In the Book of *Tehillim*, David *HaMelech* prays: שְׁגִיאוֹת מִי יָבִין מִנִּסְתָּרוֹת נַקֵּנִי, *Who can discern mistakes, from hidden faults cleanse me* (*Tehillim* 19:13). מִנִּסְתָּרוֹת נַקֵּנִי can be understood as a plea that one be cleansed of the negative influences that he cannot recall at present, but which remain in the hidden recesses of his mind. Along with this prayer, which we utter each Shabbos and *Yom Tov*, must go an active effort on our part to eradicate all forms of destructive influences from our midst.

Incredible events are transpiring in our time. It is precisely at such a time that the obligation rests heavily upon us to live in a manner that is reflective of the concepts expressed by *Mesilas Yesharim*: *Man was created only to delight in Hashem, to bask in the splendor of His Presence. . .the means which bring man to this goal are the mitzvos.*

HaKadosh Baruch Hu, in His desire to ready His creations for the coming of *Mashiach*, has caused a spirit of *teshuvah* to descend to this world. It is our duty to help those who have been awakened to *teshuvah*, and through this to awaken ourselves to spiritual improvement.

Let us cleanse our minds and hearts, and purify our lips through *shemiras halashon*. Then, the power of our *tefillos* will be awesome and we will witness the answer to our prayers that this *galus* end and the days of redemption begin.

---

4. The Steipler wrote the following in a letter regarding television: "It is quite obvious that viewing this object of *tumah* places one's entire *Yiddishkeit* in danger. Even one who views it once in a while brings a coldness upon his *emunah* and *yiras shamayim*, ל"ר. One who views it regularly becomes emptied of any trace of *emunah* and *yiras shamayim* and whatever other good he has within himself. . .

". . .There are those who allow their small children to watch [television] at neighbors' homes, saying, 'He is but a child! Let him have some fun; it will do him no harm.' This is a grave error that borders on recklessness. To the contrary: the danger is multiplied many fold with regard to small children, for they have a strong tendency to want to imitate the behavior they see in others. . .The sights a child sees become embedded in his memories. . .and his soul and *Yiddishkeit* will suffer bitterly from the abominable sights he has seen. . ." (*Kreina D'Igresa* I, p. 130).

Variations of Chesed

◄§ The Chesed of Avraham

While the *Avos*, Patriarchs, were wholesome in their spiritual perfection, each possessed one prime characteristic with which his Divine service is identified. Avraham's prime characteristic was *chesed*, kindness.

A prime form of *chesed* is *hachnasas orchim*, welcoming guests. The episode of Avraham and the three angels at the opening of *Parashas Vayeira* (*Bereishis* ch. 18) illustrates Avraham's exceptional dedication to this *mitzvah*. The angels were disguised as wayfarers, the day was unbearably hot and Avraham was recuperating from his circumcision. Yet he rushed to greet the wayfarers to invite them in, and then proceeded to serve them with classic alacrity and generosity.

Avraham's ceaseless involvement with *hachnasas orchim* is alluded to elsewhere in the very same *parashah*:

וַיִּטַּע אֶשֶׁל בִּבְאֵר שָׁבַע וַיִּקְרָא שָׁם בְּשֵׁם ה׳ אֵל עוֹלָם.

He [Avraham] planted an eshel in Beer Sheba, and there he proclaimed the Name of Hashem, God of the universe (Bereishis 21:33).

The *Gemara* (*Sotah* 10a) records a dispute between Rav and Shmuel regarding the meaning of the word אֶשֶׁל. Rav understands the term to mean *orchard*; Avraham planted an orchard from which he took food to serve wayfarers. Shmuel interprets אֶשֶׁל as an inn for lodging where Avraham maintained a supply of fruit for wayfarers.[1]

---

1. *Rashi* (*Sotah* 10a) comments that the word אֶשֶׁל is an acrostic for אֲכִילָה, *eating*; שְׁתִיָּה, *drinking*; and לְוָיָה, *escorting* — the services which a host should provide his guests.

Turning to the second half of the verse, the *Gemara* states that the word וַיִּקְרָא, *and he called*, should be understood in the causative sense, as if it were written וַיַּקְרִיא, *and he caused others to call*. After eating and drinking their fill at the אֵשֶׁל, the guests would bless Avraham, who would respond, "Bless God of Whose possessions you have eaten! Do you then think that you have eaten of what is mine? — you have eaten from that of the One Who spoke and the world came into being!" The guests would then acknowledge the beneficence of Hashem, the One and Only God. In this way, Avraham *caused others to proclaim the Name of Hashem, God of the Universe.*

Thus, the אֵשֶׁל of Avraham was at the very center of his *chesed* activities, in particular his efforts toward the greatest kindness of all — teaching others belief in Hashem. Why, then, does the Torah limit its mention of the אֵשֶׁל to a single verse while devoting numerous verses to describing the way in which Avraham welcomed the angels?

⋘ The Chesed of Lot

*P*arashas *Vayeira* details another episode of *hachnasas orchim.* When the two angels[2] — still disguised as wayfarers — entered the city of Sodom, they were met by Avraham's nephew Lot, who invited them to be his guests. Lot's behavior toward his guests was exemplary. The wicked people of Sodom had issued a decree of death for anyone who dared extend help to strangers. Lot put his life in danger and actually pleaded with the angels to accept his invitation (19:3). He prepared a feast for his guests and protected them when his neighbors demanded that they be handed over. Yet, it is not this merit that saved Lot from the fate of his neighbors.

The story is told of a man who offered generous hospitality to guests. His home was destroyed by fire and people wondered why so kind a person should suffer such a fate. The matter was brought before the *Vilna Gaon* who explained that in caring for his guests, the man had provided them אֲכִילָה, *eating* and שְׁתִיָה, *drinking*, but had failed to provide לְוָיָה, *escorting*. When the ל for לְוָיָה in the word אֵשֶׁל is removed, what remains is אֵשׁ, *fire.*

2. The angel that had come to inform Sarah that she would soon bear a child had departed after accomplishing his mission.

וַיְהִי בְּשַׁחֵת אֱלֹהִים אֶת עָרֵי הַכִּכָּר, וַיִּזְכֹּר אֱלֹהִים אֶת אַבְרָהָם,
וַיְשַׁלַּח אֶת לוֹט מִתּוֹךְ הַהֲפֵכָה. . .

And so it was when God destroyed the cities of the plain that God remembered Avraham; so he sent Lot from amidst the upheaval. . . (19:29).

"God remembered" that Lot had known that Sarah was Avraham's wife, yet when he heard Avraham telling the Egyptians that they were brother and sister [see 12:13], he compassionately kept silent. Therefore, God now had compassion on him (*Midrash Rabbah* cited by *Rashi*).

The *Midrash* makes no mention of Lot's hospitality, yet there *is* mention of his not having betrayed Avraham, who cared for Lot from the time his father died. To have betrayed Avraham would have been the epitome of ingratitude. Why was Lot's behavior in Egypt deserving of such merit?

To resolve this, we must analyze what exactly constitutes a complete *mitzvah*. As an example, let us take the *mitzvah* of *tefillin*. One can purchase a most beautiful pair of *tefillin* and carefully place them upon his head and arm each day, and yet his accomplishment may be severely wanting. As expressed in the prayer that precedes its performance, there is specific *kavanah*, intent, that should accompany the wearing of *tefillin*. "He has commanded us to put [*tefillin*] on the arm to recall the 'outstretched arm' of the Exodus and that it be opposite the heart to subjugate the desires and thoughts of our hearts to His service ... and upon the head opposite the brain, so that the soul in my brain, together with my other senses and potentials, may all be subjugated to His service, may His name be blessed." One who performs the *mitzvah* without giving thought to the above has omitted a most important aspect of this Divine command.

In a similar sense, one can perform the most magnanimous act of kindness and fall far short of carrying out the *mitzvah* in its optimum way. Moreover, two people can carry out the *identical* act of kindness, yet their deeds can be worlds apart.

People do kindnesses for a variety of reasons. Some are compassionate by nature, others may enjoy the feeling that results from helping someone else, while others may involve themselves in *chesed* simply because they were brought up that way; helping others is to them a way of life.

Lot belonged to the latter group. He had spent years in the house of Avraham, where *chesed* was a way of life. Even after joining the wicked community of Sodom, Lot did not lose the inclination toward *chesed* that had developed within him. So ingrained had this quality become that he was willing to take great personal risk for the sake of guests who were strangers.[3] *Chazal* make it clear that Lot's benevolence *was* a source of merit for him[4] — but, as is seen from the *Midrash* cited above, it was not his primary source of merit.

Lot placed himself at great personal risk by remaining silent concerning the relationship of Avraham and Sarah. Had the truth been discovered and Hashem not brought sickness upon the house of Pharaoh, Lot might have been killed along with Avraham. Here, Lot's behavior was without precedent. That he did not betray Avraham was because the appreciation and compassion he felt toward his uncle and aunt compelled him to remain silent. For this, he was rewarded measure for measure; Heaven dealt with him compassionately and he was saved.

Avraham may have had an innate tendency toward *chesed*, but this was not the driving force behind his benevolence. Avraham strove to help his fellow man because he had come to recognize his Creator's existence and he perceived that God's purpose in creating this world was "to give of His goodness unto others" (*Derech Hashem* ch. 2). Avraham realized that it is Hashem's will that man emulate His attributes. Hashem knows the needs and suffering of His every creation and provides for each according to his or her particular situation. As a parallel to this attribute, Avraham perfected within himself the quality of נוֹשֵׂא בְּעוֹל עִם חֲבֵירוֹ, *sharing his friend's burden.* When Avraham would see a wayfarer coming down the road, he imagined himself as that hungry, weary and lonely wayfarer. The way in which the wayfarer was welcomed reflected Avraham's unrelenting, incomparable pursuit of *chesed*.

---

3. HaRav Segal commented that Avraham's influence upon Lot in the area of *chesed* is a prime illustration of how the behavior of parents (or their substitutes, as was the case here) bear dramatic imprint upon their children's character.

4. *Ramban* (*Bereishis* 19:3) comments that the angels initially declined Lot's invitation so that he would urge them more strongly, and thereby increase his merit.

ᴥ Avraham and Iyov

In *Avos D'Rav Nosson* (ch. 7), Avraham's way of *chesed* is contrasted with that of Iyov:

> When suffering was visited upon Iyov, he said before HaKadosh Baruch Hu, "Master of the Universe! Did I not feed the hungry and feed the thirsty?" as it is written, "Did I eat my bread alone, did not an orphan eat from it?" (*Iyov* 31:17). "Did I not clothe the naked?" as it is written, "From the shearings of my sheep he was warmed" (ibid. v. 20).
>
> Nevertheless, HaKadosh Baruch Hu responded, "Iyov, you have not attained even half [the benevolence] of Avraham. You sit and wait in your house and guests come to you. To one who is accustomed to eating wheat bread, you feed wheat bread; to one who is accustomed to eating meat, you feed meat; to one who is accustomed to drinking wine, you give wine.
>
> "Avraham was different. He would go searching in the land until he found guests to bring home. To one who was not accustomed to eating wheat bread [for he could not afford it], he fed wheat bread; to one who was not accustomed to eating meat he fed meat; to one who was not accustomed to drinking wine he gave wine. Moreover, he built huge edifices on the roads and in them he placed food and drink. Those who entered would eat, drink and express praise of God."

Avraham's brand of *chesed* is defined by the first distinction drawn between Iyov and himself. *Avraham was different. He would go searching in the land until he found guests to bring home.* As long as he had no one to feed, Avraham knew no rest, because doing kindness was to him a Divine mission, one that put his soul in touch with every stranger that came his way.

This is why the Torah gives special attention to the episode of Avraham and the three angels. That Avraham sat outside on a day of unusually intense heat,[4] while he was weak and recuperating from circumcision, is illustrative of what motivated him toward *chesed*.

It is for us to emulate the way of our forefather Avraham. For example, when seeing a friend behaving in a negative manner, imagine yourself in his position and realize that everyone has his own personal struggles with the *yetzer hara*. Reprove him with gentle words and with respect. Show that you truly care for him and offer to study with him so that he will know what is required of him. This is a *chesed* of great magnitude.

May we merit to follow the path of Avraham and perform kindness in a manner that reflects the way of the One Above.

---

4. The Talmud (*Bava Metzia* 86b) explains that Hashem "withdrew the sun from its sheath" causing great heat, so that Avraham would not be bothered by travelers on this, the third and most difficult day of his convalescence. But after seeing that Avraham was grieved that no travelers came, Hashem sent the three angels his way.

Of course, Hashem knew in advance that Avraham would be grieved at not having guests. Many understand the above to mean that Hashem made the day unusually hot so that travelers would stay off the road and Avraham would gain added reward for his yearning to fulfill the *mitzvah* of *hachnasas orchim* despite his physical discomfort.

The Ben Sorer Umoreh

If a man shall have a wayward and rebellious son who does not heed the voice of his father and of his mother, and they chasten him and he does not heed them. His father and mother shall seize him and they shall take him out to the elders of his town and to the gate of his locale. And they shall say to the elders of his town, "This son of ours is wayward and rebellious, he does not heed our voice; he is a glutton and a drunkard." And all the citizens of his town shall stone him with stones and he shall die; and you will eradicate the evil from your midst (Devarim 21:18-21).

◆§ Fundamentals

Only a male in the first three months of adulthood can become a *ben sorer umoreh*. Among other conditions that must be met for a boy to become a *ben soreh umoreh* is that he steal money from his father and use it to purchase a specific large quantity of meat and wine which he gluttonously consumes at one time. While the case of the *ben sorer umoreh* is virtually an impossibility,[1] it is highly instructive nonetheless.

---

1. The laws of *ben soreh umoreh* are detailed in the eighth chapter of *Mesechta Sanhedrin*. According to one Talmudic opinion, the case of the *ben sorer umoreh* never occurred and never will occur. "And why was it written? [To] expound upon it, and be granted reward" (*Sanhedrin* 71a).

Chazal (*Sanhedrin* 72a)[2] comment that the *ben sorer umoreh* is killed because of what he would later become. "The Torah penetrated to his ultimate plan. In the end, he will dispose of all his father's possessions; unable to satisfy his desires, he will go to the crossroads and rob people [and kill them — *Sifsei Chachamim*]. Said the Torah, 'Let him die innocent rather than guilty.'"

Ramban (*Devarim* 21:18), before citing the above statement of *Chazal*, comments that the *ben sorer umoreh's* behavior runs contrary to fundamental Torah principles. For, in addition to acting disrespectfully toward his father and mother, the *ben sorer umoreh* has transgressed the commandments of קְדוֹשִׁים תִּהְיוּ, *You shall be holy* (*Vayikra* 19:2) and אוֹתוֹ תַעֲבֹדוּ וּבוֹ תִדְבָּקוּן, *You shall serve Him and cling to Him* (*Devarim* 13:5). *Ramban* refers us to his elucidations of these two commandments; indeed, his words describe the essence of a Jew's service of Hashem.

Ramban explains the commandment of קְדוֹשִׁים תִּהְיוּ to mean קַדֵּשׁ עַצְמְךָ בְּמוּתָּר לָךְ, *sanctify yourself with what is permitted to you.* It is possible for a person to technically avoid transgressing the Torah's prohibitions and yet be considered what *Ramban* calls a נָבָל בִּרְשׁוּת הַתּוֹרָה, *despicable person within the bounds of Torah law.* For example, one might avoid illicit relationships yet be lustful, refrain from eating non-kosher food while gorging himself with kosher food. The Torah therefore commands us: קְדוֹשִׁים תִּהְיוּ! — "Do not overindulge in that which is permissible, avoid that which is impure, and guard your mouth against gluttony and improper language. Ensure that your behavior and speech are befitting one whose life source is the Godly soul within him and who is part of the nation whom Hashem sanctified as His chosen people."

אוֹתוֹ תַעֲבֹדוּ, *You shall serve Him,* says *Ramban* (*Devarim* 6:13), defines the purpose with which a Jew should infuse his every deed.

> *That one should be at every moment like an owned servant who serves his master constantly, who makes his master's needs primary and his own needs secondary, until one reaches the point where, as they [Chazal] have put it, "All your deeds should be for the sake of Heaven" (Avos 2:12), meaning that even when*

---

2. Cited by *Rashi* to *Devarim* 21:18.

caring for one's physical needs, one will act for the sake of Hashem's service. He will eat, sleep and perform his other bodily functions to sustain his body in order to serve God. In this vein, they state (Bereishis Rabbah 9:8), " 'And behold, it was very good' (Bereishis 1:31) — this refers to sleep. Now, is sleep really something '[very] good'? Yes, for after sleeping a bit, one can then arise and toil in the study of Torah." All one's bodily functions should be performed with the words (Tehillim 146:8), "I will praise Hashem while I live, I will hymn to my God while I exist" in mind.

Thus, comments *Ramban*, the *ben sorer umoreh's* actions foretell a future that will be devoid of purity and purpose, "for we have been commanded to know Hashem in all our ways, and a gluttonous person cannot know the way of Hashem."

⤙ Good Company

The *Gemara (Sanhedrin* 70b) states that to be considered a *ben sorer umoreh*, the boy must consume his meat and wine in the company of a group that consists exclusively of boorish individuals. *Rashi* explains, ". . . for they [the boors] will accustom him to such [gluttonous] behavior. However, if there is among the group [even] one decent person, then he [the boy] will not [necessarily] continue in this way."

As mentioned above, a *ben sorer umoreh* is killed not because of what he is, but what he will ultimately become. However, he cannot be killed unless his behavior *definitely* points to a wicked future. If there is even a possibility that he might change course and mend his ways, then he must not be killed. The presence of even one decent individual at the time when he is gorging himself with food and drink might influence the *ben sorer umoreh* to ultimately find his way to the proper path.

One good person's mere presence can have a positive influence over a wayward boy who is surrounded by lowly people! Can there be a greater lesson about the effect of environment upon us and how we affect our environment?

A person can be alone and still be influenced by "good company." When one studies *mussar* with self-improvement in mind, his *neshamah* will surely be influenced in a positive way. One should not be disappointed if he does not come away feeling immediate uplift. He may rest assured that the holy words of *Sha'arei Teshuvah*, *Mesilas Yesharim* and other classic *mussar* works will leave their impression upon his soul. Consistent, sincere *mussar* study has to have a positive effect upon the student. With a *mussar sefer* in hand, one is in very good company!

৵ঌ The Power of Torah Study

In writing that the Torah "penetrated to his ultimate plan," *Talmud Yerushalmi* (*Sanhedrin* 8:7) states that the *ben sorer umoreh* is destined לְשַׁבֵּחַ אֶת תַּלְמוּדוֹ, to forget his learning. This requires explanation. Can it be that ultimate failure in Torah study should be a reason that death be decreed upon him?

In *Derech Hashem* (4:2), R' Moshe Chaim Luzzato speaks of Torah study's power to illuminate the soul of the sinner:

> *Chazal have revealed a great secret to us, that if the wicked would not forsake the study of Torah, in the end they would return to the good path ... for the words of Torah contain a spirituality that is an unchanging fact, so that one who toils over them consistently will derive a bit of spiritual awakening — a semblance of light — each time [that he studies]. Ultimately, this light will come to dominate their souls and return them to the good path. This is Chazal's intent in stating, "[Hashem said:] If only they had forsaken Me but still observed [the study of] My Torah, for its light would have returned them to the good" (Midrash Eichah, Pesichta 2).*

It would seem, however, that the above is contradicted by the *Vilna Gaon's* explanation of the comparison of Torah to rain (*Devarim* 32:2). The *Gaon* (*Even Sh'leimah* 1:11) writes that just as rain nurtures that which has already been planted, so, too, does Torah nurture that which lies within one's heart. When a heart is filled with good, then the study of Torah will cause that goodness to blossom, but when within a heart lies a "root whose fruit is gall and wormwood" (*Devarim* 29:17) then *that* is what Torah study will nurture and cause to flourish. Thus do *Chazal* state, "If one is worthy, then it [the Torah] becomes for him a potion of life; if one is not worthy, then it becomes for him a potion of death" (*Yoma* 72b).

But what of the Torah's power to return the wicked to the good path?

To resolve this, we must distinguish between sins which are *bein adam laMakom*, between man and God, and those that are *bein adam lachaveiro*, between man and his fellow. The Torah's light can illuminate the soul and help to purge one's heart of sinful desires which draw him toward the physical pleasures of this world and away from Hashem's service. This is the sort of sinner to which *Derech Hashem* refers. The *Gaon*, however, is speaking of a sinner whose soul is tainted by *midos ra'os*, destructive character traits. A person with *midos ra'os*, who studies Torah for ulterior reasons and does not seek to change himself, will not gain positively from his Torah learning. Instead, the Torah will nurture the maladies within his heart and his wicked characteristics will grow yet stronger.

The *ben sorer umoreh* is one who has shown himself to be more than just the average willful sinner. He has exhibited the most base character traits, the most despicable sort of behavior. His desire is not to change but to satisfy his lusts — and he is prepared to do anything to accomplish this. Thus, his Torah study cannot possibly affect him in a positive way. To the contrary, he is destined לִשְׁכֹּחַ אֶת תַּלְמוּדוֹ, *to forget his learning*. The Torah therefore decrees: "Let him die innocent rather than guilty."

May we merit to uproot the *midos ra'os* within ourselves and may our souls be illuminated by the brilliant light of Torah.

Shemiras HaLashon

◆§ Step by Step

נוֹצֵר תְּאֵנָה יֹאכַל פְּרְיָה

He who guards the fig tree shall eat its fruit (Mishlei 27:18).

Why is the Torah likened to a fig tree? With most trees...their fruits are harvested all at once, but the fruits of the fig tree are harvested a few at a time [for the figs ripen at different intervals]. So, too, with Torah: a little is studied today, and more tomorrow, for its wisdom cannot be learned [in its entirety] not in a year's time, and not in two year's time...(Bamidbar Rabbah 21:15).

While the *Midrash* uses the analogy of the fig tree with regard to Torah study, it can be applied to all areas of *avodas Hashem*. Spiritual accomplishments are attained in small amounts, a little at a time. Striving too much too soon can be counterproductive. Success is achieved step by step.

In this regard, we have often cited the parable of R' Chaim of Volozhin (*Ruach Chaim* 1:13), about a king who commands his servant to climb a ladder. It would be rebellion on the servant's part were he to make no attempt to ascend the ladder. However, the king would be quite satisfied to see the servant ascend one rung at a time, for this is the way that ladders are climbed. Similarly, to refrain from self-improvement is to ignore one's mission in this world. To strive toward gradual improvement is to truly serve one's Creator.

The *Mishnah* states: שַׁמַּאי אוֹמֵר: . . .אֱמֹר מְעַט וַעֲשֵׂה הַרְבֵּה, *Shammai said:. . .Say little and do much (Avos 1:15)*. This can be interpreted homiletically: When accepting *kabbalos*, spiritual resolutions, upon oneself, it is best to "speak little," that is, to accept resolutions which reflect modest self-improvement and are not difficult to fulfill. Success breeds success; when one succeeds in living up to a modest resolution, he will be inspired toward greater improvement. Through speaking "little" one will eventually "do much."

It is for us to make a sincere effort to improve; eventually, with Hashem's help, we can reach the ladder's top.

ᴥᔒ Response to the Yetzer Hara

In his preface to *Sefer Shemiras HaLashon*, the *Chofetz Chaim* writes of the *yetzer hara's* attempts to discourage us from studying the laws of guarding one's tongue. "What benefit," the *yetzer hara* asks, "will you have from studying and delving into this subject? Are you really capable of attaining its goal and guarding your tongue all your life? Let us see you do this for even a day or two! — and even then, do you really think that you can avoid *everything* that must not be spoken? Why, you are a man of the world, you have dealings with scores of people!"

The *Chofetz Chaim* responds to this argument with a passage from *Avos D'Rav Nosson* (27:3):

> R' Yochanan ben DaHavai said: Do not distance yourself from a מִדָּה that is without limit and from a labor that is without end. To what can this be compared? To someone who took water from the ocean and cast it onto dry land. The ocean did not appear any less full and the land did not become filled [with water]. The man grew frustrated. His employer said: "Foolish one! Why are you upset? Each day you will receive a gold dinar for your work."

The *Chofetz Chaim* understands the term מִדָּה to mean *trait*: "Do not distance yourself from a trait that is without limit." This trait, says the *Chofetz Chaim*, is that of *shemiras halashon*.[1] R' Yochanan's words are a response to the *yetzer hara's* arguments. "Even if you [the *yetzer hara*] would be correct [that observance of these laws for even a day or two is a difficult challenge], is this a reason to ignore the matter? Imagine a person walking along the seashore who sees that the waves have washed ashore countless precious gems. Would such a person — even if he were wealthy — refrain from picking up any because he knows that he can only remain there for a short while [and will not be able to collect all the gems]? Such an attitude is only possible if the items washed ashore are of little value. In the case of gems, however, each moment spent would earn for the man more than he would earn were he to spend one hundred days collecting items of little significance.

"This is exactly the case with regard to *shemiras halashon*. As is well-known, the *Gra*,[2] citing the *Midrash*, writes that for every moment that one refrains from speaking the forbidden, he merits a hidden light that no angel or creature can fathom. Notice that the *Midrash* does not speak of refraining from forbidden speech for a month, a week, or an hour, but for a 'moment'!"

The *Chofetz Chaim* also cites the parable of "a certain *gaon*," who was asked how one can arouse himself to concentrate on his prayers when he is near the conclusion of a given *tefillah* and has not concentrated up to that point.

> *To what can this be compared? To a young girl who is standing in the marketplace with a large basket of vegetables for sale. A thief comes up to her and begins to snatch things out of the basket. The girl is stunned and stands helplessly, not knowing what to do. A wise fellow standing some distance away calls out to her, "Why are you standing still? What are you waiting for*

---

1. *Binyan Yehoshua* understands the term מִדָּה to mean *measure*, a reference to Torah whose *measure is longer than the earth and wider than the sea* (*Iyov* 11:9). The student of Torah might grow discouraged over his inability to know all of Torah in its infinite breadth and depth. R' Yochanan, therefore, assures him that each day's study is an accomplishment for itself and earns him infinite reward.

The *Chofetz Chaim* interprets the second half of R' Yochanan's statement, "[Do not distance yourself from] a labor that is without end," as referring to Torah study.
2. An acronym for גָּאוֹן ר' אֵלִיָהוּ, the *Vilna Gaon*.

— that he should grab everything? Just as he is grabbing, so should you grab — whatever you can get will be yours!"

And so, said the *gaon*, it is with *tefillah*. As one prepares to stand before Hashem in prayer, he may be overcome by laziness and the *yetzer hara* may cause his mind to become filled with all sorts of foreign thoughts. Before he realizes what is happening, most of the *davening* has been recited without proper *kavanah*. Nevertheless, one should "grab" whatever is left before he is left with nothing, and strive to concentrate on the remainder of the *tefillah* to the best of his ability.

And so it is, said the *Chofetz Chaim*, with *shemiras halashon*. "If the *yetzer hara* overcame you today with forbidden speech, then stand opposed to him tomorrow and overcome him. And even if, *chas veshalom*, he overcomes you again, nevertheless, strengthen yourself and stand ready to do battle with him. *HaKadosh Baruch Hu* will surely assist you, so that you will be counted among the victors."

As to the *yetzer hara's* contention that it is impossible to adhere to these laws for more than a day or two, the *Chofetz Chaim* writes, "When one will ponder the matter further, he will see that this contention is entirely false. For it is a proven fact that the more one accustoms himself to being careful in this matter, the easier it becomes for him to guard his tongue. At first, when one was in the habit of saying whatever came to mind, he did not even realize that he was uttering forbidden words. Now, however, he realizes that he is about to utter something forbidden, and with a bit of effort refrains from speaking."

As to the contention that one cannot master all the laws of *shemiras halashon* and therefore, "Better to ignore this attribute, for it is a matter that is without end...", the *Chofetz Chaim* writes:

> *Would one follow such reasoning when his livelihood was concerned? For example, let us imagine that I was running somewhere to engage in some enterprise. A man asks me, "Why are you running? Do you think that this enterprise will make you one of the world's richest men, like so-and-so?" Surely, I would reply,*

"Because I can't be as rich as he, should I refrain from supporting myself?!"

If this is how one would respond when earthly matters are concerned, then what shall we say with regard to matters of the soul? The Zohar states (Parashas Chukas p. 183b) that one who guards his tongue in accordance with all relevant laws merits to be clothed in the Divine spirit. Reishis Chachmah writes (Sha'ar HaAhavah ch. 54) that R' Moshe Kordevero saw the author of Shushan Sodos in a dream, and that each hair of his beard was aglow like the light of a torch. [He revealed to him] that this was in merit of his having avoided idle chatter. [Thus, the reward for full adherence to the laws of shemiras halashon is beyond comprehension.] And if one finds himself unable to adhere to all the details of these laws [and as such, does not merit the above reward], does that mean that he should refrain from caring for his soul through guarding his tongue to whatever degree he can? For by doing so, he will not be included, Heaven forfend, among the habitual speakers of lashon hara, of whom Chazal say, "they will not merit to greet the Shechinah" (Sotah 42b).

It has been related to me that recently a man's father appeared to him in a dream and said: "It was dark for me [in the Next World], but the merit of my zealousness in matters of speech illuminated the way."

๏ For All Generations

Let no one contend that it is too difficult for us, in our lowly state, to live by the laws put forth in *Sefer Chofetz Chaim*. There were many in the *Chofetz Chaim's* days who, unfortunately, paid little attention to his works. Yet today there are, *baruch Hashem*, scores of men and women the world over who study the laws of *shemiras halashon* regularly and are meticulous in matters of speech. *Sefer*

Chofetz Chaim is original in that it is the first comprehensive code of the laws pertaining to *lashon hara*. Its content, however, is not original. These laws are as much a part of Torah as any other and are fully binding upon all Jews in all generations.

It is important that we realize the underlying basis for these laws. To speak *lashon hara* is to hurt one's fellow Jew. Such behavior runs contrary to the obligation that we seek to benefit our fellow Jew and that we love our fellow Jew as our very own selves. One who sincerely strives to live by these precepts will find that refraining from *lashon hara* is not all that difficult.

In his preface to *Sefer Shemiras HaLoshon*, the *Chofetz Chaim* writes:

> *With regard to instilling within oneself the trait of guarding one's tongue, it seems to me that there is an obvious solution: that one make sure to become fluent in all details of its laws, and to review them very, very well, so that he will know precisely what type of speech must be avoided...*

A daily calendar for the study of *Sefer Chofetz Chaim* and *Sefer Shemiras HaLashon* has been arranged and distributed worldwide for the past several years. Daily study of the laws of *shemiras halashon* and relevant Aggadic material is a primary method for refining oneself in this crucial area. It is not sufficient to complete the cycle of study once or twice. Only through *constant* study of the laws does the matter of *shemiras halashon* remain stringent in one's mind. Moreover, daily study of these laws makes a person ever vigilant in matters of speech, so that whenever confronted with a speech-related *nisayon*, test, he will always be on guard.

May the merit of studying the *Chofetz Chaim's* works shield us, and may we merit to emulate his ways and live by the teachings contained in his holy *sefarim*. If we study the *Chofetz Chaim's* works and strive to live by them, then surely the *Chofetz Chaim* will intercede on our behalf, during our lifetime on this earth and in the World to Come.

Coping with Tragedy[1]

⋖§ Man's Purpose on This World

"In truth, it is impossible for anyone of intelligence to believe that man was created merely to exist in this world. Who on this world is happy and tranquil in the fullest sense? *The days of our years among them are seventy years, and if with strength, eighty years; their proudest success is but toil and pain . . . (Tehillim* 90:10). With all sorts of suffering and sicknesses, pains and preoccupations . . .

"Moreover, if the purpose of creating man was [his existence on] the world, it would not have been necessary to have breathed into him a soul so lofty and Heavenly . . ." (*Mesilas Yesharim* ch. 1).

One comes to recognize the real purpose of the world merely by pondering creation itself. *Lift your eyes above and see Who created these* (*Yeshayahu* 40:26). The wonders of creation proclaim the infinite wisdom of their Creator and the higher purpose for which the world was intended.

Childbirth is surely one of this world's great wonders. Can the development of what the *Mishnah* calls a טִפָּה סְרוּחָה, *putrid drop,* into a fully formed baby be classified as anything but miraculous? A doctor who is a *talmid chacham* related to me that when he studied the subject of fetus development he was moved to tears out of appreciation of Hashem's wonders!

Nevertheless, the advent of childbirth brings with it many real concerns. One hopes and prays that the child will be born healthy. When the child is born healthy, one prays that he or she will merit a

---

1. The following is based on a talk given by HaRav Segal to a group of parents who had lost children, ר"ל.

long and healthy life, a life of Torah and *yiras Hashem* that will bring the child's parents *nachas* both in this world and the next.

There are times when parents' hopes are not realized, ל"ר. A baby may be born with an illness, or some other health problem. Or a child may be born healthy only to be taken from this world at a young age. How does one cope at such times?

There is but one answer:

בָּא חֲבַקּוּק וְהֶעֱמִידָן עַל אַחַת שֶׁנֶּאֱמַר: וְצַדִּיק בֶּאֱמוּנָתוֹ יִחְיֶה.

Chavakuk came and established them[2] upon one [ethical requirement], as it is written: "A righteous person will live by his faith" [Chavakuk 2:4]. (Makkos 24a).

Only with *emunah*, faith, can one cope with the travails of this world. First, one must strengthen his *emunah* in *hashgachah pratis*, in his belief that whatever occurs is a precise expression of Hashem's will. Nothing at all is left to chance.

The *Gemara* (*Bava Basra* 10a) relates that Rav Pappa slipped while climbing a ladder and nearly fell off. Rav Pappa reflected upon his brush with death and searched for a spiritual lapse that might have been its cause.[3] It was obvious to this great sage that what others might have called an "accident" was, in fact, Divinely ordained.

When a child departs this world, its parents must recognize that this could have happened only because *HaKadosh Baruch Hu*, Whose compassion is infinite, willed it to be. For what purpose was this child sent to this world and why did it have to depart so soon? No one can know for certain. However, our *emunah* that this world is merely a corridor leading to the world to come (*Avos* 4:21) makes what has occurred comprehensible in general terms. The child was a pure and lofty soul that needed to achieve a certain goal so that it could attain perfection. Perhaps its entire purpose in descending to

---

2. The *Gemara* relates that a number of great Scriptural personalities declared certain ethical requirements as a basis for fulfilling all the Torah's commandments. David listed eleven ethical requirements; Yeshayahu, six; Michah, three; and Chavakuk, one.

3. Chiya bar Rav said to Rav Pappa: "Perhaps a pauper came to you and you did not sustain him [with some *tzedakah*], for it was taught in a *Baraisa*, 'R' Yehudah ben Karchah said: If one averts his eyes from giving charity, it is as if he worships idols [for which the punishment is death].' "

this world was to perfect itself by giving its parents pleasure for the brief period that it remained with them. Viewing such occurrences in this sort of light makes it possible to cope, and go on with one's life.

While misfortune should be a cause for *teshuvah*, one must not confuse introspection with depression or guilt. Fathers or mothers who have lost a child should never blame themselves for what has happened. It is Hashem's will that we serve Him amid a spirit of joy; guilt feelings make such service impossible. Tragedy should make a person strengthen his belief in *hashgachah pratis*, that nothing is haphazard and that every deed, word and thought is significant. Such reflection will lead to strengthening of one's *avodas Hashem*.

ও Hidden Wonders

One of the true wonders of this world which is commonly overlooked is the attitude toward life that is natural to man. While the reality of death is a fact that cannot and should not be ignored, man goes about his life happy, taking pleasure in the blessings of the present. Though he may see others experiencing great difficulty and heartache in raising their children, in no way should this weaken his desire to marry and establish a family of his own. Man's natural joy of life and his desire to experience it in its fullest sense, concurrent with his knowledge of life's potential for travail and his ultimate departure from this world, is one of Hashem's great hidden miracles.

Yet another great hidden miracle is the fact that, with the passage of time, the memory of the *niftar* fades from the minds of his or her loved ones, to the point that they can be consoled and overcome their grief. This fact, say *Chazal*, is a Divine decree.[4] Of man's capacity to forget, *Chovos HaLevavos* writes:

> *The benefit of being able to forget is: Were man unable to forget, he would always be despondent, and no happy occurrence would be sufficient to drive away his despondency. He would never derive pleasure from that which should bring him joy, for he would always*

4. See *Rashi* to *Bereishis* 37:35.

remember the misfortunes that have occurred (Sha'ar HaBechinah ch. 5).

The *Gemara* (5b) relates that R' Yochanan would comfort mourners by showing them a bone from the tenth child that passed away in his lifetime. *R' Nissan Gaon* writes that this child had fallen into a vat of boiling liquid and died a horrible death. R' Yochanan would, for example, visit a grieving couple whose child had been plucked from them in his youth. The mother and father felt themselves inconsolable, that they could not possibly go on with their lives. R' Yochanan would say to them, "This is the bone of my tenth child, who died a horrible death. I have been able to overcome my grief and go on with my life, and you, too, shall overcome your grief and go on with your lives."

What is incredible is that R' Yochanan did not allow himself the benefit of the capacity to forget, which, as discussed above, is so crucial to the process of consolation. By carrying his child's bone with him, the tragedy was as vivid as ever. R' Yochanan's faith was such that he could carry his misfortune with him in a most literal sense, for the sake of bringing hope and solace to a fellow Jew. Such was the faith of the *Amoraim*, the sages of the Talmud.

⋧ Introspection

As mentioned above, misfortune should be cause for introspection, not out of guilt, but out of recognition of our purpose in this world and Hashem's exacting providence over every detail of our lives.

Introspection should focus not only on oneself, but on one's family as a whole. Effort should be expended to strengthen *shemiras halashon*, guarding one's tongue, among the family. Women should make sure that their manner of dress is in strict accordance with the requirements of *tznius*, and husbands should give careful attention to this matter as well.

Careful scrutiny of the literature that enters one's home is an absolute must. Today, there exists a plethora of English Judaica to satisfy the reading needs of family members of all ages. There is absolutely no excuse for bringing into one's home today's secular literature, which is filled with immorality and promotes outlooks which are diametrically opposed to Torah *hashkafah*.

Today's secular society scorns the idea of having large families. People read secular articles on this topic and are influenced. This matter, like any other area of Torah, is governed by the *Shulchan Aruch*. For a couple to take upon themselves to decide such matters, rather than seek the guidance of a prominent Torah authority, is sheer heresy.

The Torah's outlook is that a couple's desire should be to build a large family. Concerns over material needs are not a consideration. The *Ribono Shel Olam, Who nourishes the entire world in His goodness* (*Bircas HaMazon*), provides for each additional child.

I recall, how, many years ago, a woman wept upon learning that she was expecting another child. Years passed, and, unfortunately, the woman's husband died at a relatively young age. It was this child who bore the family's financial burden at that time.

As survivors of the awesome destruction of European Jewry, it is our responsibility to rebuild *Klal Yisrael*. We dare not look toward the gentile world for outlook on family matters. Their approach to marriage is one of lust and animalistic desire. Their offspring are products of their abominable behavior. The Torah's approach to marriage is one of *kedushah* and *taharah*, sanctity and purity. One should turn to our holy *sefarim* for guidance in these matters; heaven forfend that we seek the opinions of secularists.

Whether in time of joy or sorrow, *emunah* in Hashem and His Torah must be our guiding light. Only through *emunah* can a Jewish home become a *mikdash me'at*, a miniature sanctuary; and only through *emunah* can we overcome the vicissitudes of life and fulfill our mission in this world amid a spirit of joy.

PART III

Hespeidim / Eulogies

Rabbi Yechezkel Levenstein[1]
5644-5734 (1884-1974)

❦ Taking Matters to Heart

אַשְׁרֵי אִישׁ שֶׁיִּשְׁמַע לְמִצְוֹתֶיךָ, וְתוֹרָתְךָ וּדְבָרְךָ יָשִׂים עַל לִבּוֹ.
Praiseworthy is the person who obeys Your command-
ments and takes to his heart Your teaching and Your
word (Shacharis Prayers).

In *avodas Hashem*, practical observance is not sufficient. A person
can be very knowledgeable in Torah and have an abundance of
good deeds to his credit and nevertheless be sorely deficient in his
service if he does not take the teachings of Hashem *to his heart*.

This point is borne out in the second portion of the *Shema*. There,
the Torah speaks of the rewards merited through proper Divine
service and the punishments that may be incurred for straying from
the correct path. That chapter begins:

וְהָיָה אִם שָׁמֹעַ תִּשְׁמְעוּ אֶל מִצְוֹתַי אֲשֶׁר אָנֹכִי מְצַוֶּה אֶתְכֶם הַיּוֹם,
לְאַהֲבָה אֶת ה׳ אֱלֹהֵיכֶם וּלְעָבְדוֹ בְּכָל לְבַבְכֶם וּבְכָל נַפְשְׁכֶם.
וְנָתַתִּי מְטַר אַרְצְכֶם בְּעִתּוֹ יוֹרֶה וּמַלְקוֹשׁ, וְאָסַפְתָּ דְגָנֶךָ וְתִירֹשְׁךָ
וְיִצְהָרֶךָ. וְנָתַתִּי עֵשֶׂב בְּשָׂדְךָ לִבְהֶמְתֶּךָ וְאָכַלְתָּ וְשָׂבָעְתָּ.
And it will come to pass that if you continually hearken
to My commandments that I command you today, to
love Hashem your God, and to serve Him with all your
heart and with all your soul — then I will provide rain
for your land in its proper time, the early and late rains,

---

1. Rabbi Levenstein served as *Mashgiach* of the Mirrer Yeshivah and later of the
Ponovezh Yeshivah. His *Ohr Yechezkel* was published posthumously.

*that you may gather in your grain, your wine, and your
oil. I will provide grass in your field for your cattle and
you will eat and be satisfied.*

Ahavas Hashem, love of Hashem, is surely a most lofty attribute.
Yet the Torah makes clear that it must be complemented by a type of
service that flows from one's complete *heart and soul*. Only then can
Klal Yisrael be worthy of the rewards of which the following verses
speak. Conversely, lack of the quality of *heart* can have the most
dreadful consequences — even when one possesses the quality of
ahavas Hashem. As the Torah continues:

הִשָּׁמְרוּ לָכֶם, פֶּן יִפְתֶּה לְבַבְכֶם, וְסַרְתֶּם וַעֲבַדְתֶּם אֱלֹהִים אֲחֵרִים
וְהִשְׁתַּחֲוִיתֶם לָהֶם. וְחָרָה אַף ה' בָּכֶם וְעָצַר אֶת הַשָּׁמַיִם וְלֹא יִהְיֶה
מָטָר, וְהָאֲדָמָה לֹא תִתֵּן אֶת יְבוּלָהּ. וַאֲבַדְתֶּם מְהֵרָה מֵעַל הָאָרֶץ
הַטּוֹבָה אֲשֶׁר ה' נֹתֵן לָכֶם.

*Beware lest your heart be seduced and you turn astray
and serve gods of others and bow to them. Then the
wrath of Hashem will blaze against you. He will
restrain the heaven so there will be no rain and the
ground will not yield its produce. And you will swiftly
be banished from the good land which Hashem gives
you.*

This warning is related to the earlier promise of וְשָׂבָעְתָּ, *and you
will be satisfied:* "When you have eaten and are full, beware that you
do not rebel against Hashem. . ." (*Rashi* ibid.) Prosperity poses the
danger of laxity in *avodas Hashem* which can ultimately end in total
abandonment of Torah and *mitzvos*; hence the need for this
warning. Even one who possesses true *ahavas Hashem* is liable to
stray in a manner that may result in idol worship, ר"ל, if he will not
place these words upon his heart and soul.[2]

We are gathered here to eulogize my master and teacher, the
Mashgiach of the Ponovezh Yeshivah, of blessed memory.[3] Do you
wish to know how he developed into the *gadol* and *kadosh*, great
and holy personage, that he was? I will tell you. For some seventy

---

2. Paraphrased from v. 18.
3. HaRav Segal studied in the Mirrer Yeshivah in Poland prior to the Second World
War, at which time R' Levenstein was the yeshivah's *Mashgiach*.

years, this Jew toiled to fulfill the Torah's exhortation — וְשַׂמְתֶּם אֶת דְּבָרַי אֵלֶּה עַל לְבַבְכֶם וְעַל נַפְשְׁכֶם, *Place these words of Mine upon your heart and upon your soul.* For seventy years, he toiled over the teachings of *mussar*, the words of *Sha'arei Teshuvah, Chovos HaLevavos, Mesilas Yesharim* and other ethical works, as he strove to make them a part of his very being. Every passage in *Sha'arei Teshuvah*, every concept in *Mesilas Yesharim*, became a part of his limbs, his blood!

I am certain that when he ascended on High, a call went forth: "Clear the way for the *tzaddik*, Yechezkel ben Zlata Malka!" When the *Mashgiach* ascended Above, the holy authors of *Sha'arei Teshuvah, Chovos HaLevavos* and *Mesilas Yesharim* surely came forth to welcome him, for he was a living work of *mussar*.

✅§ In the Footsteps of His Teacher

The *Mashgiach* followed the path of his own revered teacher, R' Simchah Zissel Ziv of Kelm, זצ״ל.[4] Reb Simchah Zissel's son, R' Nachum Velvel, was once asked to portray his father's level of *yiras Hashem*. He replied, "Imagine, if you will, a man with the tip of a sword touching his heart. The slightest move will kill him. Imagine how frightened this man would be, lest he make a wrong move!" This was R' Simchah Zissel and this was his disciple, the *Mashgiach*. They were living embodiments of David *HaMelech's* declaration, שִׁוִּיתִי ה' לְנֶגְדִּי תָמִיד, *I have set Hashem before me always* (*Tehillim* 16:8). Never for a moment did they cease to be cognizant of Hashem's Presence — and their every action was predicated on the extraordinary awe which this awareness evoked.

The Torah admonishes us: *Beware, lest you forget Hashem, your God* (*Devarim* 8:11). *Rabbeinu Yonah* comments, "With this, we are cautioned to be cognizant of Hashem, Blessed is He, at every moment. A person is obligated to strive to forever acquire for himself those characteristics which such cognizance demands, such as: awe of Heaven, modesty, refinement of one's thoughts and character traits. For through such cognizance, the holy seed [of Israel] will acquire

---

4. He was a prime disciple of R' Yisrael Salanter.

every beautiful trait which is a crown upon its bearer..." (*Sha'arei Teshuvah* 3:27)

I am certain that each time the *Mashgiach* studied this passage — and it may have been a thousand times! — he pondered it well and strove to fulfill it. His every action was done with purpose, with *yiras Hashem*. We saw this with our own eyes.

⌇§ The Path to Perfection

Elsewhere in *Sha'arei Teshuvah* we find, "There are many people from whom the light of *teshuvah* is withheld, because they consider themselves pure and meritorious and give no thought toward correction of their ways — for they imagine them to be correct!" Such an attitude can exist only in one who does not study *mussar*. Only such a person can imagine that his every deed is performed for the sake of Heaven and that his ways are flawless. One who studies *Mussar*, however, will recognize that he possesses many of the *midos ra'os*, destructive character traits, about which he studies and he will strive to correct them.

When we speak of *mussar* study, we do not mean casual reading of an ethical work. This is surely not sufficient. Ponder the following: Thrice daily, all of us conclude *Shemoneh Esrei* with the prayer, "My God, guard my tongue from evil and my lips from speaking deceitfully..." Yet, there are people who speak *lashon hara* virtually the moment their prayers are concluded! It is clear that without שִׂימַת לֵב, *taking matters to heart*, no amount of prayer or study will effect any sort of change in oneself.[5]

The *Mashgiach* was a person who was never satisfied with himself. He was forever engaged in self-examination, forever demanding of himself further perfection. This he did for seventy years — and why? Because he was a true student of *mussar*.

---

5. In discussing שִׂימַת הַלֵב, HaRav Segal cited *Sefer HaChinuch's* explanation of the *mitzvah* אֶת ה' אֱלֹהֶיךָ תִּירָא, *You shall fear Hashem, your God* (*Devarim* 10:20): "One who is confronted with the opportunity for transgression is obligated to arouse his spirit and take to heart at that moment that *HaKadosh Baruch Hu* observes man's every deed."

Two themes which were forever on his lips were that of אֱמוּנָה בְּחוּשׁ, *tangible faith* and תְּפִלָּה, *prayer*. He was a living embodiment of the lofty concepts of which he spoke. To the *Mashgiach*, daily *tefillah* was an awesome service of *mussar*. When he would utter the words, *Which man desires life..? Guard your tongue from evil* (*Tehillim* 34:13-14), he would ponder the severity of *lashon hara*. When he would say, *Hashem is great and exceedingly lauded* (ibid. 145:3) he would ponder the greatness of his Creator. He would say, *He lowers the wicked down to the ground* (ibid. 147:6), and ponder the wickedness of *ga'avah*, arrogance. He would say the *Shacharis* blessing, ''Blessed are You, Hashem...Who forms light and creates darkness, makes peace and creates all,'' and ponder the fact that *Chazal* substituted the term הַכֹּל, *all*, for רַע, *evil*,[6] to avoid mentioning this concept in the daily *tefillah* (*Berachos* 11b). From this, the *Mashgiach* drew the lesson that one must always express himself in as refined a manner as possible.

This is the meaning of *tefillah b'derech hamussar*, prayer in the way of *mussar*. This was how the *Mashgiach* prayed for seventy years. Given this fact, we have at least some inkling as to the exalted spiritual level which he attained. He was a master over his every word, deed, and movement. Perhaps somewhere in the world there is to be found a Jew like the *Mashgiach*. We can be sure, however, that there are not many like him to be found.

◄§ Make for Me a Sanctuary

Nefesh HaChaim (footnote to 1:4) cites the well-known comment to the verse וְעָשׂוּ לִי מִקְדָּשׁ וְשָׁכַנְתִּי בְּתוֹכָם, *And let them make for Me a Mikdash [Sanctuary] so that I may dwell among them* (*Sh'mos* 25:8): The verse does not read: וְשָׁכַנְתִּי בְּתוֹכוֹ, *And I will dwell in it* [i.e., in the *Mishkan*], but בְּתוֹכָם וְשָׁכַנְתִּי, *And I will dwell within them*; i.e., within each and every one of them. Every Jew must transform himself into a veritable sanctuary. How is this accomplished? *Nefesh HaChaim* explains:

---

6. The verse upon which the blessing is based reads: יוֹצֵר אוֹר וּבוֹרֵא חֹשֶׁךְ עֹשֶׂה שָׁלוֹם וּבוֹרֵא רָע, *Who forms light and creates darkness, makes peace and creates evil* (*Yeshayahu* 45:7).

> *If man will sanctify himself appropriately through the observance of all the mitzvos. . .then he is a mikdash — literally — and the Divine Presence rests within him; as it is written, "The sanctuary of Hashem are they" (Yirmiyahu 7:4).*

Indeed, the *Mashgiach* transformed himself into a living *mikdash*. His every limb was sanctified for Hashem's service. We can do the same if we will strive to emulate his ways.

Each morning we say: ה' פּוֹקֵחַ עוְרִים, *Hashem gives sight to the blind* (Tehillim 146:8). When saying these words, one should ponder the gift of sight and become filled with boundless gratitude to Hashem. One should imagine how life would be were we denied this gift, ר"ל. Such pondering should naturally lead one to another thought: Am I making proper use of this precious gift? Am I careful to avoid gazing at that which a Jew's eyes must not see — in a world where immodesty is rampant? Am I careful to avoid looking at newspapers and other publications which are filled with forbidden material? One who does not exercise caution in these matters sullies his eyes and cannot possibly be considered a *mikdash*, a receptacle for the Divine Presence.

To our misfortune, television has become acceptable in certain homes. One should know that watching television is absolutely forbidden and the damage which such watching has upon the eyes and soul — particularly that of a young child — is devastating.

Thrice daily we pray: וְתֶחֱזֶינָה עֵינֵינוּ בְּשׁוּבְךָ לְצִיּוֹן בְּרַחֲמִים, *May our eyes behold Your return to Zion.* How can one who sullies his eyes and heart by viewing that which is forbidden hope to see this prayer fulfilled? How can one expect that eyes which are impure will merit to witness the glorious return of the *Shechinah* to its seat of sanctity on this earth?[7]

---

7. The *Midrash* states: "The person who guards his eyes from seeing anything unclean will surely merit that his eyes will behold the *Shechinah*. As the prophet states, *He who shuts his eyes from seeing evil . . . his eyes shall behold the King in all His beauty*" (Yeshayahu 33:15, 17).

Tur (Orach Chaim 1) observes that David *HaMelech* was so keenly aware of the importance of guarding his eyes that he composed a special supplication for it: הַעֲבֵר עֵינַי מֵרְאוֹת שָׁוְא בִּדְרָכֶךָ חַיֵּנִי, *Avert my eyes from seeing futility, through Your ways preserve me* (Tehillim 119:37).

In guarding the purity of our eyes, we must also make certain that our wives and daughters adhere to the laws of *tznius*, modesty, both in manner of dress and behavior. Unfortunately, in some homes these matters are not discussed at all, while in other homes they are not discussed sufficiently.

אִם אֵין אֲנִי לִי, מִי לִי, *If I am not for myself, who will be for me?* (*Avos* 1:14). *Rabbeinu Yonah* comments: "If I will not reprove myself and be zealous in performing *mitzvos*, who will reprove me and ensure my zealousness? For spiritual awakening through others is good for the moment, but when one awakens himself day after day, he will forever think of new ways to refine his service of Hashem..." To hear words of *mussar* is not sufficient; one must study *mussar* on his own and make a sincere effort to perfect his character traits. Those who have already left *kollel* to enter the world of business should arrange to meet together in a *beis midrash* each week for at least one half hour to study *mussar*. Were the *Mashgiach* alive, this is surely what he would demand of us.

I now take leave of you, *Mashgiach*. For forty years, I was bound to you. I beseech you to arouse Heavenly compassion on behalf of your *talmidim*, who were like your children, that we should merit to follow in your ways. We felt exceedingly close to you.

Please arouse compassion on behalf of all of *Klal Yisrael*. עֵת צָרָה הִיא לְיַעֲקֹב, *It is a time of travail for Yaakov.* May it be His will that we merit the coming of *Mashiach*, speedily and in our time.

Rabbi Moshe Schwab[1]
5678-5739 (1918-1979)

⋙ A Sublime Soul

I have come here today to eulogize my great and dear friend, יבל"ח,
the great and dear friend of us all. It is an exceedingly difficult
task. The fact that he is no longer with us has not yet registered with
me. I cannot accept the fact that R' Moshe has departed this world.
He was a flaming fire, literally . . . and now — he is gone.

The *Gemara* (*Berachos* 17a) relates:

> When R' Yochanan would complete the book of Iyov,
> he would say, "The end of man is to die, the end of the
> animal is to be slaughtered. Praiseworthy is the man
> who was brought up with Torah, whose toil was in
> Torah and who brought satisfaction to his Creator; who
> matured with a good name and who departed this
> world with a good name. Of him, Shlomo [HaMelech]
> said, 'A good name is better than good oil, and the day
> of death than the day of birth' " (Koheles 7:1).

R' Moshe was reared in an atmosphere of Torah. In his youth, he
gleaned from the wisdom and ways of R' Elchonon,[2] R' Yisrael
Yaakov[3] and R' Baruch Ber.[4] He was profoundly influenced by these
gedolim as he toiled in Torah and *mussar*.

---

1. Rabbi Schwab was *Mashgiach* of the Gateshead Yeshivah.
2. Rabbi Elchonon Wasserman, *Rosh Yeshivah* of the Ohel Torah Yeshivah in
Baranovich, Poland, before the second World War.
3. Rabbi Yisrael Yaakov Lubchansky, *Mashgiach* in Reb Elchonon's yeshivah.
4. Rabbi Baruch Ber Leibovitz, *Rosh Yeshivah* of Yeshivah Knesses Yisrael in
Kamenitz, Poland, before the war.

R' Moshe was a man who worked hard at self-perfection; indeed, he refined his character to an incredible degree. His conduct was of a type that one simply does not see.

I once suggested to him that he take a second *mashgiach* for his yeshivah. The person I had in mind was an *ish kadosh* (holy individual), one whose influence on Torah students was profound. Someone else in R' Moshe's position might have hesitated to have another person on the yeshivah administration serving in the same capacity as himself. Such hesitation was foreign to R' Moshe. His sole interest in life was to bring satisfaction to his Creator through his service of Him. His sole interest in serving as *mashgiach* was to help the *talmidim* realize their potential as *b'nei Torah*. If having another *mashgiach* in the yeshivah would be to the *talmidim's* benefit, then certainly this was what should be done! When I discussed the matter with him (and touched upon the possibility that R' Moshe might be uncomfortable with such an arrangement), he replied: "וָאס אַרט עָס מיר? עָס אַרט מיר גָארנִיט, What does it bother me? It does not bother me in the least."

His ways of benevolence were awesome. No one will ever know the full scope of his *chesed* activities. A variety of factors can impel a person to perform a given act of kindness. The lengths to which one will go to perform a kindness may well depend on the underlying source of his desire to help others. R' Moshe's way of *chesed* was a brand that may justly be called *"chesed shel Torah,"* kindness whose source is a pure desire to fulfill Hashem's will as expressed in the Torah.[5]

⋖§ R' Yochanan's Bone

A classic example of *chesed shel Torah* is the case of R' Yochanan whose ten sons past away in his own lifetime, ר"ל. R' Yochanan would carry in his pocket a bone which he would show to people who were experiencing personal grief. R' Yochanan would comfort the mourners and say, "This is the bone of my tenth son" (*Berachos* 5b). In essence, he was telling them that he had experienced tragedy

---

5. See Vol. I, discourse to *Parashas Sh'mos*.

upon tragedy in his lifetime, and with Hashem's help, had successfully overcome his grief. So, too, R' Yochanan implied, would they overcome *their* grief.

To appreciate the greatness of R' Yochanan's act, we should note that, as stated in *Chovos HaLevavos (Sha'ar haBechinah* ch. 5), Hashem granted man a great kindness in endowing him with the ability to forget. If man could not forget, then any tragedy which he would ever experience would forever remain as vivid in his mind as when it actually occurred and it would be impossible for him to overcome his grief. It is a great blessing that, as time goes on, the impact of an event fades to at least some degree, thus allowing a broken heart to be mended.

In carrying the bone of his tenth son with him, R' Yochanan was willingly taking his tragedy with him wherever he went, so that he could comfort others. He took with him an actual part of the climax of the many tragedies he had endured, so that he could comfort a grief-stricken couple in saying, "Dear father and mother: Know that I lost not one child but ten children. And yet, I am alive and well and going on with my life. You, too, shall overcome your loss and carry on with your own lives."

What impelled R' Yochanan to do this? It was not an innate desire to do kindness, for this alone could not bring a person to such an awesome act of benevolence. R' Yochanan performed kindness because it is Hashem's will that we emulate His ways and seek to perform kindness with our fellow man to whatever degree possible. This *chesed shel Torah* was what motivated R' Yochanan, and it is this which motivates the *tzaddik* in every generation to serve as teacher, father, counselor, and friend to the multitudes. This is what motivated R' Moshe Schwab.

✑§ An Expression of Gratitude

R' Moshe's feelings for others was reflected by everyone's feelings towards him. When we heard that he had taken ill, we became gripped by dread. When we heard that he had passed away, we felt as if our hearts had been torn. We did not think it possible that such a man could ever leave this world. Woe unto us! It is not for nothing that a man so great in Torah and awe of Hashem, in *chesed* and in bringing merit to the multitudes, has been taken from us.

Virtually all who are gathered here benefited from R' Moshe's kindness, either materially or spiritually. He was deeply involved in arranging *shidduchim* and in matters of *shalom bayis*, harmony between husband and wife. This is not well known because, obviously, such matters are conducted in private. We, who have gained so much from R' Moshe, can express our gratitude to him by striving to emulate his ways. Let us work to uproot the negative traits within ourselves and to replace them with *midos* that bring pleasure to Hashem and our fellow man.

It is now, while we are on this world, that we have the opportunity for *cheshbon hanefesh*, spiritual reckoning. The *Chofetz Chaim* would say that there are those who seem to think that there exists a 'club' whose members die, but that they themselves do not belong to this club! Would they consider that, indeed, their time will also come, then they would surely improve their ways.

As we strive for improvement, let us view our obligations with more than a superficial look. Take, for example, the case of a husband who goes off after supper to study Torah in a *beis midrash*, but spends much of his "learning time" engaged in idle conversation with his "study partner." His loyal wife, well aware of the Talmudic teaching that women earn their share in the World to Come through the Torah study of their husbands and sons, encourages him to maintain these sessions. Her husband, aside from transgressing the stringent sin of *bitul Torah*, disruption of Torah study, is also guilty of deceiving his wife. Would he ponder this fact, he would in all likelihood study with greater diligence.

When we contemplate the awesome matter of *shemiras halashon*, guarding one's tongue, we should examine this requirement and understand its essence. As *Rambam* writes (*Hilchos Dei'os* 7:5), the Torah prohibits us from causing our fellow man any sort of pain or damage, be it to his money, body or dignity. The basis of *shemiras halashon* is the obligation that we be zealous in regard to another person's dignity. Thus, guarding one's tongue is actually an exercise in sensitivity for the feelings of another Jew. It is possible for a person to spend an entire lifetime striving to avoid *lashon hara* and not realize this simple fact.

Let us follow the advice of *Mesilas Yesharim* (ch. 3) and think before we act. Let us complement our study of *mussar* with the study of *halachah*, for without knowledge of *halachah*, it is virtually impossible to adequately fulfill one's obligations as a Jew, be it in matters between man and God, or between man and his fellow.

R' Moshe! Your *ahavas Yisrael* was exceptional. Just as you extended yourself in your lifetime on this earth to help anyone in need, so too, now that you are on the Next World, please come to our aid. Beseech the Almighty to rescue us from our distress through the coming of *Mashiach*, speedily and in our time.

The Satmar Rav
(Rabbi Yoel Teitelbaum) 5747-5739 (1887-1979)

◊ The Aron Elokim Has Been Taken

The Book of *Shmuel* (ch. 4) recounts the events surrounding the capture of the *Aron Elokim*, Ark of God,[1] by the Philistines. The Jews and Philistines had been in the midst of battle, with the Jews suffering heavy losses. The elders decided to bring the *Aron* to the battlefront with the hope that, in its merit, the tide of battle would turn in the Jews' favor. However, such was not to be. Tens of thousands of Jewish soldiers lost their lives and the *Aron* was captured by the enemy. In addition, Chofni and Pinchas, the sons of Eili the *Kohen Gadol* (High Priest) were killed.[2] Eili sat anxiously in Shilo awaiting news from the front. Scripture relates:

> *The bearer of tidings answered and said [to Eili], "Israel has fled from before the Philistines; furthermore, the nation was greatly smitten; furthermore, your two sons, Chofni and Pinchas, died and the Aron Elokim was taken."*
>
> *And it came to pass, when he mentioned the Aron Elokim, that he [Eili] fell backwards from on his chair that was near the gate. His neck-bone broke and he died* (*I Shmuel:* 4:17-18).

1. This was the Ark which contained the *Luchos*, Tablets, and whose place was in the *Kodesh HaKadashim*, Holiest of Holies (see *Radak* to *I Shmuel* 4:4).
2. As punishment for their sins. See *I Shmuel* ch. 3-4.

Eili, who was ninety-eight years old at the time, heard the news of his nation's defeat, the deaths of tens of thousands of his people, and the deaths of his own two sons, and still maintained his composure. However, he could not maintain his composure upon hearing that the *Aron Elokim* had been captured.

Eili's daughter-in-law, the wife of Pinchas, was with child at the time. The dreadful report caused her to give birth suddenly. In her dying moments, she named her newborn son אִי כָבוֹד, meaning, *there is no honor*, for she said, *Honor has been removed from Israel, for the Aron Elokim has been taken* (ibid. v. 22). Though she had lost her own husband and was in the throes of death, the loss of the *Aron* was paramount.

In our time, *Klal Yisrael* suffered a catastrophe involving not tens of thousands, but six million. These *kedoshim* did not die in battle; rather, they were persecuted and tortured in the most horrifying ways. After the war, when the full scope of the Holocaust became known, we were still left with some source of comfort. The *Ribono shel Olam* had decreed that some should survive the deportations and tortures and among the survivors were a number of *tzaddikim*. One of these *tzaddikim* was our generation's *Aron Elokim*, the Satmar Rav. Now, the *Aron Elokim* has been taken from us. The father of our generation is gone.

✑ A Man Who Was Feared

They told R' Yochanan: "R' Chanina's soul has departed." He tore thirteen garments of silk, saying, "Gone is a man whom we feared" (Moed Katan 24a).

The Satmar Rav was an *ish emes*, man of truth, who stood watch against influences which he considered contrary to Torah. He was a staunch opponent of Zionism and even considered it forbidden to participate in their government in any way, shape, or form. Many *gedolei Yisrael* did not share this view, though they, too, strongly opposed the Zionist philosophy. Nevertheless, these *gedolim* always reckoned with the Satmar Rav's position, for they recognized both his *tzidkus* and his greatness in Torah.

The secularists themselves were well aware of his views and the influence which he wielded. More important, every Torah Jew knew his position and this made us constantly aware that the Zionist 'dream' was not our own.

"Gone is a man whom we feared!"

◄§ The Pillars of the World

"The world stands on three things — on Torah study, on service [of God], and on kind deeds" (*Avos* 1:2). The very foundations of the world are shaken when a giant of Torah wisdom departs, when a giant of *avodas Hashem* departs, or when a giant of *chesed* departs. The Satmar Rav was all three. He was a *gaon*, Torah genius, of incredible proportion. He did not cease from delving into Torah virtually his entire life. As Torah teacher to scores of *talmidim*, as *poseik*, and as brilliant expositor in both the halachic and Aggadic realms, the Satmar Rav was a great disseminator of Torah. His service of Hashem, which was manifest in the moving *tefillos* and countless tears which he offered on behalf of *Klal Yisrael*, was surely a pillar which supported us all. His acts of *tzedakah* and *chesed* were a wonder of the age.

Now, all three pillars have been taken from us. The foundations of the world are shaking!

Tur (§581 citing *Pirkei D'R' Eliezer*) writes that when Moshe *Rabbeinu* ascended to Heaven on Rosh Chodesh Elul to receive the second *Luchos* (Tablets), a *shofar* blast was sounded in the Jews' camp to place them on spiritual alert. This was done to prevent a recurrence of the terrible episode of the Golden Calf. Thus, we see that the *shofar* serves as a warning against sin. *Tur* cites the verse, *Can a shofar be sounded in a city and the people not tremble?* (*Amos* 3:6), as proof that the sound of the *shofar* can inspire *teshuvah*, repentance. These qualities serve as the basis for the custom to blow *shofar* during the month of Elul.

It seems that this year, *Klal Yisrael* was in need of much more than the *shofar* to awaken us to *teshuvah*. The *Ribono shel Olam* took the great and holy Satmar Rav from our midst only four days before Rosh Chodesh Elul. We dare not allow this call from Above to go unheeded. During this past year, many tragedies have befallen our people and a number of *gedolim* have been taken from us. As we near the Day of Judgment, it is incumbent upon us all to strengthen ourselves in Torah and *mitzvos* with renewed dedication.

⋑ "Look at Me!"

> The Rabbis taught: The pauper, the rich man and the wicked one stand in [Heavenly] judgment. The poor man is asked, "Why did you not study Torah?" If he replies, "I was poor and busy supporting myself," he will be asked, "Were you poorer than Hillel [who studied Torah despite his poverty]?" It was said about Hillel that he earned a small coin each day, half of which he would give to the watchman of the beis midrash [to gain entry] and half of which he used to support himself and his family...
>
> When the rich man comes, he is asked, "Why did you not study Torah?" If he replies, "I was wealthy and occupied with my business affairs," he will be asked, "Were you wealthier than R' Elazar?" It was said of R' Elazar ben Charsom that his father bequeathed him a thousand cities on land and a thousand ships at sea. Each day he would take a sack of flour on his shoulder and go from city to city and from province to province to study Torah...
>
> The wicked man is asked, "Why did you not study Torah?" If he replies, "I was handsome and preoccupied with my yetzer hara [evil inclination]," he will be asked, "Were you more handsome than Yosef?"...[4]
>
> Thus, poor people will be held accountable because of Hillel, the rich because of R' Elazar ben Charsom and the wicked because of Yosef (Yoma 35b).

The obvious question arises: How can the Heavenly Court bring proof against the average Jew from the likes of Hillel, R' Elazar

---

4. Who resisted the enticement of the wife of Potiphar (*Bereishis* ch. 39).

ben Charsom and Yosef *HaTzaddik*? These were men of exalted character, veritable angels clothed in human guise. Is the average Jew to be faulted for not being like them?

The answer to this must be that Hillel, R' Elazar and Yosef *HaTzaddik* were, after all, human; they possessed a *yetzer hara* and were confronted with *nisyonos*, trials, just as we are. They overcame their inclinations, surmounted their trials and dedicated themselves fully to Hashem's service. We can do the same.

Parashas Re'ei opens with Moshe saying to the people: רְאֵה אָנֹכִי נֹתֵן לִפְנֵיכֶם הַיּוֹם בְּרָכָה וּקְלָלָה, *See that I am placing before you today both blessing and curse* (Devarim 11:26). *Ohr HaChaim* interprets רְאֵה אָנֹכִי homiletically: "*Look at me!*" — i.e., look at the spiritual levels that I, Moshe, have attained, and strive to attain them as well.[5]

Our generation was fortunate to have had the Satmar Rav in its midst. We must take note of his exalted spiritual ways and strive to emulate them.

In addressing *B'nei Yisrael* in the above verse, Moshe first refers to them in the singular (רְאֵה rather than רְאוּ) and then switches to plural (לִפְנֵיכֶם rather than לְפָנֶיךָ). We may suggest that this alludes to the potential inherent in each Jew to effect changes in whole communities and even *to create* whole communities. From the efforts of a single individual can come a community of thousands of God-fearing families. This, in fact, is what the Satmar Rav accomplished after he arrived in America in 1946. Let us understand that the Rav came to America after having suffered in the death camps and after his glorious community of tens of thousands of God-fearing Jews in Hungary was destroyed. Yet he had the spiritual strength and vision to undertake the difficult task of reestablishing his community on American soil. He established his *minyan* in Williamsburg with a small group of *chassidim* and founded a yeshivah with a handful of

---

5. *Rambam* (*Hilchos Teshuvah* 5:2) states, "Every person potentially can be as righteous as Moshe *Rabbeinu.*" R' Elchonon Wasserman (*Kovetz Ma'amarim*) explains that Moshe is referred to in the Torah as עֶבֶד ה', *servant of Hashem*. A slave has no personal rights or possessions; his every act is for his master. Moshe *Rabbeinu's* every word, deed and thought was directed toward one purpose — serving his Creator. Never did Moshe have in mind personal gain or interest. He was the quintessential *servant of Hashem*. Every Jew has the capacity to serve Hashem with this same selfless devotion. This, says R' Elchonon, is the intent of *Rambam's* words.

boys. He helped thousands of survivors reconstruct their lives as his community began to take shape. Today, the Satmar *kehillah* numbers in the tens of thousands and is a fortress of Torah observance and *chesed*.

How could one person accomplish so much? There is but one answer. Along with his many other sublime attributes, the Satmar Rav was endowed with an awesome sense of responsibility. Hashem had placed him on this world to accomplish his particular mission and he would not allow personal loss and suffering to stand in the way of his goals.

After pondering this great loss that we have now suffered, we must develop our own sense of responsibility for *Klal Yisrael*. To say that this responsibility rests upon leaders such as the Satmar Rav, but not upon the average Jew, is a serious mistake. *Poor people will be held accountable because of Hillel, the rich because of R' Elazar ben Charsom* ... Every Jew has been endowed with his own unique mission in life and can accomplish much for himself, his family and his community. It is for each of us to recognize where his potential lies and to utilize his abilities to fulfill his calling.

To the Satmar Rav we say: "We are taking leave of you. Oh, what a *zechus* (merit) it was [to have had a relationship with you]! Please, go before the Heavenly throne with your illustrious grandfather, the *Yismach Moshe*, who said that he would not be silent until we are redeemed.

"We thought that you would lead us to greet *Mashiach*. Though we were not worthy of this, we pray that you will lead us to greet him from your place in the Next World. You know so well both our spiritual and physical sufferings. Arouse the Attribute of Mercy on our behalf so that the Redemption will arrive! We have no better emissary than yourself."

May Hashem *Yisbarach* have mercy on us and rescue us from this dark *galus* through the coming of *Mashiach*, speedily and in our time.

Rabbi Shneur Kotler
5678-5742 (1918-1982)

ৰ্চ Communal Loss

הַצוּר תָּמִים פָּעֳלוֹ כִּי כָל דְּרָכָיו מִשְׁפָּט, אֵל אֱמוּנָה וְאֵין עָוֶל צַדִּיק
וְיָשָׁר הוּא.

The Rock! — perfect is His work, for all His paths are justice; a God of faith without iniquity, righteous and fair is He (Devarim 32:4).

The above verse requires explanation. Is it a praise to say of someone that he is not guilty of wrongdoing? Certainly not! What, then, does the Torah mean in saying that Hashem is אֵין עָוֶל, *without iniquity?*

R' Yisrael Salanter explains that the way of Heavenly justice is unlike the way of justice in human courts. When judgments are issued on this earth, the court does not take into account the effects which the punishment will have on the defendant's wife and children. He is guilty — therefore, he must suffer the full consequences. Hashem's method of justice, however, is different. Before pronouncing judgment on an individual, Hashem takes into account how it will affect everyone whose life is touched by this person. It is therefore possible for a person to be saved from judgment on account of his wife and children. If he is a very charitable individual, he might be saved because of the effect which his death would have on the poor whom he supports. Thus, Hashem's way of justice is truly *without iniquity.*

The loss of R' Shneur Kotler, זצ"ל, is a judgment against all of *Klal Yisrael*, for all of us were touched by him in some way. He was a *gadol* of our time, great both in Torah knowledge and in *midos*. His *yiras Hashem* was outstanding, as was his overall *tzidkus*. He was a great disseminator of Torah, leader of one of the world's greatest yeshivos, and the driving force behind *kollelim* and *yeshivos* which his *talmidim* founded throughout North America and other continents. He bore upon his shoulders the needs of all of *Klal Yisrael*. It is impossible for us to fathom how one individual had the mental capacity to accomplish as much as R' Shneur did in his years as *Rosh HaYeshivah* and Torah leader.

His sweetness of personality was exceptional. What humility! He was a relatively young man, still in his sixties. What a loss, what a conflagration!

Chazal state: "If a person sees that affliction has come upon him, he should scrutinize his ways" (*Berachos* 5a). Why did *Chazal* use the term רוֹאֶה, *sees [affliction]?* Affliction is felt, not seen. It would seem that the term מַרְגִּישׁ, *experiences [affliction]*, would be more appropriate.

We may suggest that the term רוֹאֶה, *sees*, alludes to situations where one needs to perceive that the calamity was, indeed, directed at him and that he has been adversely affected by it. *If a person sees affliction*, then let him not look upon it as would an outsider viewing a happening that has affected others. Rather, let him realize that this judgment has, indeed, *come upon him* and is a warning to him that *he scrutinize his ways*. When a Torah leader such as R' Shneur is taken from our midst, we must realize that this Heavenly judgment is directed at every one of us and that we have all suffered a personal loss. If we do feel broken and distressed, then we must ponder what it is that Hashem is demanding of us. Each one of us must make his own *cheshbon hanefesh*, spiritual reckoning, and determine how he can improve his service of Hashem.

◆§ The Danger of Complacency

It is at times like this that we must ask ourselves: Are we certain that we are living our lives in such a way as to ensure ourselves a place in the World to Come? Each one of us knows the deficiencies of his own soul, the passions, desires, and negative character traits that seek to steer him toward sin. Are we doing anything to harness our desires, or to correct the destructive *midos* within ourselves?

Chazal taught, "Four groups will not merit to greet the *Shechinah* [Divine Presence]: flatterers, scoffers, liars and speakers of forbidden speech" (*Sotah* 42a). Let each of us make a personal reckoning in these four areas. For example, can one say with certainty that he is totally innocent of speaking untruths? 'Half-truths' or anything else short of absolute truth falls within the Torah's definition of שֶׁקֶר, *falsehood.*[1] Are we prepared to declare that our speech is free of שֶׁקֶר?

The *Mishnah* states: הַקִּנְאָה וְהַתַּאֲוָה וְהַכָּבוֹד מוֹצִיאִין אֶת הָאָדָם מִן הָעוֹלָם, *Jealousy, lust and glory remove a man from this world* (*Avos* 4:28). R' Yisrael Salanter notes that הָאָדָם, *the man*, is written with a definitive ה [ה' הַיְדִיעָה], alluding to *the* man of distinction. Even a man of great natural ability and intellect, a man of great knowledge and accomplishment, faces spiritual ruination if he does not expend effort at uprooting the negative traits within himself.

In one of his Divinely inspired prophecies regarding the Jewish people, the wicked Bilaam declared:

תָּמֹת נַפְשִׁי מוֹת יְשָׁרִים וּתְהִי אַחֲרִיתִי כָּמֹהוּ.
May I die the death of the upright and may my end be like his (Bamidbar 23:10).

Ramban (ibid.) explains:

> *"May I die the death of the upright" — meaning, that they [the Jewish people] are the inheritors of Gan Eden. The end of man is death, therefore, he [Bilaam] asked that he die the death of the upright — a reference to Israel ... "And may my end be like his" — like Israel, whose portion is the portion of life [i.e., the World to Come]; they are not among those who are destined for Gehinnom and obliteration.*

Bilaam perceived the pleasures of *Gan Eden* and the sufferings of *Gehinnom* with the utmost clarity — and he prayed that he merit the former. What was his end? Eternal suffering in the fires of *Gehinnom* (*Sanhedrin* 105a). How could a man who communicated with

---

1. See 'The Parameters of Falsehood' (discourse to *Parashas Mishpatim*) in Vol. I.

Hashem, to whom the World to Come was as real as life itself, fail so miserably? To anyone familiar with the relevant Scriptural and Midrashic passages, the answer is simple. Bilaam was a man of great arrogance and lust — and he made no effort to change. When he was in a prophetic state, communicating the word of the Living God, Bilaam prayed that he merit that which he knew was the greatest pleasure that exists — to bask in the glory of the *Shechinah*. When faced with temptation, however, Bilaam could not think of the true purpose of life. *May I die the death of the upright* was then furthest from his mind. At such moments, he was ruled by the *midos ra'os*, destructive traits, within himself. He sank to the level of beasts and committed the most sinful, abominable acts.

When a person falls into a routine of *mitzvah* observance and daily Torah study, he tends to become satisfied with himself and gives little or no thought to self-improvement. What of *mussar* study and introspection? That, he tells himself, is the province of *tzaddikim*; it is for the select few, not the general population. Those who subscribe to this attitude find themselves woefully unprepared when faced with any sort of spiritual test. If their pride is wounded or their jealousy aroused by their neighbor's success, they become easy prey for their evil inclination. Yesterday's lofty outlook on life is quickly replaced by a self-centered desire to satisfy one's emotional needs.

◄§ The Purpose of Death

Death was decreed upon man as a result of Adam's sin (*Bereishis* 3:19). R' Moshe Chaim Luzzato (*Da'as Tevunos*) explains that rather than a punishment, death was a necessary result of Adam's act. Had Adam not sinned, life would have been a never-ending spiral of spiritual elevation. Evil would have been an outside temptation that would not have affected man's essence. In inciting Adam to sin, the serpent succeeded in making the inclination toward evil a part of man. Now, a new process would be required to bring man back to his original state. He would have to die, so that his soul would be separated from his body, to absorb the light of the Upper World. Then, at the time of *techias hameisim*, resurrection of the dead, man's spiritual and physical selves would be joined once more. The light which the soul had acquired in Heaven would radiate from within man and restore him to the level of Adam prior to his partaking of the Tree of Knowledge.

Chazal (*Sotah* 5a) state that an arrogant person is akin to a non-believer, is fit to be uprooted like a tree of idolatry, and will not arise at the time of *techias hameisim*. It seems that the impurity which arrogance brings with it is a type that cannot be purged by the soul's ascending Above. Therefore, one who does not rid himself of this trait cannot possibly achieve spiritual cleansing and merit to arise from the dead.

It is apparent that we are far removed from a proper understanding of the destructive effects which arrogance and other negative traits have upon our souls. To our misfortune, the matter of self-refinement is woefully neglected in our day. This is only because *mussar* study is either treated lightly or totally ignored. In fact, *mussar* study is the *only* cure for character deficiency. As Shlomo *HaMelech* declared: הַחֲזֵק בַּמּוּסָר אַל תֶּרֶף, נִצְּרֶהָ כִּי הִיא חַיֶּיךָ, *Cling tightly to mussar, do not loosen your grip! Guard it, for it is your life* (*Mishlei* 4:13).

◆§ The Sages' Approach

The *Gemara* relates:

> When R' Eliezer took ill, his disciples entered to visit him. He told them, "A powerful wrath is present in the world." [He interpreted his illness as an expression of Divine wrath directed at himself — Rashi.] His disciples began to weep, except for R' Akiva, who smiled. They said to R' Akiva, "Why are you smiling?" He responded, "Why are you weeping?" They said, "A Torah scroll [i.e., their teacher] is suffering and we should not weep?" He said to them, "That is exactly why I am smiling. As long as I saw that my teacher's wine was not turning sour, that his flax was not being damaged and that his honey was not losing its consistency [i.e., that all was well with him], I thought,

'Can it be that my teacher is receiving his reward in this world, Heaven forfend?' However, now that I see him suffering, I am glad [i.e., relieved].'

R' Eliezer said to him, "Have I overlooked anything in the Torah [that you consider my suffering an atonement for my shortcomings]?" R' Akiva responded, "You have taught us, our teacher, that 'There is no man so wholly righteous on earth that he [always] does good and never sins'" [Koheles 7:20] (Sanhedrin 101a).

R' Akiva knew well the greatness of his *rebbi*, R' Eliezer. At the same time, he clearly perceived the depths of Divine judgment. He realized that suffering on this world is a cleansing of the soul which allows a person to reap his reward in the Next World.

The loss of this great *Rosh Yeshivah* for whom we mourn should serve as a reminder to us that this world is but a temporary sojourn on our journey to the World of Truth. We should utilize this moment to peer into ourselves and correct our shortcomings.

Let us bear in mind that Chapter 231 in the *Orach Chaim* section of *Shulchan Aruch* is no different from the remainder of the Jewish code of law — it is *Halachah* and no one is exempt from its requirements. That chapter concludes:

In summation: A person is obligated to turn his attention to his ways, to weigh his every deed upon the scales of his intellect. When he perceives that a given act falls within the category of service to his Creator, he should do it. If not, he should not do it. One who conducts himself in this manner serves his Creator constantly.

If a person sees that affliction has come upon him, he should scrutinize his ways. Let us engage in sincere *teshuvah*. Let us establish for ourselves fixed periods for the study of *mussar*, especially the works of the *Chofetz Chaim* which are *kodesh kadashim*, holiest of holies.

R' Shneur — we now take leave of you. We enjoyed a bond of closeness with you and we now put forth a request. You were a leader of *Klal Yisrael*, and therefore you know well our spiritual and physical situation. You know well that open hatred toward our people is intensifying and that the Torah community is few in number. True, we are witnessing a spiritual awakening and *ba'alei teshuvah* are joining our ranks, but we are, nonetheless, a very small minority. *All* of *Klal Yisrael* must become a "kingdom of priests and holy nation" (*Sh'mos* 19:6), yet we seem so far removed from such a reality. Our world is one of fear. Our people cannot place their trust in any nation and no one knows what tomorrow will bring.

We ask of you, R' Shneur: Go to your great father, R' Aharon, your grandfather, R' Isser Zalman,[2] the *Chofetz Chaim* and the six million who perished in the Holocaust. Gather them together and raise a great cry before the Heavenly Throne. Your opinion is surely reckoned with Above. There is no remedy for our situation, other than the Final Redemption. Prevail before the Heavenly Throne so that *Mashiach* will arrive!

May it be Hashem's will that we soon merit the time when all the world will recognize His sovereignty and the earth will be filled with His wisdom.

---

2. Rabbi Isser Zalman Meltzer, author of *Even HaAzel*.

The Steipler
(Rabbi Yaakov Yisrael Kanievsky)
5659-5745 (1899-1985)

◦§ Torah for Its Own Sake

The passing of any Jew is a loss to *Klal Yisrael*. The passing of a מַרְבִּיץ תּוֹרָה, *disseminator of Torah*, is of particular significance. The passing of the great מַרְבִּיץ תּוֹרָה, *tzaddik* and shepherd of our generation, the Steipler, זצ״ל, is a loss of awesome proportions.

For virtually all his life, the Steipler studied Torah לִשְׁמָה, *for its own sake*, with unsurpassed dedication, diligence and self-sacrifice. *Rosh* (*Nedarim* 51b) defines תּוֹרָה לִשְׁמָה:

> *One's every word and discussion in Torah should be for the sake of Torah; that is, to know and understand it; to add flavor and depth — without any intent toward pride or outdoing one's peers.*

One should study Torah with the goal of knowing it in its entirety: *Talmud Bavli, Yerushalmi, Halachah, Aggadah...* — not superficially, but in all its richness and depth, with a clear understanding of the fine points in any given topic. That is Torah *lishmah* and that is how the Steipler studied Torah his entire life.

In the *Gemara* we find:

> *R' Aleksandrei said: Whoever studies Torah* לִשְׁמָה *creates harmony between the Heavenly retinue and the terrestrial retinue.*
>
> *Rav said: It is as if he built a palace above and a palace below.*

R' Yochanan said: He serves as a shield for the entire
world.

Levi said: He also brings the Redemption closer
(Sanhedrin 99b).

R' Aleksandrei teaches that the study of Torah *lishmah* forges a
bond between the Heavens and this world. Rav's statement alludes to
the spiritual power inherent in a Jew's every deed, especially that of
Torah study.

◁§ The Power of Our Deeds

When one performs a *mitzvah* or commits a sin, he most likely
does not perceive himself as being any different than before.
The difference, he believes, is merely a matter of record; one good deed
or sin has been added to his slate.

This is grossly incorrect. An individual's deeds have an immediate
effect upon his soul, and moreover, all the upper and lower worlds are
affected as well. Note the following from *Nefesh HaChaim* (1:13)
regarding the power of speech:

> "For, behold! He is Molder of mountains and Creator of
> wind and He repeats to man what his conversation is"
> (Amos 4:13). . .Man is cautioned when he is now on this
> lowly world where he can neither see nor perceive the
> perfection or destruction which is effected Above
> through his every word. He is liable to think to
> himself... "Of what significance is a light word or
> conversation, that it should effect any change in this
> world?" Know then, with certainty, that every word or
> conversation which emanates from one's lips is not lost,
> and does not go to waste...

◁§ Furthermore. . .

The *Mishnah* (*Avos* 6:1) states: "R' Meir said: 'Whoever engages
in the study of Torah *lishmah* merits many things; further-

more. . .' " The term *furthermore* implies that one who studies Torah *lishmah* merits *many things* in addition to the many sublime qualities which the *mishnah* goes on to cite. What are these *many things*?

R' Chaim of Volozhin (*Ruach Chaim*) writes that *many things* refers to the infinite reward for the study of Torah *lishmah*,[1] for, while our every word and deed carries great weight in Heaven, this is especially true of Torah study. The fulfillment of this greatest of *mitzvos*, performed with proper intent, fills the upper and lower worlds with an incomparable spiritual light and sanctity. These are the 'palaces' of which Rav speaks.

Of course, there are varying degrees of Torah *lishmah*. As is obvious from *Kehillos Yaakov*, his multi-volumed work on topics in *Shas*, the Steipler's study of Torah *lishmah* was of the highest possible level. We can be sure that the Steipler's learning created an aura of *kedushah*, sanctity, which profoundly affected every one of us.

The Steipler's *hasmadah*, diligence in study, was incredible. It was common for him to learn thirty consecutive hours (except for necessary interruptions) without sleep. As is well known, his learning was exceptional not only quantitatively, but also qualitatively, for his diligence was complemented by phenomenal *ameilus*, toil, as he strained with his every ounce of energy and ability to plumb the Torah's depths.

The *Chofetz Chaim* writes (*Toras HaBayis* ch. 2) that a person is capable of speaking two hundred words in a single minute. The *Gra*[2] (*Sh'nos Eliyahu* to *Pe'ah* 1:1) writes that every word of Torah study is a *mitzvah* for itself. Can we even begin to imagine the merit which the Steipler accrued through his Torah study?

R' Yochanan said: He [who studies Torah lishmah] serves as a shield for the entire world. This applies to the Torah study of any Jew. However, there are those יְחִידֵי סְגוּלָה, *men of distinction*, who, as the greatest toilers in Torah of their generation, shield their fellow

---

1. As mentioned above, the definition of Torah *lishmah* is study for the sake of knowing the wisdom of Hashem. Of course, the primary purpose of knowing His wisdom is in order to carry out His will. "One who studies in order to practice, is given the means to study and to teach, to observe and to practice" (*Avos* 4:6). *Chazal* (*Kiddushin* 40a) tell us that when a Jew decides in his mind to do a good deed, *HaKadosh Baruch Hu* considers it as done. Therefore, writes *Shelah*, one who studies Torah *lishmah* is considered as if he has fulfilled the entire Torah.

2. גר"א is an acronym for גאון ר' אליהו, the *Vilna Gaon*.

Jews in a special way. Who knows how many tragedies were averted, how much suffering was alleviated, in the merit of the Steipler's learning?

The Torah states that one who commits murder unintentionally must be exiled to an עִיר מִקְלָט, *city of refuge*. The *Gemara* (*Makkos* 10a) cites a *Baraisa*: "If a disciple was exiled, his [Torah] teacher was exiled with him." This is derived from the word וָחָי, *and he shall live* (*Devarim* 4:22), which alludes to the obligation to provide the unintentional killer with that which will enable him to live. *Rambam* explains:

וְחַיֵּי בַּעֲלֵי הַחָכְמָה וּמְבַקְשֶׁיהָ בְּלֹא תַּלְמוּד תּוֹרָה כְּמִיתָה חֲשׁוּבִין.
The life of the masters of wisdom and its seekers without Torah is considered like death (*Hilchos Rotze'ach* 7:1).

Tzaddikim are considered alive even in death (*Berachos* 18a). The Steipler lives on. It is we to whom the term 'death' should be applied following the passing of this *gaon* and *tzaddik*. His greatness in Torah cast its glow everywhere. To his door came scores of people, day after day, people from all walks of life. Some sought his blessings, others his counsel, while still others came to pour out their troubles and benefit from his loving concern and words of encouragement. He was the *rebbi* of our entire generation; as we tried to cope with the travails of this long and bitter exile, his presence infused us with spiritual life. Now we are still in exile, while our *rebbi*, our life source, has been taken from us.

◄§ Fear of Hashem

The *Mishnah* states (*Avos* 3:31), "R' Chaninah ben Dosa said: 'Anyone whose fear of sin takes priority over his wisdom, his wisdom will endure; but anyone whose wisdom takes priority over his fear of sin, his wisdom will not endure.' "

The *Gemara* (*Shabbos* 30a) cites a verse which contains allusions to the six orders of the *Mishnah*. The verse concludes: יִרְאַת ה' הִיא אוֹצָרוֹ, *Fear of Hashem — that is its storehouse* (*Yeshayahu* 33:6). R' Chaim of Volozhin elaborates upon this teaching:

Yiras Hashem is the 'storehouse' of wisdom of the holy Torah, for through it, the Torah remains with the student. If man does not first prepare the storehouse that is yiras Hashem, then the abundant 'grain' that is Torah will be lying out in the field to be trampled by the feet of the ox and donkey, ח"ו, for it will not remain with him at all. To the above verse, the Midrash (Sh'mos Rabbah 30) states, "You may find a man who studies Midrash, Halachah and Aggadah; if he does not possess fear of sin, he does not possess anything at all..."

To the degree that one prepares his storehouse of yiras Hashem, to that degree will he be able to gather in, safeguard and retain the grain of Torah for his storehouse to hold. For when a father portions out grain to his sons, he gives each one a measurement that can be held by the storehouse that the son has prepared in advance. Even if the father will have an open hand and desire to give his son in abundance, if the storehouse cannot hold such an amount, the father will not be able to provide it. If the son will not prepare a storehouse at all, the father will not be able to give him anything, for he has nothing in which to store it.

Similarly, the hand of Hashem, Blessed is His Name, is open, as it were, to grant each one of His treasured people an unceasing flow of abundant wisdom and exceptional depth of understanding, which can remain with him and be inscribed upon his heart, and in which he will delight when he will bring it with him to the World of Tranquility. However, all this will depend upon the degree of yiras Hashem that he prepares in advance...

The Steipler's love of and dedication to Torah study was complemented by his awesome *yiras Hashem.*

One Friday night, a fly landed in his teacup. With his poor eyesight, the Steipler did not see the fly. Someone else did and stopped the Steipler from taking another sip. The Steipler thanked the person deeply, saying that he had saved him from transgressing five Torah prohibitions. The following morning, the Steipler related that he had not slept the entire night, for the thought of his having come so close to committing such a sin allowed him no rest.

An acquaintance of mine related the following which he heard directly from the person involved: One Succos in Bnei Brak, some ten years before the Steipler's passing, this person went for a walk at around midnight. His attention was drawn to a voice in the distance. He followed the voice until he found himself outside the Steipler's *succah*. The Steipler was talking to himself inside the *succah*. "What do you think, that you will live forever?" he was demanding of himself. "Eventually, you will die and they will bury you in the ground." The Steipler then described to himself the punishments of *Gehinnom* and what he feared lay in store for him when his time would come. He went on talking in this way for one half hour.

It is through such conduct that the Steipler became the *gadol* and *kadosh* that he was.

◆§ Our Obligation

The *Gemara* (*Shabbos* 153a) relates that before his passing, Rav told R' Shmuel bar Shilas, אֲחִים בְּהֶסְפְּדָאי דְּהָתָם קָאִימְנָא. *Rashi* translates: *Warm them [i.e., arouse your listeners] through your eulogy of me, for I [i.e., Rav's soul] will be present [when the eulogy will be delivered].* We may suggest another interpretation. Rav was, in effect, saying: "During my lifetime, the aura of my deeds inspired the generation to greater service of Hashem. When I die, this aura will depart along with me. Therefore, in your eulogy of me, be sure to inspire your listeners to awaken *themselves* to His service, for *I will be there*, in the World to Come, and will no longer be able to accomplish this."

To go home after a *hesped* and spend time discussing whether or not the *hesped* was a good one is to miss the point entirely.[3] One cannot go away from a *hesped* of such a *gadol b'Torah* without

---

3. Aside from the fact that the laws of *shemiras halashon* will inevitably be transgressed.

making a sincere commitment to improve in some way. Each one of us has an obligation to fill the great void created after the Steipler's passing.

We turn to the saintly *niftar* and say: We beseech you not to forget us! You know so well of all the sickness and suffering that exists among *Klal Yisrael*, ה' ירחם. Together with the *Chazon Ish*,[4] go before the Heavenly throne and arouse Hashem's compassion so that these terrible sicknesses will end. Beseech the Almighty on our behalf that we merit to become true men of spirit, that we merit to study Torah *lishmah* and fulfill the *mitzvos* in accordance with His will. We know that, "He who comes to purify himself is granted Heavenly assistance" (*Shabbos* 104a). We are in need of this assistance.

We ask that this year be one of redemption and salvation, through the coming of *Mashiach*, speedily and in our time.

---

4. The Steipler was married to the sister of the *Chazon Ish*.

Rabbi Moshe Feinstein
5655-5746 (1895-1986)

✌§ Our Loss

Our crown has fallen! We have lost the Moshe *Rabbeinu* of our generation. He was the *poseik hador*, to whom the most difficult halachic problems were brought. Incredibly, there exist *teshuvos* (halachic responsa) that he wrote seventy years ago when he was but twenty-one years of age.[1]

And what of his *midos*! His simplicity and humility! His *chesed* for each and every Jew!

In truth, we did not really know Reb Moshe. The full dimensions of his greatness are beyond us. He bore the entire world upon his shoulders.[2]

Nevertheless, it behooves us to ponder Reb Moshe's qualities as we, in our humble state, perceived them. We must attempt to understand what we had with us and what we have lost. Hopefully, this will inspire us toward *teshuvah* and emulating his ways.

---

1. Reb Moshe assumed his first rabbinic position in Uzda, White Russia, when he was but twenty years old and unmarried. During his first year as *Rav*, he wrote a thirteen-page *teshuvah* regarding a questionable marriage ceremony. Forty-four years later, Reb Moshe saw fit to include this *teshuvah* in his *Igros Moshe* (*Even HaEzer* §82).

2. HaRav Segal added: "Only two weeks ago, we lost our generation's other great leader — Rav Yaakov [Kamenetsky], who, together with Reb Moshe, guided the Torah world. Now, they are both gone — הַנֶּאֱהָבִים וְהַנְּעִימִם בְּחַיֵּיהֶם, וּבְמוֹתָם לֹא נִפְרָדוּ, [They] who were beloved and pleasant in their lifetime and in their death were not parted."

ᴈ§ The Light of Torah

The *Gemara* relates:

> R' Menacham the son of R' Yosei expounded the following: "For a mitzvah is a lamp, and Torah is light" (Mishlei 6:23) — Scripture associates a mitzvah with a lamp and Torah with [sun]light to teach us that just as a lamp illuminates only for a time, so, too, does a mitzvah shield one [from harm] only for a time; and just as [sun]light illuminates forever, so, too, does Torah shield one forever.
>
> Scripture further states [regarding Torah]: "When you walk, it will guide you; when you lie down, it will watch over you; and when you wake up, it will speak for you" (Mishlei 9:11) — "When you walk, it will guide you," refers to This World; "when you lie down, it will watch over you," refers to the time of death; "and when you wake up it will speak for you" [it will intercede on your behalf — Rashi], refers to the World to Come.
>
> This can be likened to a person who is walking alone in the blackness of night. He is frightened of thorns, briars, open pits, wild beasts and bandits — and he knows not which path to take. He comes upon a torch and is thus saved from thorns, briars and open pits, but he is still fearful of wild beasts and bandits, and he still does not know which path to take. When dawn breaks, he is saved from wild beasts and bandits, but he still does not know which path to take. When he finally reaches a crossroads, he is saved from everything (Sotah 21a).

As *Rashi* explains, the torch in the above parable alludes to *mitzvos*, which rescue a person from some forms of punishment, as represented by the thorns, briars and open pits. Daybreak represents the study of Torah, which saves a person from sin and suffering to a degree not attainable through other *mitzvos*. The *Gemara* offers three interpretations of the remainder of R' Menachem's illustration. The third is that of Mar Zutra, who explains 'and he knows not which path to take,' to mean that even after one is devoted to Torah, he cannot be certain that his conclusions in study will accord with Torah truth. He is 'saved' from this possibility when he reaches a 'crossroads,' meaning when he becomes 'a talmid chacham whose conclusions in a given topic are in accordance with the Halachah.' Rashi interprets this to mean that the Divine assistance which this person merits in his learning is manifested in his halachic opinions being accepted by his peers.

Tosafos questions Mar Zutra's interpretation, for R' Menachem states that upon reaching the 'crossroads' one is 'saved from everything.' Tosafos assumes that Torah study protects one from his yetzer hara, evil inclination, only when he is actually engaged in study. When not involved in study, one is not assured of such protection. How, then, is he 'saved from everything'?

Tosafos answers:

> To the average Torah scholar, Torah study is a primary occupation; he is involved in it and thinking into it all the time and he does not walk four amos without Torah study.

Reb Moshe epitomized the qualities mentioned above. His halachic opinions were considered the final word among Torah Jews everywhere. He merited this because he never ceased to ponder thoughts of Torah.

As is known, Reb Moshe completed the study of Shas many times. The breadth and depth of his knowledge defies description. He could not possibly have attained his awesome level of Torah scholarship without incredible hasmadah, unrelenting diligence. Indeed, it is known that Reb Moshe utilized every possible moment for Torah study. Because of this, Reb Moshe truly merited to be 'saved from everything.' The yetzer hara had no dominion over him. He was a living embodiment of humility, simplicity, kindness and every other attribute that a Jew should strive to attain.

✒ A Living Sanctuary

The Torah states: וְעָשׂוּ לִי מִקְדָּשׁ וְשָׁכַנְתִּי בְּתוֹכָם, *Make for Me a sanctuary so that I may dwell within them* (Sh'mos 25:8). *Chazal* note that the verse states בְּתוֹכָם, *[I may dwell] within them*, rather than בְּתוֹכוֹ, *within it* [i.e., the *Mishkan*]. This teaches that it is man's obligation to transform *himself* into a veritable sanctuary, to dedicate his every limb and organ and all his five senses to the service of Hashem. Then, the *Shechinah* will dwell within him.

This, too, we can say of Reb Moshe. He served Hashem with every fiber of his being, with every ounce of his strength, and in every word, deed and thought all his long life. His greatness in Torah was complemented by his boundless *chesed*. One can see the attribute of *chesed* in his *teshuvos*, where time and again, he displays a deep sensitivity and concern for his fellow man.[2]

Reb Moshe sanctified himself toward serving his Maker. He was a living *Mishkan* — and this we have lost. We must now ask ourselves: Does our service live up to that which Reb Moshe taught by example? Are we making proper use of the abilities that Hashem has granted each and every one of us? Is our intellect dedicated toward the study of Torah? Do we ponder ways through which we can help others? Do we recognize the greatness of our Creator by His awesome creations?[3] Are we perhaps guilty of letting our eyes stray, of letting our ears hear that which is forbidden? Have we perhaps used our power of speech for *lashon hara*? Can we honestly say that our lives are directed toward spiritual endeavors?

---

2. Reb Moshe once issued a *p'sak* in a very sensitive case and, as a result, was the target of verbal attack. Someone asked Reb Moshe why he had allowed himself to get involved in the matter when he knew the possible ramifications. Reb Moshe replied, "Had you seen the tears of the person who brought the case before me you would not have asked such a question."

3. In this context, HaRav Segal cited the words of Yeshayahu *HaNavi*, *Lift up your eyes and see — who created all this?* (Yeshayahu 40:26). Contemplation of the wonders of creation is, according to *Rabbeinu Yonah*, among the 613 commandments and a primary way to achieve love of Hashem, as stated by *Rambam* (*Hilchos Yesodei HaTorah* 2:2).

✑ 'Open Wide Your Mouth'

When Shlomo *HaMelech* became King of Israel, Hashem appeared to him in a dream and said, *Ask! What shall I give you?* (*I Melachim* 3:5). Shlomo replied, *Give your servant an understanding heart to judge Your people, to discern between good and evil...* Scripture continues that this request found favor in Hashem's eyes. Shlomo was told that because he had asked for wisdom, and not for wealth or long life, he would be granted unparalleled wisdom, along with wealth and honor which he had not sought.

It seems difficult to understand why Shlomo's response was deemed so praiseworthy. Was it not logical for him to request wisdom? Anyone who understands that man's existence and purpose in life transcends this world knows that wisdom, and not wealth or honor, is a most precious gift.

It seems to me that the explanation is as follows. When a person is told to request that which he desires most *and he is given time to think before responding*, then his answer will most likely reflect his understanding of what is truly important. However, when *forced to respond immediately*, one's answer will probably reflect that which he yearns for constantly and which is forever on his mind. That Shlomo in his dream immediately asked for 'an understanding heart' demonstrated that he was not a person who craved honor or wealth or any other illusory gain. Rather, he forever sought to gain wisdom, the wisdom of Torah. Thus did his response find favor in Hashem's eyes.

In a sense, every Jew is given an opportunity such as the one granted Shlomo. Hashem says to each and every one of us: הַרְחֶב פִּיךָ וַאֲמַלְאֵהוּ, *Open wide your mouth and I will fill it* (*Tehillim* 81:11). *Rashi* comments: "[Open wide your mouth] to ask of Him all your heart's yearnings." This is what the *Ribono shel Olam* offers every one of us. Unfortunately, we often squander this opportunity, as we seek wealth, honor and the like and ignore our spiritual needs.

Reb Moshe was different. He beseeched the Almighty: "Grant me greatness in Torah knowledge! Grant me greatness in *yiras shamayim*, in *midos*!" The *Ribono shel Olam* saw his "mouth open wide," and responded, "I shall fill it!" Thus did Reb Moshe merit to become a *gadol hador*, leader of the generation, upon whom the *Shechinah* came to rest.

◄§ Ponder Three Things

One of the greatest personalities of the Mishnaic era was the *Tanna*, Akavia ben Mehalalel. The *Gemara* (*Berachos* 19a) states that when the gates of the Temple Courtyard were closed on *Erev Pesach* — an indication that the huge courtyard was filled to capacity with myriads of Jews — none could be found as great in wisdom, purity and fear of Hashem as Akavia ben Mehalalel. How did he attain such greatness? A *mishnah* in *Avos* (3:1) provides a clue:

> Akavia ben Mehalalel said: Ponder three things and you will not come into the grip of sin: Know whence you came, whither you go, and before Whom you will give justification and reckoning. "Whence you came?" — from a putrid drop; "whither you go?" — to a place of dust, worms and maggots; "and before Whom will you give justification and reckoning?" — before the King Who reigns over kings, the Holy One, Blessed is He.

A person can get so thoroughly involved in his daily routine that he will ignore the fact that man does not live forever. He will seek to amass a fortune, pursue every luxury, and turn a blind eye to reality. How does one avoid falling victim to such self-destruction? Akavia tells us the answer: *Study Mussar.* Set aside a specific time each day for the study of that which will awaken you to your purpose on this earth. Through *mussar* study, you will ponder whence you came, whither you are going and before Whom you will have to stand judgment when your sojourn on this earth has ended. Through *mussar* study, you will be able to stand before Hashem at that awesome moment of reckoning and say, "I have fulfilled my mission as You desired."

∽§ Filling the Void

Thrice daily in the *Shemoneh Esrei* we beseech Hashem, "Restore our judges as in earlier times and our counselors as at first." When saying these words, we should have in mind that Hashem should bless our people with *gedolim* who can fill the tremendous void left by the passings of Reb Moshe and other Torah leaders who have departed from our midst in recent years. At the same time, each one of us must ponder what *he* can do to help produce future *gedolim*. To parents we ask: With what goal in mind are you raising your sons? Is your primary concern that your sons go on to enjoy life amid comfort and luxury, or are you instilling within them a love and thirst for Torah and a desire to dedicate themselves toward service of Hashem? This question, while addressed to all parents, is directed in particular toward parents whose sons have been blessed from Above with above-average abilities. Hashem gave your sons these abilities for the purpose of serving Him and His people. It is your obligation to guide your sons along the true path.

To students of Torah we say: Ponder well how you are utilizing your God-given abilities. Are you striving to attain your potential in Torah study? What are your long-range goals? Do you strive for greatness, and if yes, what sort of greatness do you seek?

As we are gathered here, mourning the passing of this great *gaon* and *tzaddik*, we must all become moved to sincere *teshuvah*. Let us evaluate our ways and seek to improve.

Reb Moshe: You have left this world and parted from us. I merited to visit with you. How pleasurable it was to converse with you! How vividly do I recall the sweetness of your golden personality!

Your passing has awakened us to *teshuvah*. We will strive to better our service of Hashem, in Torah study, *tefillah*, as well as in other *mitzvos*.

To Reb Moshe and Reb Yaakov we say: In your lifetime, you bore the entire world upon your shoulders. Please go now to the *Chofetz Chaim* and tell him what has transpired in your generation. Tell him that men, women and children all over the world are studying the laws of *shemiras halashon*, as codified in his classic work on this topic. Tell him how there has arisen a *ba'al teshuvah* movement in the Soviet Union whose members study Torah and observe *mitzvos* with genuine *mesiras nefesh*.

Please go before the Heavenly throne and plead before Hashem that He send us *Mashiach*, speedily and in our time.

R' Shaul Rosenberg[1]

⚜ A Lesson in Gratitude

Hashem spoke to Moshe, saying, "Exact Israel's vengeance from the Midianties; then you will be gathered in to your people" (Bamidbar 31:2).

In the above verse, Hashem orders Moshe to execute Israel's revenge against the Midianites for their having caused *B'nei Yisrael* to sin grievously and suffer terrible retribution as a result.

As *Chazal* explain, Hashem did not set a specific date for the war against Midian. He left this to Moshe, while informing him that after the war he would depart this world. According to the *Midrash* (*Bamidbar Rabbah* 21:2), Moshe could have delayed the start of the war for any length of time. He chose, however, to waste no time at all in carrying out Hashem's command. "Although Moshe knew that his death was dependent on this [i.e., on the war being fought], he carried out the command with joy and did not tarry" (*Rashi* v. 3).

Yet, for all his zealousness, Moshe himself did not participate in the battle. The *Midrash* explains:

> *Hashem told Moshe, "Take vengeance yourself," yet Moshe sent others! This was because Moshe grew up in Midian. He said, "It is not proper that I should cause distress to the nation that did good to me."*

What sort of kindness did the Midianites do for Moshe? They allowed him to live in their land as a shepherd for his father-in-law's

---

1. R' Shaul Rosenberg was president of the Yeshivah of Manchester which HaRav Segal headed. He passed away on 14 Tammuz, 5740.

flock. Moshe deemed it inconceivable that Hashem would want him to take battle against this wicked nation which had lured his own people into the depths of sin. It was Moshe's perception of the quality of *hakaros hatov*, gratitude, which impelled him to act as he did. If we find Moshe's attitude difficult to comprehend, it is because our own perception of this quality is lacking.

We have gathered here to eulogize the president of our yeshivah, R' Shaul Rosenberg, ז״ל. All of us owe him an enormous debt of gratitude. For more than forty years he bore the financial burden of our yeshivah with true self-sacrifice. It was R' Shaul who strove tirelessly day and night so that this yeshivah building in which we are gathered could be erected. It is largely because of the presence of our yeshivah that the Jewish community of Manchester has developed into a community of Torah and *yiras Hashem*. Thus, the entire community is forever indebted to R' Shaul.[2]

✥ Hillel's Self-Sacrifice

The *Gemara* (*Yoma* 35b) states that the efforts of Hillel to study Torah obligate the poor in every generation to study despite their hardships. Hillel's self-sacrifice is vividly described:

> *They said of Hillel that he used to work and earn half a dinar. Half of it he gave to the doorkeeper of the beis*

---

2. In explaining the *mitzvah* to honor one's parents, *Sefer HaChinuch* writes:

"Among the roots of this mitzvah is that it is fitting for man to recognize and bestow kindness upon one who has done him a kindness, and he should not be vile in withholding such recognition and in being ungrateful — for this is an exceedingly revolting and wicked trait in the eyes of God and men. One must take to heart the fact that his father and mother brought him into this world. It is therefore truly fitting that he grant them every honor and benefit that he can, for they brought him into this world, and toiled many toils for him in his youth."

The *Mishnah* (*Bava Metzia* 2:11) teaches that if one spots the lost object of his father and that of his *rebbi*, that of his *rebbi* takes precedence, "for his father brought him into this world, whereas his teacher who taught him wisdom brings him into the World to Come."

We may infer that if *hakaras hatov* is the underlying principle of *kibud av v'eim*, then surely the debt of gratitude owed by every student of Torah to his *rebbeim* is beyond description.

We can infer, as well, that an enormous debt of gratitude is owed also to those who make our Torah study possible.

*midrash [as his entrance fee to study], and with the
other half, he supported himself and the rest of his
family. One day, he could not earn anything and the
doorkeeper would not let him enter. Hillel climbed to
the roof and sat at the skylight so that he could hear the
words of the living God coming from the mouths of
Shemaya and Avtalyon. People say that that day was a
Friday. It was in the winter month of Teves and snow
fell on him from above. At dawn [the next morning],
Shemaya said to Avtalyon, "My brother, every day the
hall is light and today it is dark. Perhaps it is a cloudy
day?" The people looked up and saw the outline of a
man over the skylight. They went up and saw a layer of
snow three cubits thick. They brought him down,
washed him, rubbed his body with oil and sat him near
the fire. They said, "For his sake, it is proper to
desecrate Shabbos."* [3]

Hillel rose to become the leader of his generation, one of the great
figures of the Mishnaic era. Obviously, he was a man of awesome
spiritual greatness. One may wonder how his *mesiras nefesh*,
self-sacrifice, could serve as an indictment against people of lesser
spiritual stature.

The answer is simple. People will go to any lengths to attain that
which is most dear to them. A man who is driven after materialism
will work day and night and travel across the globe to attain wealth.
The glory-seeker will utilize pressure, flattery, money and any other
means to attain the honor that he so desperately seeks. Hillel
perceived that nothing in this world was comparable to the
inestimable value of Torah knowledge. It was this perception that
impelled him to go to any lengths — even at the risk of his life — to
study Torah from Shemaya and Avtalyon, the leaders of his
generation.

Thus, the indictment against the poor man is as follows: "True,
your material hardships made it difficult for you to study. But had

---

3. Hillel's life was in danger, thus making it permissible to desecrate Shabbos for his
sake. (Transgression of Rabbinic law, but not Scriptural law, was necessary.) The
people wished to call attention to Hillel's self-sacrifice for Torah, therefore they made
this pronouncement (*Ben Yehoyada*).

you perceived how imperative is the study of Torah, then you, too, would have demonstrated *mesiras nefesh* in pursuit of it — and ultimately, you would have succeeded in your quest."

Hillel serves as a model for the poor. R' Shaul Rosenberg serves as a model to us all. He grew up in Manchester and here he spent his entire life. R' Shaul's perception of Torah impelled him not only to study it himself, but to toil with genuine *mesiras nefesh* so that scores of others could study as well. In addition to his leadership of our yeshivah, he toiled for many other Torah institutions. It is incumbent upon us to learn from this man and develop within ourselves a proper appreciation for Torah study and its support.

While a person is alive, he can accrue merit for himself through Torah study and the performance of other *mitzvos*. When he departs this world, his chance for personal accomplishment has ended. However, it is possible for a person to accrue additional merit even after death. When one works for the community, his efforts continue to bear fruit long after he has departed this world. As his merits increase, he ascends to yet loftier heights in the World of Truth.

We can be certain that R' Shaul will ascend higher and higher in the Upper Worlds, for his efforts on behalf of our yeshivah and community will forever bear new fruit. Those who study at our yeshivah will raise sons and daughters who will follow the path of Torah. *B'nei Torah* also serve as an example to others with whom they come in contact. When a Torah student goes out into the world and behaves in a manner that is reflective of the Torah's teachings, he sanctifies the Name of Hashem. Each time a student of our yeshivah conducts himself in such a manner, it is a source of merit for R' Shaul.

Let us express our *hakaras hatov* to R' Shaul by bringing merit to him through our words and deeds, and by striving to appreciate the value of Torah study in the way that he did.

PART II

Thoughts on Teshuvah

Insights drawn from the discourses[1]
of HaRav Segal
to Sefer Sha'arei Teshuvah.[2]

---

1. Published in Volume Two of *Yirah VaDa'as*.
2. By *Rabbeinu Yonah* of Gerona (13th c.).

∽ The Need for Reflection

Imagine someone throwing a paper into a fire, only to realize minutes later that the paper was actually a document worth thousands of dollars. Imagine the regret and mental anguish that this person would experience. This is the sort of regret a Jew should experience upon doing that which runs contrary to God's will.

Our purpose in being on this earth is to earn our portion in the World to Come by choosing between right and wrong, a process known as *bechirah*. Would our natural instinct regarding the spiritual harm of sin be similar to that regarding physical harm, we would be denied *bechirah*, for the choice would be like deciding whether or not to place one's hand into a fire. To err would be virtually impossible.

Awareness of the gravity of sin is not a deterrent against sin. However, *pondering* the gravity of sin — through the study of *mussar* — until this reality penetrates deep into one's heart, does serve as a deterrent. As the Torah states, *"You are to know this day and **take to your heart** that Hashem is the only God ..."* (*Devarim* 4:39).

Ideally, the realization that sin distances one from Hashem should be sufficient for self-restraint to be accomplished. If it is not, then one should ponder the reckoning and retribution that he will have to face for each and every sin that is committed on this world.

Rabbeinu Yonah sums up the above as follows: "The primary aspect of repentance is חֲרָטָה, regret. One should perceive in his heart that to forsake Hashem is wicked and bitter and he should take to heart that there is punishment to be meted out for each sin" (*Sha'arei Teshuvah* 1:10).

✑ Exchanging Worlds

[When engaging in חֲרָטָה *(regret), the penitent tells himself:] "How did I exchange the eternal world for a world that is but transitory?" (Sha'arei Teshuvah 1:10).*

The sorrow of sin lies not only in the spiritual damage that it causes, but also in the loss of what could have been accomplished. The *Mishnah* (*Makkos* 23b) states: "Whoever sits and refrains from committing a transgression is given a reward like one who performs a *mitzvah*." As the *Gemara* (*Kiddushin* 39b) explains, this applies when the opportunity for sin presents itself and the person resists temptation. *Rashi* comments that restraining one's *yetzer hara* and thus refraining from sin is among the greatest of *mitzvos*. *Rabbeinu Yonah* (*Sha'arei Teshuvah* 3:9) writes that such restraint is a fulfillment of the *mitzvah* of אֶת ה' אֱלֹהֶיךָ תִּירָא, *Fear Hashem, your God* (*Devarim* 10:20).

Moreover, the time used for sin could have been utilized in a positive manner. This is implied in the *Mishnah:* "Calculate the gain of a sin against its loss" (*Avos* 2:1). Thus, when a person succumbs to sin, he exchanges eternity for the fleeting pleasures of this world.

✑ Sin's Stain

וּמַה הוֹעִילָה בְּכָל קִנְיָנֶהָ אִם רָעָה בְּעֵינֵי אֲדוֹנֶיהָ?
Of what benefit are all its [the soul's] accomplishments if it is wicked in the eyes of its Master? (Sha'arei Teshuvah 1:10).

One of the Thirteen Attributes of Mercy enumerated by the prophet Michah[1] is יִכְבֹּשׁ עֲוֹנֹתֵינוּ, *He will suppress our iniquities* (*Michah* 7:19). *Tomer Devorah* explains that Hashem does not allow sins to cancel out the effect of *mitzvos*. He does not say, "Ten sins negate ten *mitzvos*," so that the account is closed with neither punishment nor reward. Sins cannot cancel out a good deed which ascends to the highest heavens and whose reward is reserved primarily for the World to Come.

---

1. See p. 90.

However, the fact that there is no cancellation process means that just as sins do not negate good deeds, so, too, good deeds do not negate sins. No matter how many good deeds one has accrued over the course of his life, he still will be held accountable for those sins for which he has not repented — and his soul will remain tainted by them. Therefore, says *Rabbeinu Yonah*, "Of what benefit are all its [the soul's] accomplishments if it is wicked in the eyes of its Master?"

Through *teshuvah*, however, one *can* erase the sins of the past and begin anew. As *Rabbeinu Yonah* writes in *Yesod HaTeshuvah*:

> The penitent should not imagine that he can say: "Why should I labor in vain, expend my energy for emptiness and void? For how can my repentance stand up before all my sins? Whatever I can do will not avail me compared to the sins that have passed over me."
>
> Let him not say so, for the Holy One, Blessed is He, pledged through the prophet Yechezkel that his transgressions will no longer be remembered, as it is written, "As for the wicked man, if he will turn away from all his sins which he did, and safeguard all My decrees, and do justice and righteousness, he shall surely live; he will not die. All his transgressions which he committed will not be remembered against him; for the righteousness which he did, he shall live" (Yechezkel 18:21-22).

◆§ When Hot Becomes Cold

*C*hazal teach that when a person persists in committing a sin once and then a second time, it becomes to him like something permissible (*Kiddushin* 40a). This concept can be better understood in light of the following:

זָכוֹר אֵת אֲשֶׁר עָשָׂה לְךָ עֲמָלֵק בַּדֶּרֶךְ בְּצֵאתְכֶם מִמִּצְרָיִם. אֲשֶׁר קָרְךָ בַּדֶּרֶךְ וַיְזַנֵּב בְּךָ כָּל הַנֶּחֱשָׁלִים אַחֲרֶיךָ וְאַתָּה עָיֵף וְיָגֵעַ וְלֹא יָרֵא אֱלֹהִים.

Remember what Amalek did to you on the way, as you departed from Egypt. How he encountered you on the

*way and cut down the weaklings trailing behind you,
while you were faint and exhausted, and he did not fear
God (Devarim 25:17-18).*

Rashi offers an alternative interpretation of the word קָרְךָ, whose
plain meaning is *[how] he encountered you.* "It [the word קָרְךָ] is a
form of קוֹר as in קוֹר וָחוֹם , *cold and heat.* He [Amalek] 'cooled off'
your 'boiling heat.' For the gentiles were fearful of waging war
against you, until this one came along and started a war. This can be
likened to a boiling hot bath which no one dares to enter — until one
scoundrel comes along and enters it. Though he burns himself, he has
cooled the bath off for the others [by showing that it was possible to
enter it and survive]."

As long as a person is able to refrain from committing a given sin,
he sees that sin as a "boiling hot bath"; i.e., it is totally foreign to him
and he views involvement with it as something dangerous. However,
after he has succumbed to his *yetzer hara*, committed that sin *and
repeated it*, the picture changes drastically. No longer does he view
the sin with the same stringency. He has committed the sin twice and,
as far as he can see, he is the same person as before. He has not been
"burned" — or so he thinks. His new outlook, says R' Itze'le
Peterberger, will affect both the past and the future. It will be difficult
for this person to repent properly, because he has difficulty
experiencing proper regret for a sin that he longer sees as terribly
severe. At the same time, he is now much more likely to repeat the
offense again.

One should note, however, that the converse holds true as well.
When a person struggles with himself and works at uprooting the
negative tendencies within his soul, he comes to recognize sin for
what it really is. And the more he strives to improve, the stronger this
perception will grow.

◆§ Of Service and Rebellion

There is no greater praise that can be said of a Jew than to refer to
him as an *eved Hashem*, servant of Hashem. This is what the
Torah calls Moshe *Rabbeinu* and his disciple and successor, Yehoshua

bin Nun (*Yehoshua* 1:1 and 24:29). An *eved*, servant, lives solely for his master. His every action is for his master's benefit and whatever he acquires automatically belongs to his master (*Pesachim* 88b). Similarly, an *eved Hashem* lives for no purpose other than to serve *HaKadosh Baruch Hu*. His every deed, word and thought is directed toward the lofty purpose of fulfilling his Creator's will and bringing glory to His Name.

Conversely, a servant who refuses to totally subjugate himself to his master's will is a servant by title but not in practice. For a servant to approach matters, whether in action or in attitude, in a manner that is in opposition to his master's will, is a contradiction to the subservience that his position demands. This is why a Jew who scrupulously observes six hundred and twelve *mitzvos*, but ignores the six hundred and thirteenth, is considered a מוּמָר לְדָבָר אֶחָד, *apostate regarding a single commandment* (*Chullin* 4b). As *Rabbeinu Yonah* puts it, "If a servant will tell his master, 'I will heed everything you say — except for one thing,' then he has already thrown off his master's yoke and will do whatever he pleases. Regarding this does the Torah state, *Cursed is the man who will not uphold the words of this Torah, to do them* (*Devarim* 27:26), meaning: [Cursed is the man] who will not accept upon himself all the commandments of the Torah, from beginning to end . . ." (*Sha'arei Teshuvah* 1:6).

It is important to note that a person who desires to abstain from a given prohibition, but consistently succumbs to his inclination, is not deemed a מוּמָר.

Chazal state that a person who flagrantly ignores the prohibitions against speaking *lashon hara* is called a *ba'al lashon hara*. The punishment of a *ba'al lashon hara* is particularly severe (see *Sefer Chofetz Chaim* 1:3). Those who have a fixed daily study session in *Sifrei Chofetz Chaim* and *Shemiras HaLashon* cannot be classified as *ba'alei lashon hara* even if they have yet to overcome their weakness in this area, for by studying these works they demonstrate a sincere desire to improve.

R' Yisrael Salanter once said that if all a *maggid* (preacher) accomplishes with his sermons is to restrain *himself* from one sin, then his efforts were worthwhile. Similarly, if all one accomplishes in studying works on *shemiras halashon* is to refrain just once from speaking *lashon hara*, it was worth all his efforts in this regard.

Of course, the benefits of consistent study of these works are usually far more than learning to refrain from improper speech. The *Chofetz Chaim's* works on this subject can inspire one to improve all his *midos*. One can learn to overcome jealousy, enmity and other negative traits by studying the laws of forbidden speech.

◆§ "He Fashions Their Hearts"

One of the Thirteen Principles of Faith as formulated by *Rambam* is the following: "I believe with complete faith that the Creator, Blessed is His Name, knows all the deeds of human beings and their thoughts, as it is written (*Tehillim* 33:15), *He fashions their hearts all together, He comprehends all their deeds.*"

Maintaining an awareness of this principle is crucial for anyone who strives to refine his ways and attitudes. It is therefore recommended that one recite it each morning upon arising.

One should likewise bear this principle in mind when judging others. Man has been granted the wisdom to invent instruments that allow him to listen to and evaluate a person's heartbeat. However, he has not been granted the ability to determine the emotions and desires that pull at another person's heart at any given moment. Only Hashem knows this. We see a person sin and do not know that the urges which he experienced at that given moment were far greater than any urge that we might have ever known regarding that particular sin; we see him perform a seemingly simple positive deed and do not realize what sort of fortitude he mustered to perform that deed.

Conversely, we sometimes rationalize our own failure to perform a given *mitzvah* with the attitude that it was more than could be expected of us. However, Hashem, Who knows the exact limits of our abilities and potential, may well determine that, in fact, it was within our reach.

◆§ Fear Hashem

In discussing the *mitzvah* of אֶת ה' אֱלֹקֶיךָ תִּירָא, *You shall fear Hashem, your G-d* (*Devarim* 10:20), *Sefer HaChinuch* writes: "This is one of the *mitzvos temidios*, constant *mitzvos*, the obligation of which never ceases even for a moment. When one is confronted with the possibility of sin, he is obligated to awaken his spirit and take to heart at that moment that Hashem, Blessed is He, takes note of man's every deed and exacts retribution in accordance with the wickedness of his ways. One who has transgressed this precept by not taking it to heart at the appropriate time has violated this positive commandment — for such a time [i.e., when one is confronted with sin] is the precise moment for its fulfillment."

When Rabban Yochanan ben Zakkai was on his deathbed, he told his disciples, "May it be the will of Hashem that the fear of Heaven be upon you just like the fear of flesh and blood." His disciples said, "Just that?" Rabban Yochanan replied, "If only it would be that! Know that when a man sins he says, 'I hope no one will see me' " (*Berachos* 28b).

One should forever bear in mind the admonition of *Rosh* in his *Orchos Chaim* (§109): "Do not do privately that which you would be ashamed to do publicly, and do not say, 'Who sees me?' "

Were a person, at the moment of trial, to consider the loss incurred by falling into the hands of the *yetzer hara* versus the inestimable achievement of controlling one's desires, he would quite likely refrain from sinning.

❧ Anger

"**W**hoever flares up in anger will have all forms of *Gehinnom* visited upon him" (*Nedarim* 22a). The *Chofetz Chaim* explains that for each form of sin there is a particular form of punishment in *Gehinnom*. Anger, however, can lead to virtually all sins. Therefore, one who does not control his anger will, ultimately, be subject to all forms of *Gehinnom*.[1]

❧ Arrogance

Scripture states: תּוֹעֲבַת ה' כָּל־גְּבַהּ־לֵב, *Hashem despises all who are arrogant of heart* (*Mishlei* 16:5). From another Scriptural verse we learn that man's *yetzer hara* seeks to overcome him each and every day, and were it not for Hashem's help, the *yetzer hara* would prevail (*Succah* 52b). However, the arrogant cannot hope for such help, since they are despised by Hashem.

Thus, it is inevitable that an arrogant person will fall victim to the whims of his *yetzer hara*. His only hope is to engage in sincere soul-searching in order to rid himself of this terrible trait.

---

1. Rabbi Yerucham Levovitz (*Da'as Chachmah U'Mussar*, vol. III, pp.20, 252) explains that through anger the pain of *Gehinnom* becomes real even in this world. The burning emotions of anger and frustration are their own emotional *Gehinnom*.

~§ Bitul Torah

Hashem does not demand of us that we study Torah with the diligence of the *Vilna Gaon* or the *Chofetz Chaim*.[2] What *is* demanded of us is that we make proper use of the time we have available for study by learning during these periods without interruption. One who interrupts his study session to engage in idle conversation has committed an awesome sin.

The *Vilna Gaon* writes: "One should cherish the Torah very, very much, for each word that he studies is a *mitzvah* for itself . . . The rule is that one does not interrupt Torah study even for a *mitzvah* if it can be done by others. Logic mandates this, for each word [of Torah] is a great *mitzvah* for itself and is equal to them all [i.e., all other *mitzvos* combined]" (*Sh'nos Eliyahu* to *Pe'ah* 1:1).

The *Chofetz Chaim* once calculated that it is possible for a person to verbalize some two hundred words in a single minute. Think then of the eternity that is lost when one exchanges a minute of Torah study for a minute of mundane conversation. When reciting the blessing of הֲשִׁיבֵנוּ אָבִינוּ לְתוֹרָתֶךְ, *Bring us back, our Father, to Your Torah*, one should concentrate on repentance in the area of Torah study.

※ ※ ※

To the words וְדִבַּרְתָּ בָּם, *and speak of them* (Devarim 6:7), *Rashi* comments: "Your principle topic of conversation should be about them [i.e., words of Torah]. They should not be relegated to secondary importance." An עֶבֶד ה', *servant of Hashem*, is by definition one whose principle occupation is Torah study, *tefillah*, and other *mitzvos*. To become worthy of this title should be everyone's goal.

~§ Common but Severe

In *Sha'arei Teshuvah* (1:8), Rabbeinu Yonah advises that one keep a record of his spiritual stumblings and refer to it on a daily

---

2. See Volume I p. 137.

basis as he continues along the path of *teshuvah*. (This can be accomplished through the daily study of *mussar*.) *Rabbeinu Yonah* enumerates severe sins which, unfortunately, are all too common among the masses. Among them are: *uttering God's Name in vain* [הַזְכָּרַת שֵׁם שָׁמַיִם לְבַטָלָה]; *lashon hara*; *sinas chinam*, senseless hatred; and *histaklus b'arayos*, allowing one's eyes to stray. Let us discuss these items briefly.

1) There is a common misconception that one transgresses the sin of *uttering God's Name in vain* only when uttering an unnecessary or incorrect *berachah* or when one simply utters His Name for no reason, ח"ו. According to *Yesod V'Shoresh HaAvodah* (2:2), one transgresses this sin, as well as the admonition to fear Hashem (*Devarim* 10:20), whenever he utters the Name without cognizance of what he is saying. That people can be guilty of this scores of times each day, without giving the matter so much as a passing thought, is simply because they are unaware of its gravity.[3]

2) Jealousy is often the source of *sinas chinam*. One sees his neighbor being accorded the honor or status that, in his opinion, is actually due himself. He therefore resents his neighbor and resentment soon turns into hatred. The way to rid oneself of such destructive feelings is to uproot their source. Nothing in this world occurs without Hashem willing it to occur. As *Sefer HaChinuch* writes,[4] even when one has truly been wronged by his neighbor, he must realize that this, too, is His will. Of course, the perpetrator will be held accountable for his misdeed — but the pain caused to the victim could not have occurred had Hashem willed otherwise. Surely, then, there is absolutely no basis for enmity when one's neighbor is accorded honor or some other mark of distinction — for this, too, must be Hashem's will.

3) The prohibition of *histaklus b'arayos* is derived from the verse וְלֹא תָתוּרוּ אַחֲרֵי לְבַבְכֶם וְאַחֲרֵי עֵינֵיכֶם, *You shall not stray after your heart and after your eyes* (*Bamidbar* 15:39). One is not held accountable for inadvertently confronting an improper sight — but he must avert his gaze immediately. Protecting

---

3. See Volume I, p. 119.
425. See Volume I, p. 201.

one's eyes from such sights is an obligation and a prime source of *kedushah*, sanctity and *taharah*, purity. It is imperative that one be ever vigilant in this regard when walking in the street.

Let no one delude himself into thinking that laxity in this area will not affect him. *It will.* A single gaze upon a forbidden sight can cause untold spiritual harm.[5]

⋄§ Talking In Shul

One who commits sins in public desecrates the Name. He is obligated to bemoan and mourn over these deeds in the presence of others in order to sanctify the Name (Sha'arei Teshuvah 1:18).

Those who speak in *shul* during *Kaddish*, the repetition of *Shemoneh Esrei* or during the Torah reading — even between *aliyos* — is guilty of *chilul Hashem*, desecration of God's Name, aside from the essential sin of engaging in conversation at such times.

It is fitting to quote the words of the *Chofetz Chaim* on this matter (footnote to preface of *Sefer Chofetz Chaim*):

"In discussing the stringent sin of idle conversation in the *beis haknesses*, I deem it proper to mention how great is the resultant harm of such talk. Unfortunately, such talk often begins with one man relating stories to his neighbor that are laced from beginning to end with *lashon hara* and *rechilus*.[6] Such conversation usually begins

---

5. R' Aharon Kotler would visit various American cities on fund-raising missions for his yeshivah. Once, he and a student who was accompanying him returned to their hotel suite after a local visit. R' Aharon excused himself and went alone into the suite's adjoining room. The student became concerned when a long time passed without R' Aharon reappearing. The student made his way to the other room, knocked and then entered. He found R' Aharon crying bitterly. R' Aharon explained:

When the elevator had opened in the lobby where they were waiting, a woman wearing improper attire left the elevator and passed in front of them. R' Aharon was weeping for the fact that Heaven had not protected him from seeing that terrible sight (heard from the student himself).

6. *Rechilus* is *lashon hara* which causes ill feelings between Jews. The prohibition of this severe form of forbidden speech is found in *Vayikra* 19:16.

prior to the Torah reading — but when the reading commences, the *yetzer hara* incites the person to continue his narrative, so that he continues speaking *lashon hara* even as the Torah reading is in progress. Often, this person is among the distinguished members of the congregation whose seat is at the eastern wall, so that his sin is committed in full view of everyone. In this way, one is guilty of desecrating Hashem's Name in public, meaning among ten Jews, and this sin is far greater than the average sin of *chilul Hashem*.[7]

"... See how many prohibitions this man has transgressed: 1) The sins of *lashon hara* and *rechilus*, aside from numerous other commandments both positive and negative [which one might transgress when speaking *lashon hara*.][8] 2) The sin of *You shall not desecrate My Holy Name* (*Vayikra* 22:32), which he has transgressed in the presence of ten Jews. 3) He has ignored the Torah reading; even if he has missed a single verse or even a single *word*, his sin is too great to bear. For even with regard to one who leaves the synagogue while the Torah reading is in progress, Scripture states, *Those who forsake Hashem will perish* (*Yeshayahu* 1:28; see *Berachos* 8a); how much more does this apply to one who is present in the *beis haknesses* whose craving for idle conversation and *lashon hara* causes him to ignore the word of the Living God! Often, this occurs on Shabbos, when the sin is far greater than on a weekday, as is stated in many holy *sefarim*.

"Similarly, one who is in the habit of conversing in the *beis midrash* and *beis haknesses* will often finish his story during *Kaddish*, thus refraining from answering *Yehei Shemei Raba* ..., an exceedingly exalted declaration. *Chazal* teach that even one who has within himself a bit of heresy will be forgiven [when uttering this declaration]. Even when [the one involved in idle conversation] does utter *Yehei Shemei Raba* ... he usually utters it too late, which relegates his declaration to the category of אָמֵן יְתוֹמָה, *an orphaned amein*,[9] which can cause one's children to become orphaned, ר"ל — for even if one's *amein* is delayed by indolence, this curse applies

---

7. The *Chofetz Chaim* refers the reader to *Sefer HaMitzvos* of the *Rambam* §63.

8. In his preface to *Sefer Chofetz Chaim*, the *Chofetz Chaim* enumerates seventeen negative commandments and fourteen positive commandments which one is liable to transgress when speaking *lashon hara*.

9. See *Shulchan Aruch, Orach Chaim* 124:8.

nonetheless, as the commentators make clear. How much more so when its delay is caused by *lashon hara* and *rechilus*!

"To all of the above is added the sin of engaging in idle conversation in the *beis haknesses* or *beis midrash*, which is a great sin, as stated in *Shulchan Aruch*[10] — and certainly when such conversation is in the form of *lashon hara* and *rechilus*. In his holy letter, the *Gra* [*Vilna Gaon*] writes of the terrible punishments for which one is liable for every forbidden word he utters, and no word is overlooked."

---

10. *Orach Chaim* 151:1.

∽§ Hashem's Goodness

W e are obligated to ponder Hashem's goodness in granting us the process of *teshuvah* to atone for our sins. A person who brazenly defies the will of an earthly king cannot hope for the king's mercy. Surely he will have to suffer the consequences of his rebellion. Even when one has broken the law inadvertently, he cannot hope to be pardoned unless he is entirely blameless. The King of kings, however, forgives both שׁוֹגֵג, *inadvertent transgression* and מֵזִיד, *willful transgression*, through *teshuvah*. As *Rabbeinu Yonah* writes in *Sha'arei Teshuvah* (1:9), "For all forms of repentance [i.e., for any sort of sin], one can gain forgiveness."

David *HaMelech* said: כִּי עִמְּךָ הַסְּלִיחָה לְמַעַן תִּוָּרֵא, *For with You is forgiveness, that You may be feared* (*Tehillim* 130:4). *Ibn Ezra* explains that were it not for *teshuvah*, many a sinner, with no hope to make amends, would stray completely from the proper path. The possibility of *teshuvah*, however, gives one reason to fear Hashem and ultimately repent.

Thus, *teshuvah* not only atones and purifies, but also serves as an impetus toward *yiras Hashem*.

∽§ "Abundantly Cleanse Me"

R abbeinu Yonah writes:

> There are many levels of repentance by which one draws closer to the Holy One, Blessed is He. Although

every type of repentance brings about some sort of forgiveness, the soul cannot become completely purified to the extent that the sins are regarded as never having been committed, unless the heart is cleansed and the spirit is properly conditioned, as it is written, "Praiseworthy is the man to whom Hashem does not account iniquity and whose spirit is without deceit" (Tehillim 32:2). The soul may be compared to a garment that needs cleansing. A little washing will suffice to remove the surface dirt, but only after repeated washings will it become entirely clean. Therefore, it is written that the penitent [David HaMelech] said (Tehillim 51:4), "Abundantly cleanse me from my iniquity [and from my sin purify me]" (Sha'arei Teshuvah 1:9).

David pleaded that Hashem accept his repentance to the point that his soul be totally purified from any taint of sin. This goal is the essence of our prayer each Shabbos and *Yom Tov:* וְטַהֵר לִבֵּנוּ לְעָבְדְּךָ בֶּאֱמֶת, *and purify our heart to serve You in truth.* This goal is within everyone's reach, and those who sincerely strive for it are granted the Heavenly assistance they need.

To the words אַשְׁרֵי אִישׁ יָרֵא אֶת ה', *Praiseworthy is the man who fears Hashem (Tehillim* 112:1), the *Gemara (Avodah Zarah* 19a) comments: Praiseworthy is the man who fears Hashem בְּעוֹדוֹ אִישׁ, *when he is still a man,* meaning when he is young and in possession of all his energies so that he can engage his *yetzer hara* in battle and emerge victorious *(Sha'arei Teshuvah* 1:9). The spiritual tests of youth are far greater than those confronting man in his old age when his physical strength has waned. The greater the test, the greater the victory. Spiritual struggles of youth can bring a person to awesome heights of purity and sanctity.

Nevertheless, *teshuvah* can accomplish until the very end of a person's life. As *Rambam* writes *(Hilchos Teshuvah* 2:1): "Even if a person has sinned all his days and repents on the day of his death, and dies amidst repentance, all his sins are forgiven."

⇜ Men and Women Alike

In *Tehillim*, David *HaMelech* proclaims: ,אַשְׁרֵי אִישׁ יָרֵא אֶת ה'
Praiseworthy is the man who fears Hashem (*Tehillim* 112:1). The
Gemara (*Avodah Zarah* 19a) asks, " 'Praiseworthy is the *man*' —
and not the woman?" Rather, explains the *Gemara*, the term אִישׁ,
man, conveys the vigor of youth, ". . . that he should hasten to
perceive his Creator before the days of old age" (*Rashi*).

It was clear to *Chazal* that the verse could not imply an exclusion
of women from among the God-fearing, for *yiras Hashem* is
something that every Jew must attain. Therefore, says R' Yisrael
Salanter, though women are excluded from the *mitzvah* to study
Torah for the sake of study alone,[1] they are not excluded from the
study of *mussar*. "The study of *mussar* is not like other Torah study,
for the obligation with regard to other study does not encompass all
Jewish souls. Women are exempt from the *mitzvah* to study Torah
. . . but such is not the case with *mussar* study . . . for the 'battle'
encompasses all human beings. The battle of which we speak is that
of [the soul versus] the *yetzer hara* and its machinations, its desires
and schemes, in whose net one can become ensared to the point that
he will be unable to rise, ח"ו.

"The obligation to study *mussar* encompasses everyone — no one
is exempt" (*Ohr Yisrael* §3).

It is proper for every man to study *mussar* with his wife. There is
nothing shameful about this. Who among us is greater than the great
Rav of Jerusalem, Rabbi Yosef Chaim Sonnenfeld, who studied
halachah with his *rebbetzin* each day for one half hour?

⇜ True Men of Wisdom

"If you see a *talmid chacham* sin at night, do not think
negatively of him by day, for surely he has already repented"
(*Berachos* 19a). One can explain the terms "night" and "day" as
referring to periods of spiritual darkness and illumination. If a *talmid*

---

1. Women are, of course, required to be knowledgeable of the *halachos* that pertain
to their observance of *mitzvos*.

chacham is gripped by the darkness of his evil inclination, one can be sure that before long he will recover from this lapse; he will once again perceive the "light" of spiritual strength and make amends for his mistake.

In citing this teaching, *Rabbeinu Yonah* comments, "Tarrying in matters of repentance is found only among the *amei ha'aretz*, the ignorant masses, who are in a state of spiritual slumber and who lack the knowledge and understanding needed to hurry to save their souls" (*Sha'arei Teshuvah* 1:3).

Rabbeinu Yonah provides us with new insight into the meaning of the term "*talmid chacham.*" To be worthy of this title, it is not sufficient to have acquired significant knowledge of Torah. A *talmid chacham* is one who engages in *cheshbon hanefesh*, soul-searching; he regularly takes stock of his deeds and wastes no time in refining and repenting for them when necessary.

Conversely, a veritable genius who is fluent in all of *Shas*, but does not live with *cheshbon hanefesh*, is classified as an *am ha'aretz*.

◄§ The Way of a Tzaddik

It is true that there are tzaddikim who stumble in sin on occasion, as it is written, "For there is no man so wholly righteous on earth that he always does good and does not sin" (Koheles 7:20). However, they subsequently contain their evil inclinations — if they sin once they do not repeat it; they struggle with themselves and repent (Sha'arei Teshuvah 1:6).

The key to the *tzaddik's* ability to refrain from repeating past mistakes is his recognition of sin's destructiveness. It is this awareness which impels him to establish personal safeguards so that he will not commit that sin again. Moreover, in the aftermath of sin, the *tzaddik* engages in deep personal struggle. He demands of himself, "How did it come to pass that I committed such an act? Where did I go wrong? Why did I not overcome my inclination?" Such soul-searching brings to light the root cause of what has transpired and is a prime factor in the process of *teshuvah*.

◦§ The Light at the End of the Tunnel

In *Sha'arei Teshuvah* (1:2), *Rabbeinu Yonah* writes that Divine wrath and retribution will progressively increase toward one who is cognizant of his misdeeds but makes no use of the gift of *teshuvah*. He cites a Midrashic parable by way of illustration:

> This is likened to a band of robbers who had been imprisoned by the king but managed to dig a tunnel [for their escape]. They broke through and fled — except for one man [who chose to remain behind]. When the prison warden discovered the tunnel and saw that this man had stayed behind, he began to beat him with his stick. "Hapless one!" he screamed. "The tunnel was open in front of you! Why did you not save yourself?" (*Koheles Rabbah* 7:32).

The parable can be understood as follows: The man who remained behind did not need to expend great effort at creating an avenue of escape — it was there before him, waiting to be used. All that was needed was for him to crawl through the tunnel and he would have found himself in the open air of freedom. His inaction conveys more than mere foolishness. The fact that he did not make use of a golden opportunity to escape indicates that he is unafraid of the impending judgment against him.

With regard to our sins, we need not feel overwhelmed by the task of transforming ourselves from bad to good. The path to full repentance is already paved before us. All that is required of us is that we embark on the path and demonstrate a sincere desire to change. Then *HaKadosh Baruch Hu* will lead us by the hand along the road of return. However, failure to engage in *teshuvah* indicates a lack of fear of Divine retribution. The "tunnel" is open before us — why don't we save ourselves?

◦§ Don't Despair

מִן הַטּוֹבוֹת אֲשֶׁר הֵיטִיב הַשֵּׁם יִתְבָּרֵךְ עִם בְּרוּאָיו, כִּי הֵכִין לָהֶם
הַדֶּרֶךְ לַעֲלוֹת מִתּוֹךְ פַּחַת מַעֲשֵׂיהֶם . . .

Among the kindnesses which the Blessed One has done for His creations is that He prepared for them [i.e. mankind] the way to ascend from within the snare of their deeds . . . (Sha'arei Teshuvah 1:1).

Each *mitzvah* that a Jew performs endows his *neshamah* with added sanctity. This is evident from the text of the blessings which precede the performance of most *mitzvos*: "אֲשֶׁר קִדְּשָׁנוּ ... בְּמִצְוֹתָיו, ...Who has sanctified us with His *mitzvos* ... " The converse is true of sin. "Sin sullies the heart of man" (Yoma 39a). The deeper one's involvement in sin, the deeper he sinks into the morass of *tumah*, spiritual impurity.

Nevertheless, one should not give way to despair, for it is never too late for *teshuvah*. Moreover, through *teshuvah* one can attain awesome spiritual heights, as *Chazal* state, "The level attained by *ba'alei teshuvah* cannot be attained even by perfect *tzaddikim*" (Berachos 34b). This truth is alluded to in *Rabbeinu Yonah's* reference to *teshuvah* as a means לַעֲלוֹת מִתּוֹךְ פַּחַת מַעֲשֵׂיהֶם, *to ascend* from *within the snare of their deeds.*

יֵאוּשׁ, *despair*, is a prime tool of the Satan in quelling thoughts of repentance that enter one's heart. This truth is alluded to in the *Maariv* prayer: וְהָסֵר שָׂטָן מִלְּפָנֵינוּ וּמֵאַחֲרֵינוּ, *And remove spiritual impediments* [שָׂטָן] *from before us and from behind us.* It is Satan who awakens within us the desires which lead to sin [מִלְּפָנֵינוּ], and it is Satan who, after we sin, seeks to have us believe that our waywardness has precluded any possibility of *teshuvah* [מֵאַחֲרֵינוּ].

The Chassidic master R' Aharon Karliner said, "Despondency is not a sin in and of itself — but the sins to which despondency can lead, no sin can cause."

⋑§ Hashem Calls to Us

"Reuven returned to the pit" (Bereishis 37:29). From where did he return? ... He had been preoccupied with his sackcloth and fasting [in repentance for the sin of moving his father's bed] (see ibid. 32:22). Said HaKadosh Baruch Hu to him: "Since the beginning of

*time, no one ever came before Me to repent[3] — you are
the one who 'opened' the way of teshuvah. By your life,
your descendant will open the way of teshuvah." This
descendant was Hoshea, who declared [in the name of
Hashem] (Hoshea 14:2), "Return, Israel, to Hashem,
your God, for you have stumbled because of your sins"
(Bereishis Rabbah 4).*

In what way was Hoshea the one "who opened the way of
teshuvah"? R' Itze'le [Peterberger] explained (*Kochvei Ohr* §73):
Hoshea taught that Hashem calls to us, as it were, to return to Him,
for it is His desire to draw us close and shower us with His goodness.
Later, the prophet Yirmiyahu echoed this concept: *Return, wayward
children, I shall heal you from your waywardness* (Yirmiyahu 3:22).
HaKadosh Baruch Hu calls to the Jewish people, imploring us to
make use of the gift of *teshuvah* and return to Him. He assures us
that through *teshuvah* our souls will be healed of the spiritual
maladies that sin has wrought.

Yet, Hashem insists that the initial step toward return come from
within ourselves, without His assistance. "Open for Me an opening
like the eye of a needle, and I will open for you an opening like that
of a hallway." In *Sha'arei Teshuvah* (1:1), *Rabbeinu Yonah* writes,
"Even if their rebellion is great and they behave [toward Hashem]
treacherously, He does not close the gates of *teshuvah* before them."
Note that the text reads, ". . . He does not close the gates," rather than,
"He allows the gates of *teshuvah* to remain open." One must take the
initial step and "knock" on the gates of *teshuvah*. Having knocked,
he can rest assured that the gates will open. Hashem will grant him
the opportunity and Heavenly assistance that is needed for
repentance to succeed.

◆§ Don't Delay

*When a sinner delays his repentance, the retribution
that he will incur becomes greater with each passing
day (Sha'arei Teshuvah 1:2).*

---

3. Adam and Kayin repented after being told by Hashem that they would be
punished for their sins. Reuven was the first to repent on his own initiative (*Yefei
Toar* and *Maharzu*).

To tarry with regard to *teshuvah* is not merely to postpone something of paramount importance. Each day that repentance is delayed, sins are inevitably repeated. Moreover, the possibility lies open for the sinner to engage in sins that he has not encountered or desired previously. All this leads to more טִמְטוּם הַלֵּב, *numbness of the heart*, which makes the possibility of *teshuvah* even more remote.

One who delays engaging in *cheshbon hanefesh*, introspection, is in essence refraining from embarking on the path of genuine *teshuvah*. To have embarked on the path of *teshuvah*, one must make a sincere commitment to improve. This does not mean to undertake to fast or to engage in other forms of affliction, but to correct one's life in some small positive way.

◄§ Out of Love, Out of Pain

> *Teshuvah is accepted even when the sinner repents because of his many afflictions — and certainly if he repents out of awe and love of Hashem (Sha'arei Teshuvah 1:1).*

In truth, every person should be inspired to *teshuvah* out of *hakaras hatov*, gratitude to Hashem for the abundant kindness which He has bestowed upon him from the moment he entered this world. However, even when one repents because he has become afflicted with illness or other forms of suffering, ר"ל, his *teshuvah* is accepted. For even when *teshuvah* is born of adversity, the penitent has nonetheless shown that he believes his suffering to be Divinely ordained. When one turns his heart to the One Above out of recognition that whatever happens to him is from Hashem, he engages in *teshuvah*.

◈§ Suffering

תָּשֵׁב אֱנוֹשׁ עַד דַּכָּא, וַתֹּאמֶר שׁוּבוּ בְנֵי אָדָם.

You reduce man to pulp, and You say, "Repent, O sons of man" (Tehillim 90:3).

When Hashem visits suffering upon a person, He is speaking to him, as it were, imploring him to improve. As *Rashi* comments to the above verse, "Through the means of affliction, Hashem tells the people, 'Return, O sons of man, from your wicked ways.'"

Of suffering, *Rabbeinu Yonah* (*Sha'arei Teshuvah* 2:4) writes: "When a person accepts upon himself God's reproof and corrects his ways and thoughts, it is fitting that he rejoice over his suffering, for through it he has attained exalted accomplishments. It is therefore proper for him to offer praise unto Hashem, Blessed is He, as he would for his other successes. Thus it is written, *I will raise the cup of salvation and invoke the Name of Hashem* (Tehillim 116:13); and . . . *Trouble and sorrow I would find — then I would invoke the name of Hashem* (ibid. 3-4).

Midrash Tanchuma (Yisro 16:1) states:

> One should rejoice at personal suffering more than for the [obvious] good, for even if a person has had only good all his life, his sins will not be forgiven — and through what will they be forgiven? Through suffering.
>
> Rabbi Eliezer said: One should feel a sense of gratitude toward HaKadosh Baruch Hu when suffering comes upon him. Why? Because suffering draws a person close to Him, as it is written, "Hashem reproves the one whom He loves" (Mishlei 3:12).
>
> When suffering comes upon a person, he should accept it and withstand [the test] — for its reward is infinite.

✒ "Ba'al Teshuvah"

There are many levels of *teshuvah*. As we have mentioned elsewhere, elementary *teshuvah* is comprised of חֲרָטָה, *regret;* עֲזִיבַת הַחֵטְא, *abandoning the sin;* and וִדּוּי, *confession.* Shlomo HaMelech states: וּמוֹדֶה וְעֹזֵב יְרֻחָם, *And one who confesses and abandons [his sin] will be granted compassion (Mishlei 28:13).* "Confession," to have any validity, must be accompanied by regret. Thus the verse refers to one who has utilized the three basic components of *teshuvah.* "He will be granted [Divine] compassion, for he is a *ba'al teshuvah,* though there are many levels of *teshuvah"* (*Sha'arei Teshuvah* 1:19).

Thrice daily in the *Shemoneh Esrei* we beseech Hashem to return us before Him בְּתְשׁוּבָה שְׁלֵמָה, *in perfect repentance.* Reaching the highest level of *teshuvah* should be our goal, but we must recognize that even the most minimal level of *teshuvah* achieves some degree of atonement and makes us worthy of the title *"ba'al teshuvah."*

אַשְׁרֵי אָדָם מְפַחֵד תָּמִיד, וּמַקְשֶׁה לִבּוֹ יִפּוֹל בְּרָעָה, *Praiseworthy is the man who is forever fearful, but one who hardens his heart will fall into evil (Mishlei 28:14).* With these words, says *Rabbeinu Yonah* (*Sha'arei Teshuvah* 1:20), Shlomo HaMelech delivers a two-fold message to the *ba'al teshuvah:* "Strive ever higher on the ladder of repentance, and forever be alert to the enticements of the *yetzer hara,* lest it renew itself with added strength as it seeks to undo your spiritual attainments. Moreover, never cease to repent, for one can never be sure that his level of *teshuvah* thus far is sufficient."

As we have stated on other occasions, such "fears" must not be confused with sadness, nervousness or despair, which have no place in *avodas Hashem.* It is *HaKadosh Baruch Hu's* desire that we serve

Him with joy. The fear to which Shlomo refers is spiritual alertness, a constant vigilance against temptation.

Rabbeinu Yonah offers positive steps through which such vigilance should be expressed. "He should increase the awe of Hashem within his soul, and forever pray to Hashem that He help him along in his *teshuvah* and rescue him from his inclination." When praying, in the fifth blessing of *Shemoneh Esrei*, that Hashem bring us near to Him as we repent, one's thoughts should focus on the fact that only through Divine assistance can we overcome our evil inclination[1] — and only if we sincerely seek to improve will that assistance be granted.

Among the Torah's commandments is the *mitzvah* to help a person unload his animal's burden (*Sh'mos* 23:5). The *Gemara* (*Bava Metzia* 32a) explains that one is only required to *assist* his neighbor; however, if the animal's owner leaves the person to struggle with the burden alone, then he is not required to do the work.

Similarly, Hashem helps those who endeavor to help themselves.

◆§ Prime Deterrent

הִתְבּוֹנֵן בְּרָעַת הַמִּתְאַחֵר מִן הַתְּשׁוּבָה, כִּי רַבָּה הִיא
Ponder the wickedness of one who defers repentance,
for it [his wickedness] is great (Sha'arei Teshuvah 1:4).

Without a doubt, sincere *teshuvah* is in itself a prime deterrent to subsequent sin. This can be likened to a man who has been hospitalized for an extended period of time after having eaten a food that was harmful to his health. The ramifications of his action will in all probability deter the man from eating that food again, at least for a while. Similarly, the regret, sorrow and soul-searching which are essentials of *teshuvah* serve as a deterrent to future sin.

Each night before retiring, we recite the words of *Tehillim*: רִגְזוּ וְאַל תֶּחֱטָאוּ אִמְרוּ בִלְבַבְכֶם עַל מִשְׁכַּבְכֶם וְדֹמּוּ סֶלָה. According to *Rabbeinu Yonah* (*Sha'arei Teshuvah* 1:4), the word רִגְזוּ means *be agitated*. The

---

1. One interpretation to the blessing's phrase וְהַחֲזִירֵנוּ בִּתְשׁוּבָה is *influence us to return [in perfect repentance before You].*

verse is thus translated, "Be agitated and sin not; reflect in your hearts while on your beds, and be utterly silent." *Rabbeinu Yonah* comments:

> Ponder the wickedness of one who defers repentance, for it [his wickedness] is great. If he would not delay, but would repent immediately, sighing in bitterness of heart, in agitation and anxiety, his eyes overflowing in sorrow, then, when his evil inclination would encounter him a second time and set sin before him, he would conquer his inclination. He would recall his experience with the cup of bitterness and would not drink from it again, as it is written, רִגְזוּ וְאַל תֶּחֱטָאוּ, "Be agitated and do not sin," meaning, become agitated and pained in that you sinned and sin no more .... This interpretation is borne out by the term רְגָזוּ as in אַל תִּרְגְזוּ בַּדָּרֶךְ, Do not become agitated on the way (Bereishis 45:24) and וְתַחְתַּי אֶרְגָּז, I grow agitated where I stand (Chavakuk 3:16). This term signifies extreme remorse over the past and the present. It is precisely for this reason that the word רִגְזוּ was chosen here, as opposed to יִרְאוּ, fear, or גּוּרוּ, cower.

⧫§ Measure for Measure

> [A primary principle of teshuvah is that] one better his deeds in the very areas in which he sinned. If he was guilty of gazing at immoral sights, he should accustom himself to keeping his eyes cast downward. If he sinned through lashon hara, let him toil in Torah study. With every limb with which he sinned, let him strive to fulfill mitzvos (Sha'arei Teshuvah 1:35).

Sin brings spiritual impurity to the limbs through which it is accomplished. *Mitzvos*, on the other hand, bring sanctity. The impurity of sin can only be eradicated by the sanctity of *mitzvos*. In the words of *Chazal* (quoted by *Rabbeinu Yonah*): "Tzaddikim, through the very thing with which they sin, they seek appeasement [before God]."[2] Therefore, if one sins with his eyes, he must sanctify them by consciously avoiding forbidden sights; if he used his lips for forbidden speech, he should use them instead for the study of Torah.

◄§ Varying Orders

The process of *teshuvah* is not fixed; one's order of repentance will depend on the nature of his sin(s).

In one place, *Rabbeinu Yonah* discusses the order of *teshuvah* for a sinner who falls victim to temptation and commits an act which is normally foreign to him. "The beginning of this man's repentance is חֲרָטָה, *regret*, to experience distress in his heart over his sin and feel in his soul the bitterness of gall. After that, he should increase his fear of Hashem each day ... until his heart will be correct, trusting in Hashem" (*Sha'arei Teshuvah* 1:11).

Rabbeinu Yonah tells us here that while חֲרָטָה is the initial step in this man's process of *teshuvah*, the penitent must not allow himself to be destroyed by feelings of guilt. Dwelling on one's sins can lead to despair and make it impossible to serve Hashem properly. Therefore, one should set aside a fixed time each day to ponder his past mistakes and אַחֲרֵי כֵן, *after that*, he should increase his fear of Hashem, as he goes from strength to strength as a beloved servant of the One Above.

Rabbeinu Yonah goes on to discuss the case of the habitual sinner, the person who consistently transgresses a given *mitzvah* or demonstrates a form of negative behavior.

> *The process of repentance [for this man] can be likened to one who still grabs hold of the sheretz[3] as he*

---

2. The *Midrash* states: "Moshe said before Hashem [after the Jews crossed the Sea of Reeds]: 'I know that I sinned with the word אָז, as it says, *And from when* [מֵאָז] *I spoke to Pharaoh You caused this people to suffer even more* (Sh'mos 5:23). Now that You have sunk Pharaoh in the sea, I will praise You with the word אָז,' as it says, אָז יָשִׁיר מֹשֶׁה, *then Moshe sang* ...

"Such is the way of the righteous, through the very thing with which they sin, they rectify their sin. So, too, Moshe provoked Hashem with the word אָז, and with the word through which he sinned, he rectified his sin."

3. One of the eight small animals that are contaminated when they are dead and which convey their *tumah*, contamination, to people and objects. See *Vayikra* 11:29-31.

*seeks to immerse himself [in a mikveh] and become
purified. First he must let go of the sheretz and only
then can he immerse himself, for as long as the sheretz
is in his hand, immersion will accomplish nothing.*

*Abandoning one's contemplation of sin [עֲזִיבַת
מַחֲשֶׁבֶת הַחֵטְא] is akin to letting go of the sheretz, while
regret over the sin [חֲרָטָה], confession [וִדּוּי] and prayer
parallels immersion (Sha'arei Teshuvah 1:11).*

The source of habitual sin is a lack of perception of the seriousness
of sin and a reluctance to struggle with one's *yetzer hara* — which
makes personal refinement impossible. It is some sort of perception of
the gravity of sin and a sincere will to begin to struggle with oneself
which *Rabbeinu Yonah* terms עֲזִיבַת מַחֲשֶׁבֶת הַחֵטְא, *abandoning one's
contemplation of sin*. When one's introspection effects a real change
in attitude, the process of *teshuvah* has begun.

This order is implied in the words of the prophet: יַעֲזֹב רָשָׁע דַּרְכּוֹ
וְאִישׁ אָוֶן מַחְשְׁבֹתָיו וְיָשֹׁב אֶל ה' וִירַחֲמֵהוּ וְאֶל אֱלֹהֵינוּ כִּי יַרְבֶּה לִסְלוֹחַ, *May
the wicked one forsake his path and the deceitful man his thoughts,
and let him return to God Who will show him mercy, and to our God,
for He is abundantly forgiving (Yeshayahu 55:7).* "The initial step of
repentance for this man is to abandon his wicked way and thought,
and resolve to uphold and accept upon himself not to sin again. Then,
he should regret his corrupt actions and return to Hashem" (*Rabbeinu
Yonah*).

⚜ Changing Strategies

Even after completing the *teshuvah* process, one must forever be
alert to the workings of his inclination. The *Gemara* (*Berachos*
61a) likens the *yetzer hara* to a fly. The *Chofetz Chaim* explained
that when swatted at, a fly will find itself another spot upon which
to settle. Similarly, when the *yetzer hara* loses a battle, it returns to
test the individual in some other way.

In combating one's *yetzer hara*, one must realize that different
situations require different tactics. A *ba'al mussar* illustrated this
point by citing two Aggadic teachings regarding arrogance. In one
place (*Sotah* 5a), *Chazal* state that an arrogant person is likened to an

idol worshiper, while elsewhere (*Bava Basra* 98a), they teach that even one's immediate family will find his arrogance offensive. It would seem that the power of the first teaching should make the second superfluous. In truth, however, this is not so. There are some who view the comparison between arrogance and idol worship as an abstract, philosophical concept and have difficulty relating to it. They might be shaken, however, by the realization that arrogance might earn them the revulsion even of their immediate family. Knowledge of this practical consequence could bring about a complete transformation in their behavior.

The above concept is found in the Torah itself. With regard to the *yefas to'ar*, the captive gentile woman (see *Devarim* 21:10-14), the Torah commands that a number of steps be taken to make her appear very unattractive. This is done in the hope that she will thus lose favor in the eyes of her captor who desired her as a wife (*Ibn Ezra*). Of course, for obvious reasons, marriage to such a woman (even after her conversion) is fraught with spiritual danger. The Torah, however, addresses the problem of a man who has been overcome by passion and will not be easily swayed by philosophical discussion. For him, it is necessary to make the woman appear repulsive in an attempt to quell his desires.

In struggling with one's *yetzer hara*, one must be prepared to alter his battle plan, depending on the particulars of a given situation. As we have mentioned elsewhere, a primary method of *mussar* study is to select an appropriate verse or statement of *Chazal* and repeat it with feeling many times. In doing so, one should select that which will best address his particular emotions and attitudes.

✥ Afflictions

It is not for us to engage in personal fasts or other forms of physical affliction as a way of *teshuvah*. An appropriate method of affliction for our generation is that of a *ta'anis dibur*, to designate a significant part of a day to refraining from speech, save for Torah and *tefillah*. This, writes the *Chofetz Chaim* (*Shemiras HaLashon* p. 53), is more effective than a fast and is considered as if one had wept exceedingly over his sins. A word of caution: such undertakings should not be done at the expense of others (as when it will cause them distress).

Another accepted method of affliction is to eat in such a way that one does not satisfy his cravings. However, this must be done carefully and in a way of *hatznei'a leches*, without attracting attention.

In his *Yesod HaTeshuvah*, *Rabbeinu Yonah* writes:

> He [the penitent] should not satisfy all his desires, neither in food nor drink. So said Rabbi Avraham ben David [the Ra'avad], who was one of the most devout people in the world, "The greatest, finest, and most wondrous barrier [to sin] is to refrain from foods." This is how he explained his words: "Let one not refrain completely from eating meat or drinking wine, for what the Torah prohibited is enough. Rather, while one is eating and still desires to eat, let him — in honor of the Creator — set aside some of his desires, and not eat according to his appetite. This method will prevent him from sinning, and remind him more than a weekly fast to love the Creator, for this is every day, continuously, whenever he eats and whenever he drinks, to set aside part of his desire in honor of the Creator."

In truth, self-restraint is a necessary component of *avodas Hashem*; in no way is it limited to the process of *teshuvah*. As *Rabbeinu Yonah* himself puts it:

> When a person overcomes his desires for things which are permissible, he causes his soul to succeed [in its lifelong struggle]; this attribute brings satisfaction to the soul, for through it, man's intellect becomes uplifted and prevails [over his passion].
> ... Those who foolishly do not seek to overcome their physical desires, and instead forever pursue earthly indulgences, will not turn away when their passions are confronted by sin or anything that can be termed wicked (Sha'arei Teshuvah 1:31).

A fundamental rule of child rearing is that children should not be given everything they ask for. A parent who never says "No!" to a child is molding an individual who will never be satisfied unless his every desire is granted him. Many adults fail to realize that it is likewise beneficial to tell *themselves* "No!" occasionally when their desires are awakened for that which is permissible.

The human soul is forever engaged in a struggle with its evil inclination. By engaging in self-restraint regarding that which is permissible, one prepares himself for those moments when the *yetzer hara* seeks to entice him to sin. However, one who is untrained in the art of self-restraint will be unprepared when the moment of trial is upon him.

Moreover, one who pursues his earthly desires is never satisfied. In the words of *Ramban*:

> For when the heart of a satiated soul, which does not crave what is bad for it, is possessed by a bit of craving and it satisfies that craving — then the soul will have an increased craving and be exceedingly thirsty for that thing ... and it will desire bad things for which it originally had no craving at all (Ramban, Devarim 29:18).

A Jew should forever bear in mind *Ramban's* understanding of the Torah's command of קְדוֹשִׁים תִּהְיוּ, *You shall be holy* (Leviticus 19:2): קַדֵּשׁ עַצְמְךָ בְּמֻתָּר לָךְ, *Sanctify yourself in that which is permitted to you.*

◆§ A Humble Spirit

Among the fundamentals of *teshuvah* is that one be of modest and humble spirit. In the Psalm which *Rabbeinu Yonah* calls פֶּרֶק הַתְּשׁוּבָה, *the Chapter of Repentance*, David proclaims: *The offerings of God are a broken spirit; a heart broken and crushed, O God, You will not despise* (Tehillim 51:19). This means that though a sinner is deserving of disgrace for having flouted his Creator's commands, nevertheless, one who humbles himself out of remorse is assured that he will not be despised by God.[4]

---

4. *Rabbeinu Yonah* (1:33) explains that the term נִשְׁבָּר [לֵב], *[a heart] broken*, connotes a modest and humble spirit, while נִדְכֶּה, *crushed*, connotes the breaking of physical lust, for the heart is the seat of man's desires.

Ga'avah, arrogance, stems from a feeling that one is superior and deserving of accolades (*Mesilas Yesharim* ch. 11). Humility flows from the opposite feeling. As *Rabbeinu Yonah* puts it: "The highest level of humility, which the path of *teshuvah* dictates, is that one make great and glorious Hashem's service. One should not congratulate himself for his accomplishments; rather, everything should be seen as insignificant as compared to what is demanded in service of Hashem. Therefore, he should make himself humble and go about his service privately, and he should not seek honor for his noble deeds. He should not pursue glory for his praiseworthy deeds, but should conceal them from others to the best of his ability" (1:24).

Later, *Rabbeinu Yonah* cites the famous teaching of the prophet Michah: *It has been told to you, O man, what is good and what it is that Hashem seeks of you — only to do justice and love kindness and to walk humbly with Hashem, your God* (Michah 6:8).

Rabbeinu Yonah also cites the words of the prophet Yeshayahu:

> *He [God] says: "Pave a road, pave a road! Clear a path! Lift up the obstacle from My people's path." For so says the exalted and uplifted One, Who abides forever and Whose Name is holy, "I abide in exaltedness and holiness — but am with the contrite and lowly of spirit, to revive the spirit of the lowly and to revive the heart of the contrite"* (Yeshayahu 57:14-15).

The prophet exhorts us in Hashem's Name to *pave a road* of goodness and proper behavior, and to *lift up the obstacle* placed in our path by the *yetzer hara*. The *obstacle* referred to is the thought which brings one to commit a sinful act (*Rashi*).

When a sinful thought enters a person's mind it is his obligation to divert his thoughts to other matters. In this way, the *obstacle* is removed before harm has been done. Quickly diverting one's thoughts away from sin is the only way to deal with מַחֲשָׁבוֹת רָעוֹת, *sinful thoughts*. One should take note that when a person struggles with himself to drive away such thoughts, he is engaging in a service of Hashem that can truly be called הַצְנֵעַ לֶכֶת, *walking humbly*, for no one but the *Ribono shel Olam* is privy to the workings of man's thoughts.

❧ ❧ ❧

Humility in practice: One should accustom himself to speak gently, as it is written (Mishlei 15:1): מַעֲנֶה רַּךְ יָשִׁיב חֵמָה וּדְבַר עֶצֶב יַעֲלֶה אָף, *A soft answer turns away wrath, but a distressing word stirs up anger (Sha'arei Teshuvah 1:29).*

The opening of *Iggeres HaRamban* reads: "Accustom yourself to speak gently to all people at all times, and with this, you will be saved from anger, which is a most wicked trait to influence man toward sin." An important principle of *avodas Hashem* is that man's inner self is profoundly influenced by his own external actions. Speaking gently has a soothing effect on one's heart; it quiets inner anger and inspires humility.

This volume is part of
THE ARTSCROLL SERIES®
an ongoing project of
translations, commentaries and expositions
on Scripture, Mishnah, Talmud, Halachah,
liturgy, history and the classic Rabbinic writings;
and biographies, and thought.

For a brochure of current publications
visit your local Hebrew bookseller
or contact the publisher:

Mesorah Publications, ltd

4401 Second Avenue
Brooklyn, New York 11232
(718) 921-9000